Law, Policy and the Environment

Edited by
Robin Churchill, John Gibson
and Lynda M. Warren

Basil Blackwell

ISBN 0 631 18166 0

First published 1991

Published simultaneously as Vol. 18, No. 1
of Journal of Law and Society ISSN 0263-323X

Basil Blackwell Ltd.
108 Cowley Road, Oxford, OX4 1JF, UK.

Basil Blackwell Inc.
3 Cambridge Center,
Cambridge, MA. 02142, USA.

British Library Cataloguing in Publication Data
Law, policy and the environment.
  1. Great Britain. Environment. Policies of government
  I. Churchill, R. R. (Robin Rolf) II. Warren, Lynda III.
Gibson, John
  333.70941

  ISBN 0-631-18166-0

Library of Congress Cataloging in Publication Data applied for.

Printed on recycled paper

Typeset by Megaron, Cardiff, Wales.
Printed in Great Britain by Whitstable Litho, Kent.

LAW

Contents

Introduction

ROBIN CHURCHILL, JOHN GIBSON AND LYNDA M. WARREN*

A 'green revolution' is said to be taking place and the United Kingdom Government professes to be a participant.[1] Recent months have seen the enactment of the Environmental Protection Act 1990 and the publication of the White Paper on the Environment.[2] The question must be asked, however, whether the rhetoric is being matched by corresponding action. The White Paper is long on words and short on proposals for action. It remains to be seen how well the Environmental Protection Act and other recent legislation will be implemented and enforced. Environmental goals also run counter to much of the Government's own philosophy, especially deregulation and privatization.

This special issue of the *Journal of Law and Society* examines current environmental policy in the United Kingdom and considers the role of law in the implementation of that policy. There is, in reality, no readily identifiable discrete body of environmental law. The main fields of environmental legislation, pollution control, conservation and land-use planning, are dealt with as separate issues by legislators and administrators alike.

Indeed, as Robin Grove-White contends in his paper on land use, there is no clear environmental agenda for the law to work on. To a large extent, progress in the field of environmental protection has been reactive, with the issues that appear topical and politically useful attracting the attention of government and non-governmental organizations alike.

This fragmentation of interest is also a consequence of our system of government in which issues are compartmentalized within different government departments with little feel for the need for co-operation. This lack of integration at central government level would seem to be a crucial failing in the development of a United Kingdom general environmental policy. Time and again the management of different sectoral concerns leads to conflicts of interest, as is illustrated in this volume by the papers on agriculture by Michael Winter and nature conservation by Lynda Warren. Even where there is no direct conflict between activities, the consequences of the failure to incorporate environmental objectives as a fundamental part of policy are evident in the critiques of energy and transport presented by John Woodliffe and Stephen Joseph respectively. On publication of the White Paper, the

* Cardiff Law School, University of Wales College of Cardiff, PO Box 427, Cardiff CF1 1XD, Wales

1

Government announced that a minister would be appointed in each central government department to follow through the White Paper initiatives.[3] Although a ministerial committee, chaired by the Prime Minister, has been charged with the function of co-ordinating the Government's approach to environmental issues, it is difficult to envisage how these arrangements will work in practice given the confrontational nature of a cabinet government.

There has, however, been some progress, notably in the Government's commitment to integrated pollution control in the Environmental Protection Act 1990, Part I, as described by John Gibson. The legislation addresses one of the major problems inherent in any attempt at pollution abatement, namely the danger of transferring a pollution burden from one medium to another, and also provides a framework for a system of quality objectives and emission standards. There is not, however, integration of the administration of pollution control measures. In relation to water this may present problems over the division of responsibilities between Her Majesty's Inspectorate of Pollution and the National Rivers Authority, which was set up under the Water Act 1989. This legislation, introduced to provide for the privatization of the water industry, has also served to separate the pollution control functions of the old water authorities from service functions relating to water supply and sewerage. The merits of the new system are addressed by William Howarth in his paper on water. Improvements have also been made to the law relating to waste regulation, as discussed by Neil Hawke. Part II of the Environmental Protection Act tightens up the law, and introduces a measure of separation of powers between polluter and enforcer that was absent under the Control of Pollution Act 1974.

Despite the claimed green credentials of the Government, it cannot be denied that much of the initiative for progress on environmental protection has originated as a result of pressures from outside the United Kingdom. David Freestone describes the legal basis for environmental policy in the European Community, and goes on to discuss the impact of the European Community in shaping United Kingdom policy and legislation on environmental issues, especially in the fields of pollution control and nature conservation. On an international level, the United Kingdom is party to several conventions that impose environmental obligations. Robin Churchill analyses the development and implementation of international environmental law in the areas of pollution control and nature conservation.

Ultimately, what governments do about the environment and, indeed, their very understanding of the word 'environment', is a reflection of society's attitude towards the issues. In the opening paper, Kay Milton analyses the administration of environmental protection from a social scientific viewpoint, and illustrates the hidden constraints that dictate government positions on different environmental issues. Her analysis draws out a point hinted at by several contributors to *Law, Policy and the Environment*, namely that, whatever the rhetoric, in reality there is no government environmental policy as such in this country, but rather a loose collection of policies in relation to disparate environmental issues. Nevertheless, the last three years have seen

2

more legislation and administrative changes in relation to the environment than have been made for many years. The Government White Paper prompted policy documents from the opposition parties,[4] and there is every sign that the environment will figure prominently in the political debate in the next few years.

NOTES AND REFERENCES

1   See, for example, Margaret Thatcher's speech to the Royal Society on 27 September 1988 in which she referred to the need to nurture and safeguard the environment.
2   *This Common Inheritance: Britain's Environmental Strategy* (1990; Cm. 1200).
3   The names of the ministers concerned were announced in a Department of the Environment press release 1990/515.
4   The Labour Party, *An Earthly Chance* (1990); Liberal Democrats, *What Price Our Planet?* (1990).

Interpreting Environmental Policy: A Social Scientific Approach

KAY MILTON*

Any discerning participant in the environmental debate very quickly realises that there is more at issue than the question of how to solve environmental problems. There are underlying disagreements over how problems are defined, their degree of seriousness, who is responsible for solving them, and how amenable they are to solution. These disagreements run deep; they are based on different moral principles, different values, different assumptions about how the world operates, and they are found not only at the international level, where cultural diversity is to be expected, but at all levels, within a single society or organization, and within the actions and policies of a single corporate group.

The current debate over British environmental policy provides plenty of evidence for this kind of diversity. The Government claims that its concern for the environment is genuine, that it takes seriously the threat of global warming, that it places high priority on the conservation of wildlife and countryside. But many of the Government's policies appear to contradict these claims; the nuclear industry receives government support despite the dangers of toxic waste, important wildlife habitats continue to be destroyed by development, international efforts to tighten environmental controls are resisted.

In everyday life we make sense of such apparent contradictions in the same way as we interpret all our actions, by placing them in context; by identifying them as part of a wider complex of strategies, motives, and ideas. One important function of social science is to assist this process of interpretation by identifying the appropriate context, that in which the actions concerned make the most sense. In this paper, I use a model of cultural diversity developed originally within social anthropology, to throw light on some of the apparent inconsistencies within current British environmental policy.

THE GRID/GROUP MODEL OF CULTURAL DIVERSITY

The grid/group model, formulated by Mary Douglas[1] and developed further

* Lecturer in Social Anthropology, Queen's University of Belfast, Belfast BT7 1NN, Northern Ireland

by social scientists in several different disciplines, is a way of classifying cultural perspectives. It is based on the premise that different ways of seeing the world are linked to different forms of social organization. A person's assumptions about how the world operates, their values and their moral judgements depend upon the kinds of social relationships and interactions in which they engage. Social relationships (the 'group' dimension) are represented by a continuum that runs from strong individualism to strong collectivism. At one end of this continuum, a person's social identity is based on their position in an ego-centred network; at the other end it is based on membership of a social group. Social interaction (the 'grid' dimension) is represented by a continuum that runs from restriction to independence. At one extreme actions are prescribed, at the other they are open to individual choice.

The combination of these two dimensions produces four different forms of social organization which are characterized by four institutionalized ways of thinking and acting (see figure 1):

(i) The entrepreneur: the result of high levels of individualism and independence. Personal profit (material or otherwise) is the main motivation, the market the principal mechanism through which it is achieved. Gains are maximized, losses are minimized.

(ii) The egalitarian: produced by a high degree of independence and strong group membership. People belong to collectives which define their own membership criteria and make their own rules. Personal profit is less important than the general good.

(iii) The hierarchist: produced by high levels of collectivism and prescription. People belong to groups whose actions are prescribed by others or by 'the system'. There is a strong emphasis on central control; procedures are more important than end results.

(iv) The fatalist: produced by high degrees of individualism and prescription. People's freedom of choice is restricted and they lack the support of bounded groups. They feel manipulated by a system over which they exercise no control.

This model provides a framework for analysis at different levels. It enables us to classify individuals; people belong to one or other category depending on how they perceive their social world and operate within it.[2] It can be used to classify different sectors of a culturally diverse society[3] or to identify different levels within a single organization[4] or to build a typology of whole societies, each of which may be spread over one or more sectors of the model.[5] It can also, I would suggest, be used to classify actions, policies, and strategies which may be based on one or other cultural perspective.

DEVELOPING THE MODEL

The grid/group model is outlined above in its simplest form. Through its application it has undergone several developments.[6] One of these is

5

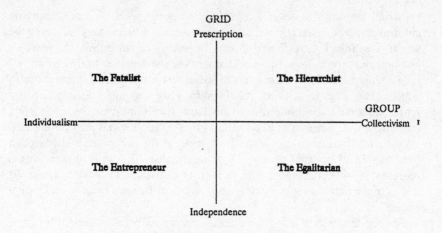

Figure 1: The Grid/Group model of cultural diversity

particularly relevant to the analysis of environmental policy. Through the use of the model in the study of ecological management,[7] the four perspectives have been identified with four ways of perceiving nature. These 'myths' of nature are represented by images of a ball in a landscape (figure 2).[8]

(i)   Nature is robust: represented by a ball at the bottom of a deep hollow. Push it up the side and it will always return to a stable position at the centre. This myth forms the basis of an entrepreneurial approach, which encourages the exploitation of nature for individual gain.

(ii)   Nature is fragile: the view held by the egalitarian, represented by a ball on top of a rise. Push it in any direction and it may roll down the slope. Stability, once lost, is difficult to regain.

(iii)   Nature is robust within limits: represented by a ball in a valley between two hills. If pushed a short distance up the side, it will return to a position of stability, but push it too far and it will topple over the edge. This is the myth held by the hierarchist, and promotes caution, based on sound scientific knowledge, imposed through central control.

(iv)   Nature is capricious: the fatalist's view, represented by a ball on a flat plain. It might roll in any direction, thus prediction and planning are impossible.

APPLYING THE MODEL

It has been claimed that the four institutionalized cultural perspectives are mutually contradictory.[9] At the level of logic, this is not difficult to accept. The entrepreneurial assumption that nature is tolerant of any exploitation is clearly incompatible with the assumption that it will tolerate no interference, or only some interference, or is totally unpredictable. Each of the other

6

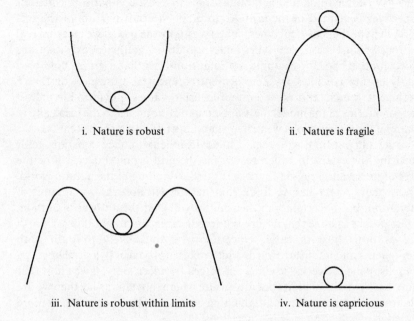

i. Nature is robust

ii. Nature is fragile

iii. Nature is robust within limits

iv. Nature is capricious

Figure 2: The four myths of nature

perspectives similarly precludes the other three. At the levels of common sense understanding and everyday action, the picture is less clear. The claim that the perspectives are mutually contradictory seems to deny the possibility of an individual or group simultaneously holding more than one. This in turn makes it difficult to envisage how cultural change involving a switch from one perspective to another might occur, given that change is generally not instantaneous but involves a period of transition.

People are continually acting in ways that might appear contradictory in terms of the grid/group model. For example, the same individual might buy a more expensive phosphate-free washing powder, on the grounds that the good of the environment should take precedence over personal profit (egalitarian); use a car rather than suffer the inconvenience of public transport (entrepreneurial); and lobby the government for tighter pollution controls (hierarchist). Entrepreneurial industrialists might donate a proportion of their profits to environmental charities. If they do this ultimately for personal gain (to reap the benefits of a green image) it is entirely consistent with their entrepreneurial strategy. If they do it out of a sense of duty, or to salve their consciences, their entrepreneurial perspective begins to look rather shaky.

The fact that people's everyday actions do not fit neatly into the analytical boxes we construct for them is not a problem; it is fundamental to the nature of social scientific analysis. Models are constructed, not as accurate descriptions of the way people think and act, but as tools to assist comparison. The four perspectives generated in the grid/group model are not mirrors of the real world but hypothetical ideal types. When we apply the model we measure real situations against these ideal types and, in so doing, compare real situations with each other. So, for example, we might observe that a group holding a broadly egalitarian ideology employs entrepreneurial strategies, or that a government which expresses entrepreneurial values pursues hierarchist policies. In terms of the model these appear as deviations from the ideal, and in explaining those deviations we arrive at an understanding of the reality.

I would suggest that, with regard to environmental policy, a major factor influencing the extent to which reality fits the grid/group model will be the degree of uncertainty present in people's understanding of the natural world. Entrepreneurs might like to think that nature will absorb any amount of exploitation, but uncertainty in their minds will lead them towards caution. Fatalists might assume that nature is unpredictable, but might think it worth being cautious 'just in case'. Uncertainty is thus likely to push both entrepreneurs and fatalists towards a hierarchist approach. In a similar way, a hierarchist perspective will itself be reinforced by uncertainty; if we know that nature is robust within limits but are unsure where those limits lie, then we are likely to be even more careful, tightening central controls, demanding more knowledge on which to base our decisions.

Egalitarians, on the other hand, may be pushed towards a hierarchist approach by practical considerations. Given that some use of natural resources is essential for survival, a lifestyle which avoids all exploitation of nature will be untenable in many contexts. For practical purposes, many people who act in an egalitarian fashion in some contexts, act like hierarchists in others. In addition to making environmentally-friendly choices in their daily lives, they campaign for greater central control to minimize environmental damage.

BRITAIN'S ENVIRONMENTAL POLICY

How can the grid/group model help us to interpret the Government's current environmental policy? I suggest that by classifying specific policies in terms of the model we can see them in their wider context and highlight some of the factors that shape them. Lowe and Flynn have pointed out that there is no environmental policy as such in Britain, but rather a series of 'pragmatic and incremental responses to specific problems'.[10] These responses have given rise to the complex array of legislative, administrative and other mechanisms through which our environment is managed. During 1989 and 1990 a more co-ordinated approach has emerged. The Environmental Protection Act covers a wider range of issues than any previous piece of environmental legislation, and the Government's current thoughts and intentions on environmental matters have been brought together in the recent White Paper.[11] For the analysis that follows, I have selected three areas of environmental concern; global warming, wildlife and countryside conservation and pollution. Page references to the relevant parts of the White Paper are given in parenthesis.

BRITAIN'S RESPONSE TO GLOBAL WARMING

The White Paper presents Britain's role in the control of global warming as part of a communal obligation, shared by all nations, in which everyone can and should play a part (64). The Government sees its own role as one of encouraging and enabling individuals, companies and other organizations to accept this obligation and act upon it. Government defines the framework and provides initiatives; the success of those initiatives depends on decisions made by individuals (71). The broad framework consists of two targets: to phase out the production and consumption of chlorofluorocarbons (CFCs) (weight for weight the most powerful greenhouse gases) by the end of the century, and to stabilize emissions of carbon dioxide (by far the most common greenhouse gas) at 1990 levels by the year 2005 (68). Measures are also being taken, through changes in agriculture and waste disposal policies, to reduce emissions of methane.

The potential for reducing emissions of carbon dioxide is discussed in relation to two main areas: energy and transport. Energy production is expected to become increasingly efficient as a result of the privatization of the electricity industry, under the Electricity Act 1989 (68). This legislation also guarantees at least a limited future for nuclear energy, which remains in the public sector, and renewable energy, by obliging electricity suppliers to contract for specified amounts of electricity from non-fossil fuel sources until 1998 (205). Research and development in renewable energy sources will be aimed at increasing their commercial viability (72). Energy conservation will be promoted through grants to householders for energy-related improvements, development of energy efficiency technologies and assessment techniques, and the possible strengthening of building regulations (70).

Transport policy is directed at meeting current and projected demand for private travel, the Government's attitude to which is clearly favourable:

> ... the Government welcomes the continuing widening of car ownership as an important aspect of personal freedom and choice. The speed and flexibility of motoring make it indispensable for much business travel, which in turn is vital for the economy.(73)

Accordingly, the extensive road building programme is presented mainly as an economic strategy, but one which will bring environmental benefits by reducing congestion and therefore increasing fuel efficiency (74). Market-based measures to limit the environmental impact of motoring include tax incentives to use more fuel-efficient cars and less polluting fuel. The inclusion of an emissions check in the MOT test is the only regulatory measure proposed. The environmental benefits of public transport are acknowledged but policy is directed at meeting current demand and increasing cost-effectiveness. The possibility of reducing the overall demand for travel is

9

addressed only as a long-term measure (76). The possibility of meeting current and projected demand for mobility by switching that demand from private to public transport is not considered at all.

BRITAIN'S APPROACH TO WILDLIFE AND COUNTRYSIDE CONSERVATION

The Government's policy on wildlife and countryside conservation can be described as a mixture of carrots and sticks. The carrots take the form of financial incentives for habitat creation and management available to landholders through various schemes (the farm diversification grant scheme, set-aside, woodland grant and farm woodland schemes, environmentally sensitive areas, and so on (98–102)). Financial incentives for some conservation measures are available within National Parks. A new countryside initiative is under consideration, which might offer grants to landholders in England for the re-creation or management of landscapes for public enjoyment (103).

The sticks take the form of legislative measures for the protection of wildlife and countryside. Some of these operate through the planning system; development controls implemented by local authorities in Great Britain and by the Department of the Environment in Northern Ireland (82–84), which include the requirement for certain development proposals to be accompanied by an environmental impact assessment (87).[12] Government has accepted that this requirement should be extended, 'in appropriate cases', to developments proposed through private Bills (90). Other legislative measures operate through the Wildlife and Countryside Act 1981 and the equivalent legislation in Northern Ireland,[13] which provide for the designation of protected areas (national nature reserves, marine nature reserves, sites/areas of special scientific interest (SSSIs/ASSIs))[14] and for the wider protection of some species of animals and plants. Government policy also includes the designation of areas protected under international laws and conventions, such as special protection areas under the EC directive on the conservation of wild birds (79/409/EEC), and wetlands of international importance under the Ramsar Convention (110).

In addition the various government agencies, such as the Countryside Commissions, the Nature Conservancy Council,[15] the Ministry of Agriculture and the relevant government departments in Scotland and Northern Ireland, offer advice and information to landholders on a wide range of things to do with wildlife and countryside conservation. In this area, perhaps more than any other, the Government envisages a prominent role for the voluntary sector (104). In general terms, the Government clearly hopes that private landholders will accept a degree of personal responsibility for the protection of wildlife and countryside, and some new initiatives, such as community forests and a new national forest, are intended to be financed from the private and voluntary sectors (101). But economic considerations remain paramount and a prosperous rural economy is presented almost as a precondition for a healthy and diverse countryside (96).

10

The most striking feature of the Government's policy on pollution is the extent to which it is dictated by EC directives. Air quality standards, for example, are set by the EC in relation to smoke, sulphur dioxide, lead, and nitrogen dioxide (143).[16] Several of the measures announced in the White Paper are intended to ensure that Britain meets those standards; for instance, the banning of straw and stubble burning in England and Wales by 1993 (146) and the control of vehicle emissions through the MOT test (145). Pollution from motor vehicles is targeted in separate EC directives which will require all new cars to be fitted with catalytic converters from the end of 1992 (150). Pollution from large combustion plants is also controlled through an EC directive, under which the Government has made legally binding commitments to reduce sulphur dioxide emissions by up to sixty per cent of 1980 levels by 2003 (149). Full compliance with EC standards on smoke emissions is required by April 1993. Air quality standards on radon and methane in buildings, not governed by EC legislation, will be controlled through building regulations (158–9).

The quality of drinking water and bathing water is also the subject of EC legislation.[17] Under the 1989 Water Act the control of water quality will be the responsibility of the National Rivers Authority (NRA), which will advise government on the standards to be set by law (163). Standards in drinking water will be monitored by the Drinking Water Inspectorate (164). The NRA will be responsible for regulating pollution from farm effluent. Improvements in sewage treatment and the use of long sea outfalls are being introduced in order to comply with the EC bathing water directive (165). The dumping of various substances in the sea, including liquid industrial wastes, sewage sludge, and stone waste from coal mining, will be phased out by the end of 1998 (171). The use of polychlorinated biphenyls (PCBs), which are highly toxic and accumulate in the marine food chain, will be banned from the end of 1999 (178). The principle of separating the roles of producer and regulator, which led to the formation of the NRA, will also be applied to the management of controlled waste; the Environmental Protection Act will create Waste Regulation Authorities to monitor the activities of waste disposal companies (139).

A major innovation presented in the White Paper and in the Environmental Protection Act is the policy of integrated pollution control (IPC). The release of highly polluting substances to water, air, or land will be regulated by Her Majesty's Inspectorate of Pollution (HMIP) in England and Wales and Her Majesty's Industrial Pollution Inspectorate (HMIPI) in Scotland.[18] Processes to be controlled in this way will be prescribed by the Secretary of State for the Environment and anyone wishing to operate such a process will require authorization from HMIP or HMIPI. Authorization will only be given subject to the polluter using the best available techniques not entailing excessive cost (BATNEEC) to minimize damage. The inspectorates will charge potential polluters for authorizations in order to recover the costs of implementing IPC (138). As well as establishing the policy of IPC, the Environmental Protection

Act sets tighter controls and stiffer penalties for pollution and provides for public access to information held by pollution control authorities (221).

COMPARING THE POLICIES

The Government's policies in these three areas are made up of two main mechanisms: economic measures and regulation. Economic measures – tax incentives and deterrents, grants and loans – are ways of intervening in the market to influence individual choice.[19] They therefore belong to a broad entrepreneurial approach, since their successful operation depends upon people acting as entrepreneurs, to maximize personal gain and minimize loss. This approach is used quite extensively and explicitly in wildlife and country-side conservation, but to a lesser degree in policies on global warming, where market intervention is expected in the long term (68), but where few firm pro-posals are made. The much publicised 'polluter-pays principle', which was examined in some detail in the Pearce Report[20] and was expected to form the cornerstone of the Government's policy on pollution, is presented in the White Paper mainly as a longer term possibility still under consideration (271–8).

Regulatory measures set the limits within which individual choice can operate and are central to a hierarchist approach. They play a major part in the Government's policies on pollution and a significant, though smaller, part in policies on wildlife and countryside conservation. The Government's policies on global warming are virtually free of such measures. The only clear regulatory proposals are for emissions tests on vehicles, possible changes in building regulations (70) and the non-fossil fuel obligation (72, 205). Global warming policy appears to be characterized instead by a *laissez-faire* approach, which neither regulates individual choice nor attempts to influence it significantly. The Government might claim that the privatization of the electricity industry (under the Electricity Act 1989) can itself been seen as an environmental measure, since it is intended to increase efficiency and therefore to help control carbon dioxide emissions. Whatever the case, this is clearly an entrepreneurial approach. The Government's expectation, at least in the short term, is that market forces, given a free rein, will go some way towards achieving the desired goals.

A simple comparison of these three areas of government policy therefore reveals that the approach to global warming is almost entirely entrepreneurial, that the approach to pollution is predominantly hierarchist, and that the approach to wildlife and countryside conservation is a mixture of the two. This is partly, but not entirely, what we would expect from a government whose principal aim has been to create an entrepreneurial atmosphere in all areas of social and economic activity, and whose overriding strategy has been 'to shift the burden of effort and payment from the state to the private sector'.[21] We would expect such a government, faced with a choice between entrepreneurial and hierarchist policies, always to opt for the former. Why, then, has the dominant ideology of Thatcherism been expressed so unevenly in

12

environmental policy? Why has a hierarchist approach been allowed to dominate policies on pollution, and why has it not dominated other environmental policies to the same extent? The main reasons are both historical and structural in nature.

THE HISTORICAL LEGACY

No government inherits a clean slate on which to write its policies; it has to pursue its aims by modifying what already exists. In 1979 the Thatcher Government inherited 'an accretion of common law, statutes, agencies, procedures and policies'[22] relating to various aspects of environmental conservation. Some legislative and administrative structures were well established, but these were not evenly distributed over the full range of environmental concerns. Pollution control already had a long history, with important legislation dating from the middle of the nineteenth century, and a number of protective measures having been introduced since the Second World War, including the Clean Air Act in 1956 and the Control of Pollution Act in 1974.[23] Control over land use was a more recent introduction, but was extensive. The Town and Country Planning Act of 1947 effectively nationalized the right to use land[24] and the concept of land as a communal resource was reinforced in the National Parks and Access to the Countryside Act of 1949. This Act also provided for the conservation of wildlife through the designation of nature reserves and SSSIs. Otherwise, legislation to protect wildlife was directed mainly at birds and a few other selected species.

The Thatcher Government's efforts to reduce obstructions to growth have been directed mainly at the land-use planning system, with the increased zoning of areas where constraints are reduced, and the use of mechanisms such as special development orders and private Bills, which by-pass normal planning controls.[25] Wildlife conservation has also suffered from these measures, but the most significant move in this field has been the break up of the Nature Conservancy Council (NCC) under the Environmental Protection Act. Many conservationists fear that this will considerably weaken the implementation of the legal provisions for nature conservation.[26] Pollution control, in contrast, has suffered little from the effects of 'Thatcherite reformism and deregulatory zeal'.[27] On the contrary, it has been strengthened in Great Britain by the setting up of bodies such as HMIP and the NRA[28] and by the measures introduced in the Environmental Protection Act. The differential impact of the Conservative Government's entrepreneurial intentions on these areas of environmental concern needs to be understood within the wider political context.

THE WIDER STRUCTURE

The British Government is not, of course, an independent agent, but part of a hierarchical system within which its actions are, to some extent, prescribed; it fits firmly into the hierarchist sector of the grid/group diagram. From one side, its actions are constrained by the need to keep the support of the electorate. From the other, they are constrained by the various international bodies to which Britain belongs, of which the most important in the environmental context is the European Community. Although the Treaty of Rome imposed no environmental obligations on member states, the EC has, since 1973, implemented four successive action programmes on the environment. The Single European Act has amended this position and made environmental protection a necessary component of all EC policies.[29] EC environmental policies have been implemented mainly through directives. These define objectives which each member state is legally obliged to meet through its domestic legislation. The Government is therefore obliged to adopt hierarchist policies, those which impose central control, in areas covered by EC directives.

The influence of EC legislation on Britain's pollution control policy has already been commented upon. Pollution is the subject of more EC directives than any other environmental issue.[30] In 1986 there was a clear demonstration of how this legislation can curb the Government's entrepreneurial zeal. The original plans to privatize the regional water authorities would have placed pollution control in the hands of private companies. Legal advice taken by the Council for the Protection of Rural England (CPRE) indicated that this would have been against EC law. The National Rivers Authority was established as a result of the need to modify these plans.[31] The British Government has also felt the heavy hand of the EC as a result of its failure to comply fully with the directive on bathing water (164), and of the delay in implementing EC directives in Northern Ireland.[32]

Similar pressure has been exerted in other areas. The revision of Great Britain's wildlife law, which produced the Wildlife and Countryside Act in 1981, was necessary in order to implement the EC birds directive and to enable closer compliance with the Berne and Bonn Conventions.[33] The United Kingdom remained in breach of the birds directive until the Northern Ireland legislation was revised in 1985, by which time the European Commission had begun proceedings against the United Kingdom Government by issuing a 'reasoned opinion'.[34] The Government is currently under pressure to comply more closely with the directive by introducing a licensing system for the control of pest species. The EC directive on environmental impact assessments (85/337/EEC), which covers wildlife and landscape, climate, pollution, and cultural heritage, has increased the control of the planning system over the environmental effects of some forms of development.

EC influence is not only the major factor in determining the hierarchist nature of the Government's policies on pollution control, wildlife protection and, to a lesser extent, land-use planning. It is also indirectly responsible for the entrepreneurial aspects of wildlife and countryside conservation. The financial incentives offered to landholders for the creation and management of wildlife habitat and amenity landscapes are a by-product of the reform of the EC's Common Agricultural Policy. They are designed primarily to reduce agricultural production by diversifying the use of rural land.

14

What, then, of Britain's policy on global warming, which is predominantly entrepreneurial in character? Why has the Government's entrepreneurial ideology so far been allowed freer expression in this area than in any other? The underlying reason is that global warming has been defined as an urgent problem only within the last few years. So there were no ready-made legal or administrative structures for dealing with climate control, to restrict the Government's hand. For the same reason, prescriptive international agreements on climate control have not yet been developed. The only prescriptive measure in place is the requirement that environmental impact assessments (under EC directive 85/337) take effects on climate into account,[35] but international guidelines for doing so have not been agreed. Most EC member states want to stabilize carbon dioxide emissions at 1990 levels by the year 2000; Britain has agreed to do so by 2005.[36] The Inter-Governmental Panel on Climate Change (IPCC)[37] is primarily a research body which can make recommendations, but has no legislative powers.

For the present, then, governments have a relatively free hand to tackle the problem of global warming as they see fit. International pressure is strong but remains informal, while debates on the most appropriate measures continue.[38] The British Government has made its view quite explicit, saying that 'the best way to act on global warming is through an international framework convention setting a broad strategy' (67). They suggest that negotiations for such a convention should begin more or less immediately, and that the work of the IPCC provides a sound scientific basis for agreement. But they also point out that this work is in its infancy and that a thorough analysis could take fifteen years (67). In the meantime, they urge other industrial nations to develop their own strategies for dealing with the problem. Such an approach, if it succeeds, will suit the Government's entrepreneurial intentions very well. An international convention setting a broad strategy, rather than one setting narrowly defined targets and guidelines, would allow sufficient scope for entrepreneurial domestic policies to be used. The longer it takes to agree such a convention, the more time current domestic policies will have to develop unhindered by hierarchist international influence.

CONCLUSIONS

The Thatcher Government's broad strategy, over a wide range of policy areas, has been to create the social conditions which encourage an entrepreneurial perspective. Entrepreneurs operate through ego-centred networks rather than groups. They forge contacts with individuals and exchange costs and benefits in a free market. Participation in a network, in which the dominant motive is personal gain, can often be in direct conflict with membership of a group, in which the main driving force is often the good of the group as a whole. It is not surprising, then, that some of the Government's policies have been aimed at weakening institutions such as trades unions, which uphold egalitarian principles. This is sound thinking in terms of the grid/group model: weaken the groups and the networks will have the chance to flourish. The process of network-building occupies the left-hand side of the grid/group diagram (figure 1). It is a process which produces both winners and losers. The winners maintain and increase their options and, in so doing, restrict the options of the losers. In theory, then, conditions designed to produce an entrepreneurial way of operating will result in a society made up of entrepreneurs and fatalists.[39]

Running through the Government's thinking on environmental matters is a line of argument which appears inconsistent with this broad approach. A message expressed clearly and repeatedly in the recent White Paper is that the protection of the environment is the responsibility of us all, and that each individual has a part to play in creating a safer and greener world (16, 34, 268–70). In terms of the grid/group model this is a theoretical impossibility. People are being expected to act like egalitarians in a social system which is designed to produce only entrepreneurs and fatalists.

Of course reality, as we know, is not like that. Even if it wanted to, the British Government could not, under present conditions, create a society consisting solely of entrepreneurs and fatalists; its policies are too heavily constrained by the hierarchical system of which it is a part. The reality is that entrepreneurial, fatalistic, hierarchist, and egalitarian perspectives are all alive and well, and interact with each other to produce the subtle complexities of the environmental debate, and of any other cultural discourse. But the grid/group model highlights trends which have important practical implications for environmental protection in the United Kingdom. It indicates, for instance, that where egalitarianism flourishes it does so in spite of, not because of, current government policies, and implies that if it is to continue to flourish, then the entrepreneurial trend must not be allowed to engulf the environmental lobby. The alternative course of action is the one towards which the British Government has so far taken only a few tentative steps; to ensure that the environment can be protected through market forces. This could only be achieved if the personal rewards for protecting the environment were considerably greater than the Government has so far been prepared to make them.

NOTES AND REFERENCES

1   M. Douglas, *Natural Symbols* (1970).
2   J. Hampton, 'Giving the Grid/Group Dimensions an Operational Definition' in *Essays in the Sociology of Perception*, ed. M. Douglas (1982).
3   P. James, P. Tayler, and M. Thompson, *Plural Rationalities* (1987) (Warwick Papers in Management, no. 9).
4   M. Thompson and A. Wildavsky, 'A Cultural Theory of Information Bias in Organizations' (1986) 23 *Journal of Management Studies* 272–86.
5   op. cit., n. 1, pp. 86–91.
6   D. Ostrander, 'One- and Two-dimensional Models of the Distribution of Beliefs', and M. Thompson, 'A Three-dimensional Model', both in *Essays in the Sociology of Perception*, ed. M. Douglas (1982).

7 W.C. Clark and R.E. Munn (eds.), *The Sustainable Development of the Biosphere* (1986).

8 M. Thompson and P. Tayler, *The Surprise Game: An Exploration of Constrained Relativism* (1986) (Warwick Papers in Management, no. 1); James et al., op. cit., n. 3; M. Douglas, 'A Typology of Cultures' in *Kultur und Gesellschaft* (1988).

9 op. cit., n. 4, p. 281.

10 P. Lowe and A. Flynn, 'Environmental Politics and Policy in the 1980s' in *The Political Geography of Contemporary Britain*, ed. J. Mohan (1989) at p. 256.

11 *This Common Inheritance* (1990; Cm. 1200).

12 This requirement was introduced to comply with the EC directive on the assessment of the effects of certain public and private projects on the environment (985/337/EEC O.J. 05.07.85 L. 175).

13 The Wildlife (Northern Ireland) Order 1985 and the Nature Conservation and Amenity Lands (Northern Ireland) Order 1985 (and its 1989 amendment).

14 Area of special scientific interest (ASSI) is the Northern Ireland equivalent of site of special scientific interest (SSSI).

15 The Nature Conservancy Council is to be split into three separate agencies for England, Scotland, and Wales under the Environmental Protection Act 1990, and will be combined with the Countryside Commissions in Scotland and Wales.

16 Directives 80/779 O.J. 30.08.80 L. 229; 82/884 O.J. 31.12.82 L. 378; and 85/203 O.J. 27.03.88 L. 87.

17 Directives 80/778 O.J. 30.8.80 L. 229, and 76/160 O.J. 05.02.76 L. 31.

18 In Northern Ireland industrial pollution is controlled by the Northern Ireland Alkali and Radiochemical Inspectorate, but there is no indication in the White Paper that this body will adopt the policy of IPC. Rather, it would appear that the Government feels such a policy is unnecessary in Northern Ireland (op. cit., n. 11, p. 262).

19 D. Pearce, 'In the market for action' *The Guardian*, 7 December 1990.

20 D. Pearce, A. Markandya, and E.B. Barbier, *Blueprint for a Green Economy* (1989).

21 T. O'Riordan, 'Nature Conservation Under Thatcherism: the Legacy and the Prospect' (1989) 10(4) *ECOS* at p. 4.

22 op. cit., n. 10, p. 256.

23 D. Vogel, *National Styles of Regulation* (1986) 31–44.

24 id., p. 35.

25 op. cit., n. 10, pp. 263–4.

26 I. Prestt, 'Comment: Unanswered Questions' *Birds Magazine*, Winter 1989; D. Ratcliffe, 'The Nature Conservancy Council 1979–1989' (1989) 10 (4)*Ecos* 9–15.

27 op. cit., n. 10. p. 265.

28 These agencies do not operate in Northern Ireland, where pollution control is considerably weaker than in Great Britain (see House of Commons Environment Committee, *Environmental Issues in Northern Ireland, Session 1989–90* (1990; H.C. 39).

29 N. Haigh, *EEC Environmental Policy and Britain* (1987) 9–11.

30 id. Haigh lists fifty-one EC directives, plus a number of amendments and other instruments, dealing with air, water, waste, and chemicals.

31 op. cit., n. 10, p. 267.

32 op. cit., n. 28, p. xiv.

33 The Convention on the Conservation of European Wildlife and Natural Habitats (Berne), and the Convention on the Conservation of Migratory Species of Wild Animals (Bonn).

34 op. cit., n. 29, p. 297.

35 id., p. 350.

36 Friends of the Earth, *How Green is Britain? The Government's Environmental Record* (1990) 210–4.

37 Established in 1988 under the auspices of the United Nations Environment Programme, and the World Meteorological Organization (see op. cit., n. 11, p. 66).

38 J. Goldemberg, 'Policy Responses to Global Warming' in *Global Warming: The Greenpeace Report*, ed. J. Leggett (1990) 174–83.

39 Compare Thompson and Tayler, op. cit., n. 8, p. 5.

The Integration of Pollution Control

JOHN GIBSON*

INTRODUCTION

The White Paper on the Environment,[1] published in September 1990, declares the current policy on pollution control adopted by the Government of the United Kingdom. It maintains that the Government takes a precautionary approach to the control of pollutants, relating the scale of effort to the degree of risk. This basic principle is said to be guided by a number of additional aims: to prevent pollution at source; to minimize the risk to human health and the environment; to encourage and apply the most advanced technical solutions, while recognizing the integrated nature of the environment and the need to achieve the best practicable environmental option; to apply a 'critical loads' approach by assessing the levels of pollutant that local environments can tolerate; and to ensure that the polluter pays for the necessary controls. The White Paper states that these principles are united in a new system of 'integrated pollution control'.

This essay examines the concept of integrated pollution control, and evaluates the extent to which the system introduced by the Government justifies the use of that accolade. It also analyses the role of the law in the establishment of integrated pollution control, and discusses the relationship between law and administrative policy in the implementation of a new method of environmental protection.

THE BACKGROUND TO INTEGRATED POLLUTION CONTROL

The historical development of pollution control in England and Wales has been a piecemeal process with separate legal and administrative regimes governing discharges to air, water and land. Since the nineteenth century, the control of air pollution has been divided between national and local bodies: the Alkali Act 1863 created a national inspectorate to regulate emissions of hydrochloric acid gas from alkali works, while the Public Health Act 1875 empowered local authorities to abate nuisances caused by smoke. This division of responsibility was preserved under subsequent legislation, so that

* Cardiff Law School, University of Wales College of Cardiff, P.O. Box 427, Cardiff CF1 1XD, Wales

18

industrial air pollution remained the responsibility of national inspectors,[2] whereas smoke, dust, and grit from domestic chimneys and combustion processes were policed by local authorities.[3] Local authorities were also originally responsible for controlling water pollution under the Rivers Pollution Prevention Act 1876, but their functions were transferred successively to river boards,[4] river authorities,[5] and water authorities;[6] those regional bodies were replaced in 1989 by a single agency, the National Rivers Authority, which now regulates water pollution throughout England and Wales.[7] In contrast, the management of waste disposal on land is a comparatively modern development, and is administered on a local basis. Although local authorities have long possessed powers under public health legislation to remove refuse and abate nuisances from the accumulation of noxious matter, it was not until the implementation of the Control of Pollution Act 1974 that they were given comprehensive responsiblities for dealing with domestic and industrial waste.

Thus, the traditional British approach to pollution control has been to divide the environment into sectors, and allocate the custodianship of each to one or more local, regional, or national authority. However, in recent years, it has increasingly been recognized that air, water, and land are in fact interdependent, and that substances discharged into one medium may have damaging impacts in another. For example, chemical fertilizers and sewage sludge spread on agricultural land or toxic waste buried in land-fill disposal sites may leach into watercourses. Sulphur dioxide (SO_2) and oxides of nitrogen (NO_x) emitted into the atmosphere from conventional power stations, large industrial combustion plants, and motor vehicles can produce acid rain that erodes buildings and kills trees and fish. Likewise, atmospheric emissions of carbon dioxide (CO_2) from the burning of fossil fuels contribute to the greenhouse effect, which may lead to global warming and a consequent rise in sea level. Again, the release into the air of chlorofluorocarbons (CFCs) from aerosols, refrigerators, solvents, and air conditioning systems may deplete the ozone layer, resulting in increased ultraviolet radiation that may cause skin cancers, damage crops and harm the marine food chain. Moreover, unless pollutants can be eliminated altogether, they are simply transformed or transferred elsewhere, and measures taken to reduce pollution in one environmental medium may create problems for another. For instance, when flue gas desulphurization equipment is fitted to power stations in order to reduce air pollution from emissions of sulphur dioxide, the 'scrubbing' process produces by-products of contaminated water and lime that must be discharged into the aqueous environment or disposed of as waste on land. It is clearly desirable, therefore, that all the potential polluting effects of an activity should be taken into account before it is permitted to take place. Yet, the role of the regulatory authorities has in the past been confined to protecting the particular medium entrusted to them, and their insularity has been compounded by the public law doctrine of *ultra vires*, which precludes them from acting for purposes beyond their statutory brief.

In 1976, the Royal Commission on Environmental Pollution recommended[8] that the Alkali Inspectorate, which was then responsible for controlling air pollution from the industrial processes that presented the most difficult problems, should be subsumed into a new unified body with widened responsibilities across the whole environment. This recommendation was belatedly adopted by the Government eleven years later. In April 1987, Her Majesty's Inspectorate of Pollution (HMIP) was formed from a combination of the existing Industrial Air Pollution Inspectorate (successor to the Alkali Inspectorate), the Radiochemical Inspectorate and the Hazardous Waste Inspectorate; it was also given new functions in the control of water pollution.

The Royal Commission had also proposed the principle that wastes should be disposed of according to the 'best practicable environmental option' (BPEO),[9] and in 1984 the Government declared its acceptance of this idea.[10] The meaning of the 'best practicable environmental option' was elaborated by the Royal Commission in a further report published in 1988:[11]

> A BPEO is the outcome of a systematic consultative and decision-making procedure which emphasizes the protection of the environment across land, air and water. The BPEO procedure establishes, for a given set of objectives, the option that provides the most benefit or least damage to the environmental as a whole, at acceptable cost, in the long term as well as the short term.

This concept is fundamental to an integrated approach to environmental protection.

THE ENVIRONMENTAL PROTECTION ACT 1990

In July 1988, the Department of the Environment produced consultative proposals for the introduction of a system of 'integrated pollution control' (IPC) incorporating the BPEO principle.[12] These proposals formed the basis of the major legislative reforms now enacted in Part I of the Environmental Protection Act 1990, under which certain industrial processes that discharge significant amounts of harmful substances to air, water, or land will be prescribed by the Secretary of State for the Environment, and their operation will require the prior approval of Her Majesty's Inspectorate of Pollution.[13] It is expected that about 5,000 industrial installations will be affected. In addition, there will a related system of air pollution control by local authorities over less harmful processes, which will only be concerned with atmospheric emissions. This will replace powers previously exercised by local authorities under the Public Health Act 1936, which enabled them to abate statutory nuisances due to air pollution, but had the disadvantage that the remedy was only available after the event.

1. *Prescribed processes and substances*
The scope and effectiveness of integrated pollution control necessarily depends upon the identity of the particular processes and substances to which it will be applied. Regulations[14] prescribing these are expected to be made in April 1991, but the Department of the Environment gave advance indication of their

likely content in draft schedules prepared during the passage of the Environmental Protection Bill. The list of prescribed processes will be divided into two parts; those in one part will be regulated by Her Majesty's Inspectorate of Pollution, while those in the other will be under local authority air pollution control. The regulations will also contain lists of prescribed substances for each environmental medium; the list for air will apply to both integrated pollution control and the local authority air pollution regime, while those for water and waste on land will be applicable to integrated pollution control alone.

The processes discharging to air were the subject of two consultation exercises in 1986[15] and 1988,[16] and the list will be based on a reclassification and rationalization of the works scheduled under the previous system of industrial air pollution control; whereas past practice adopted a process-oriented approach to the identification of scheduled works, the new format will concentrate not only on the type of process involved, but also on the product manufactured. Six main categories of industry will be covered, namely 'fuel and power', 'metal', 'mineral', 'chemical', 'waste disposal', and 'other industries', with over thirty detailed classes under these headings. The intention is to make the new schedule easier to apply, and to align it with the provisions of the EC air framework directive.[17]

In relation to water, the prescribed processes will be those that discharge substances included in the 'Red List' drawn up by the Department of the Environment. The 'Red List', which was announced in Parliament in April 1989,[18] consists of twenty-three dangerous substances selected for priority action. The catalyst for the creation of the 'Red List' was the United Kingdom's commitment at the Second International Conference on the Protection of the North Sea[19] to achieve a fifty per cent reduction between 1985 and 1995 of inputs via rivers and estuaries of substances that are persistent, toxic, and liable to bioaccumulate. Although the European Commission had previously identified 129 chemicals as candidates for control under the EC dangerous substances directive,[20] the United Kingdom considered it more efficient to concentrate its efforts instead on a narrower range of targets. The selection method adopted by the Department of the Environment involved measuring a limited number of properties and inputs of the substances on the EC candidate list, and assigning them to categories as either high, medium, or low.[21] These classifications were then applied to decision trees representing different scenarios in order to determine whether the substances emerged as priority candidates. The 'short term scenario' was intended to indicate the concentration of a substance that might cause acute toxic effects, the 'long-term scenario' dealt with chronic toxic effects, and the 'food-chain scenario' covered substances that might be toxic to higher organisms by accumulation through the food chain; a 'carcinogenicity scenario' was subsequently added to study whether the properties of a substance suggested that its presence in the aquatic environment might cause cancer. This approach is, however, open to criticism because the categorization of attributes inevitably involves generalizations and arbitrary judgments. Moreover, uniform laboratory tests were adopted in order to provide standardized criteria without ecotoxicological studies; for example, toxicity to higher organisms was measured according to the lethal dose for rats. Thus, the results of such tests may not necessarily correspond to the effects of the same substances in the aquatic environment. These criteria have also been used to select a 'priority candidate list' of additional substances to be given first consideration for 'Red List' status; these would be subject to a second-stage scrutiny, which would include consideration of their quantity, patterns of use, and presence in the environment, but no changes are expected to be made to the 'Red List' for at least two years.[22]

Integrated pollution control will also apply to processes generating large amounts of 'special waste'. 'Special waste' is currently defined in the Control of Pollution (Special Waste) Regulations 1980,[23] which provide for a system of consignment notes warning disposal authorities of waste that may be dangerous or difficult to dispose of; these regulations are under review, and the definition of 'special waste' is expected to be revised.[24] The new definition will make it clear that 'special waste' includes substances that are liable to become dangerous or difficult to dispose of if they are not processed or treated, and it will take account of definitions in the 1989 Basel Convention on the Control of Transboundary Movements of Hazardous Wastes and their Disposal[25] and the draft EC directive on hazardous waste.[26]

The Environmental Protection Act[27] also empowers the Secretary of State for the Environment to set statutory emission limits, restricting the concentration of any substance that may be released by a prescribed process, and enables him to establish quality objectives and standards for any environmental medium. This is a development of the concept of statutory water quality objectives introduced by the Water Act 1989,[28] although the utilization of that provision has itself been deferred until autumn 1992.[29] The Secretary of State will also be able to make national plans for the progressive improvement of emission limits and quality objectives; such plans may also limit the total amount of substances that can be discharged within the United Kingdom, and allocate quotas to industrial operators.

2. *The Authorization of Processes*
Once integrated pollution control has been implemented, it will be illegal to carry on a prescribed process without an authorization from Her Majesty's Inspectorate of Pollution, who must be satisfied that the applicant will be able to comply with the conditions imposed.[30] In the case of processes under local authority air pollution control, the authorization must be obtained from the district council in whose area they are conducted.[31] An authorization is required[32] to contain such *specific* conditions as the enforcing authority considers appropriate to achieve various objectives, including compliance with national plans, statutory emission limits and quality standards, and European and international environmental obligations. In particular, conditions must ensure that the *best available techniques not entailing excessive cost* (BATNEEC) will be used to prevent and minimize the release of

prescribed substances, and to render harmless any that are released. Furthermore, in the case of releases to more than one environmental medium from processes under central control by Her Majesty's Inspectorate of Pollution, conditions must ensure that the *best practicable environmental option* is adopted to minimize pollution of the environment as a whole; the BPEO principle is thus given explicit recognition for the first time in British legislation.

In addition, a general condition will be implied in every authorization that, in relation to any aspect not regulated by a specific condition, the operator must nevertheless use the *best available techniques not entailing excessive cost*. In a prosecution for breach of this general condition, the onus will be placed on the accused to prove that there was no better available technique not entailing excessive cost than was in fact used;[33] since this involves the logically questionable task of proving that something does not exist, the burden of proof will be difficult to discharge. The new approach combining express requirements with a residual duty contrasts with the previous system of industrial air pollution control, where the operators of processes registered under the Alkali etc. Works Regulation Act 1906 were not subject to specific conditions, but had a statutory duty to 'use the *best practicable means* for preventing the emission into the atmosphere from the premises of noxious or offensive substances and for rendering harmless and inoffensive such substances as may be so emitted.'[34] The advantage of conditions is that they dictate precise technical measures, and compliance can more easily be monitored and enforced. On the other hand, conditions may not be comprehensive, and may be overtaken by technological developments, whereas the standards implicit in a general duty evolve with the passage of time. The approach adopted by the Environmental Protection Act is therefore an attempt to realize the benefits of both methods.

3. *Relationship with Other Authorities*
A special limitation is placed on the scope of conditions in relation to processes generating controlled waste.[35] Her Majesty's Inspectorate of Pollution is not permitted to impose conditions regulating the final deposit of such waste on land, which is instead a function of waste regulation authorities. Thus, the Inspectorate is limited to dealing with prior considerations such as waste minimization by requiring, for example, the use of clean technology. This means that pollution control is not completely integrated, since the ultimate destination of the waste produced is outside the discretion of the inspectorate.

Another complication concerns the relationship between integrated pollution control and the system of consents for discharges to water operated by the National Rivers Authority. The National Rivers Authority was established by the Water Act 1989 to assume the regulatory role of the water authorities when their utility functions for water supply and sewerage were transferred to privatized water companies. Its creation on 1 September 1989 was, therefore, a political necessity to facilitate the privatization of the water

23

industry, and could not have been postponed until the introduction of integrated pollution control. This means, however, that discharges of 'Red List' substances to water, which are scheduled for integrated pollution control, are already subject to regulation by the National Rivers Authority. The solution adopted by the Environmental Protection Act[36] is to oblige Her Majesty's Inspectorate of Pollution in such circumstances to incorporate in its authorizations any conditions required by the National Rivers Authority; this is a minimum stipulation, and the Inspectorate could still impose more onerous conditions. However, an authorization may not be granted at all if the National Rivers Authority certifies that it would result in a failure to meet a water quality objective. This fragmentation of responsibility for the same environmental medium is arguably anomalous, and is unlikely to have arisen without the demands of water privatization. The two regulatory bodies are obvious candidates for amalgamation, but the Government prefers instead that they should be given time to settle down and establish their credibility.

4. *The Meaning of 'BATNEEC'*

The meaning of the phrase 'best available techniques not entailing excessive costs' is clearly fundamental to the success or failure of integrated pollution control. The term is derived from the EC air framework directive,[37] although this strictly refers to 'technology' rather than 'techniques'; the Department of the Environment considers that 'techniques' are wider in scope, since they cover operational factors as well as hardware. The Environmental Protection Act provides little elucidation, apart from explaining that BATNEEC includes not only technical means and technology, but also the personnel employed in a process and the buildings in which it is carried on.[38] During the passage of the Bill, however, the Department of the Environment produced general guidance on its own interpretation of the term.[39] This suggests that 'best' means the most effective at dealing with polluting emissions; the effectiveness of a technique must have been demonstrated, but there may be more than one that meets the requirement. 'Available' is defined as procurable by any operator of the class of process in question; this does not imply that the technology is in general use, but it does require general accessibility. Sources may be located outside the United Kingdom, and there need not be more than one, but, if there is a monopoly supplier, the technique must be available to all operators. 'Techniques' embrace both the process used and how it is operated, and include its concept and design, the components of which it is made up and the manner in which they are connected together.

The most controversial aspect is inevitably the proviso 'not entailing excessive costs.' According to the Department of the Environment, although there is a presumption that the best available techniques will be used, this may be rebutted if it can be shown that the costs would be excessive in relation to the environmental protection to be achieved. The example is given of one technology that reduces the emission of a polluting substance by ninety per cent and another that achieves an additional reduction of five per cent at four times the cost; in such a case, the Department suggests that the extra expense

24

may be unjustified unless the emissions are particularly dangerous. Inevitably, there is a strong element of subjectivity in such cost-benefit analyses, although the potential for placing economic values on environmental gains and losses has recently been explored in the Pearce Report.[40] The Government believes that 'action on the environment should be proportionate to the costs involved and the ability of those affected to pay them.'[41] Not surprisingly, there are fears that the requirement to employ the best available techniques may be undermined for reasons of financial expediency. It is also important that the test should apply uniformly, and should not be used to permit lower standards for less affluent operators.

Since BATNEEC is embodied in the legal requirements for authorizations, its interpretation should in theory be a matter for the courts. In practice, however, a great deal will depend on the opinion of the enforcing authorities who decide the conditions to be imposed. Moreover, the Department of the Environment will publish a series of guidance notes for particular processes, giving generic information about discharge limits and preferred technologies; these will be similar in concept to the *Notes on Best Practicable Means* issued under the previous system, which set out the Inspectorate's views on the minimum standards necessary to satisfy legal requirements, and stipulated presumptive emission limits, breach of which would be regarded as evidence that the 'best practicable means' were not being used.[42] The meaning of 'best practicable means' was not judicially determined, although there were some analogous cases dealing with similar terminology.[43] The scope of executive discretion is thus likely to remain very considerable.

5. *The Implementation Programme*

The introduction of integrated pollution control and local authority air pollution control will be phased. In April 1990, the Government stated that the first measures would be implemented at the beginning of 1991,[44] but that schedule has already been extended by four months. The current timetable, which was announced in November 1990,[45] envisages that integrated pollution control will be applied to new plant, processes undergoing substantial changes and existing large combustion plants in April 1991. The latter category is included in order to comply with the EC large combustion plants directive,[46] which imposes a series of targets for reducing atmospheric emissions of sulphur dioxide and oxides of nitrogen. Other existing processes will not be subject to integrated pollution control until April 1992. However, the granting of authorizations will take another four years to complete, and interim consents reflecting the best available performance from installed equipment will initially be given to existing dischargers. Likewise, local authority air pollution control will be introduced in three stages: some new and existing processes, including waste oil processes, will be controlled from April 1991; another group will be brought under control in October 1991, and the remainder will be incorporated in April 1992. To that extent, therefore, the full benefits of both these new systems will be delayed for administrative reasons. It is an unfortunate characteristic of environmental law that

25

legislative reforms often fail to fulfil their immediate promise by remaining dormant on the statute book.

6. *Cost Recovery Charges*

The Environmental Protection Act[47] empowers the Secretary of State to make a charging scheme, prescribing fees that enforcing authorities must charge for applications for the grant or variation of an authorization, and also the charges payable during its subsistence. Separate schemes may be made for integrated pollution control and local authority air pollution control, but they must recoup the relevant expenditure attributable to authorizations. In July 1990, the Government explained its intention to introduce a cost recovery charging scheme, covering the expenses directly related to the regulation of firms, but not those that serve wider objectives such as policy development.[48] It is proposed that Her Majesty's Inspectorate of Pollution should make an initial charge for each application for a new authorization under integrated pollution control, and an annual charge to cover the ongoing costs of compliance monitoring and enforcement. Charges would be based on the number of defined 'components' within a process, and would thus vary according to its size and complexity. In contrast, a standard charge would be made for all processes under local authority air pollution control, except that a lower fee would apply to small waste oil burners. Although this system accords to some extent with the 'polluter-pays principle', it fails to reflect the environmental costs resulting from the polluting effects of authorized processes.

7. *Resource Implications*

A major factor in the effectiveness of any regulatory system of environmental protection is the adequacy of the resources devoted to its administration. In the explanatory and financial memorandum to the Environmental Protection Bill, the Government estimated that the implementation of integrated pollution control would only require an extra fifteen staff within Her Majesty's Inspectorate of Pollution. The notional staff complement of the Inspectorate had been increased from 219 to 240 in October 1989, and an additional ten posts were approved for 1990–91.[49] These numbers seem surprisingly small to oversee 5,000 industrial installations. However, in May 1990, there were still forty-four vacancies, despite a twenty-eight per cent increase in salaries.[50] There had been reports of discontent and resignations within the Inspectorate since its reorganization in 1987,[51] and there was further controversy surrounding the suicide of its director.[52] Moreover, the prospect of new technological requirements for industry inevitably creates a competing demand from industrialists for the same kind of qualified scientists as are needed by the Inspectorate. There have thus been serious difficulties in recruiting and retaining the staff necessary for the administration of integrated pollution control.

About three quarters of the expenditure incurred by the Inspectorate in operating integrated pollution control is supposed to be met through the cost recovery charging scheme. The Government estimates that this annual chargeable expediture should amount to between £3.1 million and £3.2 million at 1988 prices. Charges are also intended to reimburse most of the district councils' costs arising from local authority air pollution control, which the Government considers should broadly match their expenditure previously incurred in enforcing the Public Health Acts. Since the new controls are regarded as streamlining local authorities' existing functions, no increase in public sector staffing is acknowledged to be necessary. These assumptions seem optimistic, and their accuracy remains to be tested. Consequently, there must be some doubts as to whether the new central and local regimes will be sufficiently staffed and financed.

8. *Public Access to Information*
The Royal Commission on Environmental Pollution recommended in 1984 that there should be a presumption in favour of unrestricted public access to information obtained by pollution control authorities.[53] This recommendation was accepted by the Government,[54] and, in 1986, the Department of the Environment reported on the measures necessary to implement it.[55] In addition, the Environment and Safety Information Act 1988, which originated as a Private Member's Bill, established public registers of certain formal notices issued under environmental protection statutes. There has also been a recent EC directive on freedom of access to information on the environment.[56] In 1989, consultative proposals were published by the Department of the Environment for a system of registers for integrated pollution control and local authority air pollution control.[57] The proposals were widely criticized because the registers would have contained only summary information about compliance with authorizations, which could have concealed the most serious instances of pollution by recording annual average performances. Accordingly, the Government later undertook to ensure full disclosure of such data.[58]

The Environmental Protection Act[59] requires both Her Majesty's Inspectorate of Pollution and each district council to maintain registers containing particulars of applications, authorizations and other specified information, which must be open to free public inspection. In order to aid accessibility, a register kept by a district council will include not only details of the processes controlled by itself, but also those in its area under central control by the Inspectorate. There are, however, two important circumstances in which relevant data may be suppressed. First, the Secretary of State can direct that information affecting national security should be kept off the register. Second, a person who is required to supply information may apply to the enforcing authority to have it excluded from the register on the ground that it is commercially confidential. This might happen where details of a secret new process or material might otherwise be revealed to rival companies. The Government insists that an exception will only be allowed if the applicant can convincingly demonstrate that disclosure would harm his or her commercial interests to an unreasonable degree.[60] Nevertheless, the scope of administrative discretion means that the potential exists for a significant limitation of the public right of access to environmental information.

27

9. *Enforcement*

Another important development under the Environmental Protection Act[61] is the introduction of stiffer penalties for offences, and the maximum fine on summary conviction has been increased from £2,000 to £20,000. The deterrent effect of this measure will, however, depend upon the likelihood of prosecutions being brought. The former Industrial Air Pollution Inspectorate rarely prosecuted offenders, but instead cultivated close links with industry, relying on persuasion and co-operation. This relationship was sometimes thought to be too cosy. There is some evidence that Her Majesty's Inspectorate of Pollution is now adopting a more detached stance, and the chemical industry has even complained that it was not involved in the drafting of new guidance notes.[62] However, the enforcement record of the Inspectorate has so far reflected traditional practice, and there were only three successful prosecutions for air pollution in 1987–88 and two in 1988–89.[63] It is, therefore, crucial to the success of integrated pollution control that a more assertive policy towards enforcement should be adopted.

CONCLUSION

The White Paper on the Environment[64] describes the promotion of integrated pollution control as the most important feature of the Environmental Protection Act, and boasts that the United Kingdom is going further than any other European country in introducing it. There can be little doubt that, in principle, it is a development to be welcomed, although it would be wrong to claim that pollution control in the United Kingdom will as a result be fully integrated. The structure of integrated pollution control reveals its ancestry as a development of the previous system of industrial air pollution control, on to which have been grafted mechanisms for dealing with emissions to other environmental media. Like its predecessor, the new regime is selective in the industrial processes to which it may be applied; nor can it dictate the final disposal of waste on land, and, in the case of 'Red List' substances discharged to water, it has an unwieldy overlapping relationship with the National Rivers Authority.

Despite the enhanced role of Her Majesty's Inspectorate of Pollution, there are still many other regulatory bodies concerned with environmental protection. Not only is there the new system of local authority air pollution control, but local authorities are also responsible for waste regulation on land. The control of water pollution from land-based sources is the province of the National Rivers Authority, but the disposal of waste at sea is administered by the Ministry of Agriculture, Fisheries and Food. Furthermore, pollution from offshore installations is controlled by the Department of Energy, while pollution from ships and emissions from vehicles are the responsibility of the Department of Transport.

Not surprisingly, there have been repeated demands for further integration of the regulatory functions of at least some of these bodies. Both the Labour

Party and the Liberal Democrats are committed to the establishment of an Environmental Protection Executive or Agency.[65] In November 1989, the Earl of Cranbrook introduced a Private Member's Bill[66] in the House of Lords, proposing the creation of an Environment Protection Commission with a separate executive arm; although the bill was withdrawn, it served the purpose of stimulating debate about the issues involved. However, the Government believes[67] that any benefits of amalgamation would not outweigh the disadvantages of further administrative upheaval so soon after the establishment of Her Majesty's Inspectorate of Pollution and the National Rivers Authority. It does, however, propose that the Inspectorate, which is currently part of the Department of the Environment, should be given greater independence by becoming a separate executive 'Next Steps' agency, albeit still remaining within that department. In addition, it is considering the possibility of creating an umbrella organization to oversee the pollution control work of both the Inspectorate and the National Rivers Authority, and has suggested that the Inspectorate should perhaps be given the leading responsibility for the regulation of waste disposal.

Clearly, then, the introduction of integrated pollution control should not be regarded as the last word on environmental protection. While it certainly constitutes a worthwhile improvement on previous arrangements, it is a partial solution rather than a complete answer to the problems. The legal recognition of the interdependent nature of the environment and the use of the 'best practicable environmental option' are, of course, greatly to be welcomed. Less desirable are the ambiguous economic qualifications in the standard of 'best available techniques not entailing excessive costs.' Much will depend, however, on the manner in which the new powers are applied. Legislative prohibitions on pollution may give an appearance of stringency, but the discretion of the executive to authorize discharges that would otherwise be unlawful makes administrative practice more important than the letter of the law. The role of Her Majesty's Inspectorate of Pollution, which has had a chequered history, is therefore fundamental. Only if the Inspectorate is provided with adequate resources and fired with sufficient political will can integrated pollution control justify at least some of its optimistic expectations.

NOTES AND REFERENCES

1 *This Common Inheritance: Britain's Environmental Strategy* (1990; Cm. 1200) 136.
2 Alkali etc. Works Regulation Act 1906; Health and Safety at Work etc. Act 1974.
3 Clean Air Acts 1956 and 1968.
4 River Boards Act 1948.
5 Water Resources Act 1963.
6 Water Act 1973.
7 Water Act 1989.
8 *Fifth Report of the Royal Commission on Environmental Pollution* (1976; Cmnd. 6371; chair: Sir Brian Flowers) ch. 9.
9 id., para. 271.

10   Department of the Environment, *Controlling Pollution: Principles and Prospects* (1984; Pollution Paper no. 22) para. 10.

11   *Twelfth Report of the Royal Commission on Environmental Pollution* (1988; Cm. 310; chair: Sir Jack Lewis) para. 2.1.

12   Department of the Environment/Welsh Office, *Integrated Pollution Control: A Consultation Paper* (July 1988).

13   A similar system will also apply in Scotland, where it will be administered by Her Majesty's Industrial Pollution Inspectorate and the river purification authorities.

14   Made under the Environmental Protection Act 1990, s.2.

15   Department of the Environment/Scottish Development Department/Welsh Office, *Air Pollution Control in Great Britain: Review and Proposals: A Consultation Paper* (December 1986).

16   Department of the Environment/Scottish Development Department/Welsh Office, *Air Pollution Control in Great Britain: Follow-Up to Consultation Paper Issued in December 1986* (December 1988); Department of the Environment/Scottish Development Department/ Welsh Office, *Air Pollution Control in Great Britain: Works Proposed to be Scheduled for Prior Authorisation: A Consultation Paper* (December 1988).

17   Directive 84/360, OJ 16.7.84 L188.

18   150 *H.C. Debs.*, Written Answers cols. 405–6 (10 April 1989); 506 *H.L. Debs.*, Written Answers cols. 121–3 (10 April 1989).

19   Second International Conference on the Protection of the North Sea, Ministerial Declaration (1987) para. xvi.

20   Directive 76/464, OJ 18.5.76 L129. The candidate substances are listed in OJ 14.7.82 C176.

21   Department of the Environment/Welsh Office, *Inputs of Dangerous Substances to Water: Proposals for a Unified System of Control* (July 1988).

22   Department of the Environment, *United Kingdom North Sea Action Plan 1985–1995* (1990) para. 13.

23   S.I. 1980 No. 1709.

24   Department of the Environment/Welsh Office, *Control of Pollution Act 1974, The Special Waste Regulations 1980, A Consultation Paper: Special Waste and the Control of its Disposal* (January 1990).

25   Cm. 984 (1990).

26   COM(88) 391 final; COM(89) 560 final.

27   s.3.

28   s.105.

29   143 *H.C. Debs.*, col. 401 (7 December 1988).

30   Environmental Protection Act 1990, s.6.

31   id., s.4.

32   id., s.7.

33   id., s.25.

34   Health and Safety at Work etc. Act 1974, s.5(1).

35   Environmental Protection Act 1990, s.28.

36   id.

37   op. cit., n. 17.

38   Environmental Protection Act 1990, s. 7(10).

39   See 518 *H.L. Debs.*, cols. 767–8 (26 April 1990).

40   D. Pearce, A. Markandya, and E.B. Barbier, *Blueprint for a Green Economy* (1989) 51–95.

41   op. cit., n. 1, p. 13.

42   Her Majesty's Inspectorate of Pollution, *Best Practicable Means: General Principles and Practice* (1988; BPM 1).

43   *Scholefield* v. *Schunck* (1855) 19 J.P. 84; *L.C.C.* v. *Great Eastern Railway Co.* [1906] 2 K.B. 312; *Manchester Corporation* v. *Farnworth* [1930] A.C. 171; *Adsett* v. *K. & L. Steelfounders and Engineers Ltd.* [1953] 2 All E.R. 320; *Martin* v. *Boulton and Paul (Steel Construction) Ltd.* [1982] I.C.R. 366; *West Bromwich Building Society* v. *Townsend* [1983] I.C.R. 257.

44   op. cit., n. 39.

45   Department of the Environment News Release 665 (28 November 1990).

46 Directive 88/609, OJ 24.11.88 L336. See Department of the Environment/Scottish Development Department/Welsh Office/Department of the Environment for Northern Ireland, *Implementation of the Large Combustion Plants Directive: The Proposed Statutory Plan for Reductions of Emissions of Sulphur Dioxide and Oxides of Nitrogen from Existing Large Combustion Plants in the United Kingdom* (18 September 1990).

47 s.8.

48 Department of the Environment/Welsh Office, *Pollution Regulation: Cost Recovery Charges* (July 1990). See also Department of the Environment/Welsh Office, *Cost Recovery Charging for Integrated Pollution Control: A Consultation Paper* (April 1989).

49 164 *H.C. Debs.*, Written Answers col. 96 (18 December 1989).

50 173 *H.C. Debs.*, Written Answers col. 103 (22 May 1990).

51 *The Times*, 31 October 1989, p. 9; *The Times*, 1 November 1989, p. 2; *The Times*, 18 November 1989, p. 4.

52 *The Times*, 28 February 1990, p. 6.

53 *Tenth Report of the Royal Commission on Environmental Pollution* (1984; Cmnd. 9149; chair: Sir Richard Southwood) para. 2.77.

54 Department of the Environment, *Controlling Pollution: Principles and Prospects* (1984; Pollution Paper no. 22) para. 21.

55 Department of the Environment, *Public Access to Environmental Information* (1986; Pollution Paper no. 23).

56 Directive 90/313, OJ 23.6.90 L158.

57 Department of the Environment/Welsh Office, *Integrated Pollution Control and Local Authority Air Pollution Controls: Public Access to Information* (August 1989).

58 *The Times*, 30 January 1990, p. 5.

59 ss.20–22.

60 op. cit., n. 58.

61 s.23.

62 *The Times*, 31 July 1990, p. 7.

63 op. cit., n. 49.

64 op. cit., n. 1, pp. 137, 139.

65 The Labour Party, *An Earthly Chance* (1990) 17–18; Liberal Democrats, *What Price Our Planet?* (1990) 73.

66 Environment Protection Bill.

67 op. cit., n. 1, p. 232.

Land Use Law and the Environment

ROBIN GROVE-WHITE*

I

The emergence of the environment as a mainstream political issue in Britain during the 1980s cannot be understood without an appreciation of the role of the land-use planning system. This system – best seen as the constantly evolving web of law, policy and convention which regulates and orders a range of land uses in the United Kingdom[1] – has been a powerful influence on the distinctive form in which environmental issues have emerged in a British context. This has been so not simply because of the regulatory constraints the system has provided, but also because of the 'cultural' framing created by the discourse and idioms of town and country planning law. These have helped shape certain of the forms in which environmental tensions have been conceptualized and have found public expression.

Hence, the purpose of this paper is to throw light on how, in recent years, land use planning law and its institutional forms have been exploited as an *arena*, in the process helping to frame and shape elements of a distinctively *British* environmental agenda.

Underlying this approach is the author's belief that in particular national cultures, environmental issues and, more generally, political agendas about the environment are not simply 'givens' to be found existing objectively in nature as, so to speak, a set of instantly recognisable physical issues. To be sure, they tend to be manifested in particular physical problems, but the issue of *which* issues emerge as environmentally significant in particular cultural contexts, *why*, and in *what* forms, is not explicable only in terms of objective physical observation. Rather, such questions are social and cultural. Indeed, notions of 'the environment' in particular contexts have been social constructions, the products of frequently turbulent processes of social 'negotiation' in complex cultural settings, rather than self-evident sets of unproblematically identified physical problems for which 'solutions' must then be sought.[2]

Legal commentaries on the relationship between law and the environment[3] tend to take the range and nature of environmental problems as self-evident or given. The key questions then become whether, given these 'problems', legal

* *Senior Research Fellow in Environmental Research Policy, Lancaster University, Lancaster LA1 4YN, England*

instruments and institutions are contributing usefully or effectively to their mitigation. Important and illuminating as this approach is – not least because some of the problems we now face, nationally and globally, really are increasingly serious – it neglects the role of the law as itself a social institution, exerting a major influence on the ways in which our particular society may be able to conceptualize and frame its understanding of what is at stake when we speak of environmental issues.

To illuminate the general point with a familiar example – the costs of access to the courts and the restrictive rules of *locus standi* applying to, say, litigation under the Town and Country Planning Acts ensure that legal precedents are set on the basis of arguments by certain classes of 'interest' rather than others. Crucially, the wider social signals given by such judgments are not simply legal. They are also cultural and normative. They communicate messages, diffused throughout society, that certain kinds of interests and arguments, not others, will have purchase with the courts, thus encouraging future actors to allow for such limitations in comparable instances. In other words, the legal precedents concern not simply juridical substance, but also social framing.

Indeed, one consequence of the messages communicated in this particular case may be to lead those seeking justice in cognate fields to avoid altogether direct recourse to the courts for relief or improvement; instead they may tend to be propelled towards other, surrogate, avenues of redress, in forms not readily recognisable to the legal analyst – for example, apparently 'irrational' political protest, or partisan manoeuverings within the subterranean complexities of administrative practice in a particular field, or even, less constructively, discontented acquiescence, of a kind corrosive to the social authority of the legal system itself.[4]

In the case of the town and country planning system, the legal framework offers a range of opportunities and constraints which can help or hinder the emergence of environmental tensions. The strong *local* territorial base of the system's development plan and development control provisions, the pervasive rhetoric (and practice) of public participation in land-use planning arrangements, the adaptable, indeed protean, character of public inquiry mechanisms under the Planning Acts, and the constant frictions between local and central government on land-use priorities – all of these have afforded nodes for the potential articulation of public concerns, frequently on issues different from (or broader than) those thought appropriate by professionals in the field, be they local authority planners, Department of the Environment (DoE) administrators, or members of the planning bar. Indeed, an important implication of the argument developed in the central section of this paper is that the undue fixation of many commentators on the relationships between the principal 'formal' interests in the legal system – DoE, local planning authorities, the courts, planning applicants and appellants, and (just occasionally, but always residually) third parties – may have helped mask some of the system's most interesting and significant 'environmental' implications over the past two decades, since these have tended to arise outside any such formal matrix.

Overall then, the arguments that follow reflect a particular view of the role of planning law in relation to the environment in the United Kingdom. It is not enough to ground discussion of this role on positivistic definitions of particular environmental problems, and then to proceed from there. Rather, the importance of planning law lies also in the way in which it has contributed in practice – frequently inadvertently – to the manner in which the United Kingdom society's definitions of these problems *have actually been constructed.*

The development of analyses of this kind has a potentially wide social importance. Unless society and, in particular, our political and administrative systems can understand better where their definitions in the environmental sphere are coming from, and especially the social forces and contingencies which are driving those definitions, we will have little collective ability to learn from past experience or to generate the social consensus now needed in this increasingly diffuse and controversial field.

II

The modern era of environmental politics in the United Kingdom can be dated conveniently from 1969–70. Friends of the Earth UK was set up in London in late 1969, the most dynamic of a new wave of environmental groups, and something of a catalyst for the reinvigoration and refocussing of certain of the older, more established groups like the Council for the Protection of Rural England (CPRE) and the Royal Society for the Protection of Birds (RSPB). Furthermore, 1970 saw the publication of the first-ever White Paper on the environment,[5] as well as the creation of the Royal Commission on Environmental Pollution,[6] and, towards the end of the same year, the establishment of the Department of the Environment itself.[7] The latter took place after the election of a new Conservative Government, but the Whitehall preparations had been put well in hand by the preceding Labour administration, which would have taken broadly the same step.[8]

The roots of each of these institutional developments – which proved influential, collectively, for the ways in which environmental tensions developed in the 1970s and 1980s – lay in escalating public concerns in western countries, focussing on the impacts of the pursuit of undifferentiated economic growth as the dominant priority of public policy. The responses to one of the most conspicuous manifestations of these impacts – widespread pollution of environmental 'commons' – reflected a new social dynamic, with 'the environment' as its focus. However, because the problems were pictured officially as largely matters for technical and scientific administration, it was a dynamic which for the most part by-passed the country's mainstream political parties – until the late-1980s when they found themselves forced to take a deeper interest.

Some of the resulting activity, it is argued below, found expression through the planning system, or rather exploited the planning system as one of its

34

several outlets. However, for much of the period, key professional actors within the system remained highly selective in their responses to the emerging phenomenon of new patterns of public environmental concern.

There were several reasons for this. By 1970, the planning system in broadly its modern form was already more than twenty years old. It had developed a powerful culture and internal preoccupations of its own, framed by the aims and distribution of powers and duties in the landmark Town and Country Planning Act 1947. The statutory definitions of 'development,' on the basis of which planners were required to operate the system, excluded afforestation and agricultural land uses; the controls had only indirect purchase on such national policy fields as energy and transport; and the system treated 'pollution' concerns as largely exogenous. Moreover, the avowedly olympian, neutral perspective of planning professionals, encouraged deliberately by their patterns of specialist training and education, encouraged a sense of themselves as above partisan wrangles between 'developers' and 'members of the public', notwithstanding an admirable range of local authority initiatives to extend 'public participation' in the 1970s, in the light of the 1969 Skeffington Report.[9]

Moreover, in their relations with central government, local authority planners faced a continuing set of tensions which were both a legacy of the pattern of relationships and expectations set in motion by the 1947 Act and the result of new social and physical configurations affecting town and country alike. Thus, by the mid-1960s, there was widely shared dissatisfaction with the operation of the development plan system; this led to the Planning Advisory Group report of 1965,[10] and in the early 1970s to the creation, under the Town and Country Planning Act 1971, of the new system of structure and local plans. Changing patterns of transportation – in particular the continuing escalation in levels of dependency on road freight and private car ownership in the 1950s and 60s – were central to the need for this development, and also helped trigger both the massive convulsion of Peter Walker's local government reorganization of 1972 and the extended motorway programme which he sanctioned in 1971.[11] (The Department of Transport was at the time one element in the newly consolidated Department of the Environment.)

Hence, during the 1970s, the planning system faced adjustment to a range of major structural challenges which were, to a considerable extent, distinct from the preoccupations and drives which underlay the public concerns now beginning to be defined and crystallized in an environmental 'movement'. This was true even of the motorway issue, which gave rise to a succession of highly controversial public inquiries under the Highways Acts in the mid-1970s – including the M42, M3 and Aire Valley proposals.[12] Indeed, the purpose of the 1971 motorway programme, as well as of the restructuring of the development plan system in 1971 and of the local government reforms of 1972, was to intensify and streamline the processes of economic growth and expansion on orthodox lines, 'handling' any 'amenity' or 'landscape' side-effects as residuals of these primary priorities. There was little identification by planners with arguments of the kind advanced with increasing sophistication

35

at public inquiries by Friends of the Earth, the Conservation Society, CPRE local branches, and others in opposition to new motorway proposals in the mid-1970s, that the traffic forecasts on which such new plans rested were destructive and unacceptable and that the patterns of development and community disruption they would encourage were socially unfair and unsustainable.[13] Indeed, the reverse was the case. For the most part, local planning authorities saw themselves as bound to assist the implementation of central government attitudes and policies on these matters, seeking only to mitigate the worst local impacts of any new developments that resulted.

Significantly too, there was little enthusiasm within the planning profession for embryonic moves toward more synoptic statutory systems of environmental impact assessment (EIA) in the United Kingdom, based on the European Commission's reinterpretation of the EIA provisions in the United States of Amercia's National Environmental Policy Act of 1970. DoE planners over the period responded negatively to the Commission's intentions[14] and it was not until a directive became inevitable (in the early 1980s) that official attitudes towards the prospect of EIA began grudgingly to change.

1979 was a watershed for planners, as for many other public sector professionals. They encountered the full force of the new Conservative Government's ambition to reduce bureaucratic obstacles to the freer working of 'markets' in the early 1980s. The Local Government, Planning and Land Act 1980 continued the process of strengthening district councils at the expense of the counties, and, in a series of speeches aimed at discouraging supposed local authority restraints on needed developments, Michael Heseltine (then, as now, Secretary of State) made clear the new Government's intention radically to recalibrate and refocus the planning system to encourage the freer and more creative play of market forces.[15] The drive towards claimed internal efficiency within DoE itself was a parallel Heseltine concern in the same mode; the introduction of his MINIS form of management appraisal of policies within the Department[16] and the slashing of DoE's staff complement by one third were two particular achievements. But Heseltine was far from exclusively concerned with reducing bureaucracy. His pioneering role in attempts to revive the prospects of Liverpool in the wake of the 1981 Toxteth riots, and his introduction of urban development corporations, most notably on Merseyside and in the London Docklands, were major moves aimed at by-passing supposed local authority obstructionism, as were subsequent experiments with enterprise zones and simplified planning zones.

In such a turbulent climate, in which long-held assumptions were being challenged almost daily, the planning profession was increasingly unsettled and disoriented.[17] Just as the major legislative changes of the early 1970s had posed enormous adjustment challenges to local authorities, rendering them in the process relatively unresponsive to new patterns of environmental perspective which could not be digested within their revised arrangements of duties and responsibilities, so ministers' assaults of the early 1980s and the continuing pressures on local government finance marginalized all but the most imaginative local authority planning professionals from important

36

developing undercurrents in public awareness of the kind represented by the now increasingly dynamic environmental pressure groups. As we shall see below, this provided the environmental groups with opportunities of which they were not slow to take advantage.

All of these developments shifted formal responsibility in the planning sphere downwards to district council level as the 1980s advanced, whilst in reality moving strategic power and control upwards to central government. The processes were reinforced through a succession of DoE circulars to local authorities,[18] aimed at narrowing the basis on which planning permissions might be refused and in particular at encouraging more relaxed local authority attitudes towards new housing and industrial development. The tensions triggered by these trends by the mid-1980s were considerable, as can be seen from the case studies below. At this stage, it is sufficient to note that central government's inconsistency towards the strategic planning functions of local authorities, particularly at county level, and DoE's *dirigiste* tendency to planning by appeal as the decade progressed, created swelling grass-roots resentments and tensions on which environmental groups were exceptionally well-positioned to capitalize, particularly in the Tory heartlands of the south-east.[19]

However, the crucial dramas surrounding these tensions were played out less in the formal contexts of the courts or Parliament than in the interstices of the planning framework itself – in public inquiries, and in intense disputes about the wording of proposed advice to local planning authorities in circulars, or about demographic assumptions used to underpin housing availability studies; or about the significance of numbers of planning appeals granted over the heads of local authorities.

The actual subject matter of the disputes was thus frequently arcane. Part of the reason they became so pungent politically lay in the increasingly intense development pressures in Conservative constituencies in the south of England. But this would not have become so, had not the planning issues become entangled in the drives and imperatives of the environmental movement which was consolidating in the 1980s. It is necessary now to turn to this dimension.

Whilst, as has been seen above, the principal preoccupations of planning professionals about the efficacy of the planning system in the 1970s and early 1980s flowed from central government pressure to adjust a long-established legal framework to meet changed economic and social perceptions and priorities, this was far from the case for much of the wider public taking advantage of the opportunities offered by the system for debate of public issues.

Before discussing two illuminating controversies within the planning system in the mid-1980s, it is useful to understand the distinctive attitude to the system which had evolved within the national environmental groups in the 1970s and early 1980s.

From the mid-1950s onwards, the planning system and, in particular, Whitehall's land-use decision processes had become slowly more open to public view. Administrative reforms following the Crichel Down débâcle of 1954,[20] and the 1957 Franks report on tribunals and inquiries[21] encouraged progressively greater public expectations of involvement and transparency in planning decisions, challenging 'Whitehall knows best' attitudes.[22] Developments like the creation of the Civic Trust, following the 1957 Civic Amenities Act, encouraged the spread of local amenity societies, and the 1960s were punctuated by a series of *ad hoc* controversies about land-use issues, in which such societies played major roles.[23]

In the new phase of environmental concern from 1970 onwards, the opportunities for involvement in land-use issues presented by the planning system helped a distinctive social movement to begin defining itself. Not only did the system offer opportunities for direct public participation not available in other spheres, such as pollution control,[24] but its structural biases tended to encourage a focus on *specific* land-use developments rather than on 'planning' in the broader, more conceptual sense. This forced groups exploiting the system's opportunities to focus their arguments on individual development proposals. Moreover, because of the lack of clarity in the relevant legislation about the legitimate scope of 'planning' itself – a source of continual tension between the courts, Government, and planners – the system had the flexibility to accommodate some of the more novel articulations of environmental groups, encouraging them to insinuate progressively more strategic and long–term arguments into the discussion of individual developments.[25]

The public inquiry system – whether under the Town and Country Planning Acts, or more industry-specific instruments like the Highways or Electricity Acts – became a particularly important focus. Groups like Friends of the Earth and the Conservation Society, groping for influence and an effective public presence in such fields as energy policy and nuclear power, or the now-proliferating motorways programme, discovered quickly that whilst public inquiry decisions seldom went their way, the system provided nevertheless highly visible entry points for reaching a potentially sympathetic public constituency. Their experience interacted with that of long-established groups like CPRE and others in relation to the energy, minerals, and water industries, and with *ad hoc* local action groups and societies fighting particularly contentious proposals (Windscale, the M3, the M40–M42, the Roadford reservoir, and a dozen other instances could be mentioned).

Indeed, the processes of tactical planning, intellectual preparation and increasingly sophisticated forensic argumentation entailed in this exploitation of the opportunities afforded by the public inquiry system over the period can be said to have played a significant role in the self-definition of the UK's environmental movement. In important respects, the initial consolidation of a domestic environmental agenda became itself a function of the opportunities for public argument afforded by that system.

This reflected, increasingly, a distinctive 'cultural' perspective on public inquiries not shared by planning professionals, administrators, putative developers or the courts. Thus where the latter tended to see inquiries as residual (if individually complex) elements in broader processes of development planning and control, environmental groups were drawn increasingly to public inquiries for their *theatrical*, quite as much as for their forensic, opportunities.[26] Increasingly, the system became used as an arena for public argument, in which complex issues of policy could be dramatized in terms of individual developments, in a fashion which the all-important news media could digest – and moreover in a context in which public rights were to some extent safeguarded by the courts. This was as true of the processes leading up to an inquiry, as of inquiries themselves. In the 1970s and early 1980s, environmental groups – whose processes of interaction through London-based national campaign staffs were increasingly sophisticated – gravitated increasingly towards these opportunities, notwithstanding their complaints about the disadvantages they faced relative to major developers, public or private, in particular cases.[27] Through these processes, they honed their definitions of some solid and reliable 'enemies', such as the nuclear industry and the 'roads lobby'.

Indeed, it is no coincidence that when, in the period 1975–85, intensive agricultural policies and their cumulatively devastating impacts on traditional landscapes and wildlife habitats became a target of campaigning by bodies like CPRE, the RSPB and, subsequently, Friends of the Earth, calls for the integration of the industry into the planning system, making it subject to the patterns of development control and public inquiry to which other industries were subject, formed a central campaigning plank.[28] There could be no better illustration than this emphasis of the confidence such key campaigning groups felt in the opportunities presented by the system for focusing media interest and winning public and political sympathy.

The exploitation of the inquiry system in these new ways caused considerable anxiety in some official quarters. Nevertheless, conscious of the political desirability of containing as much argument as possible within the discipline of an inquiry framework, ministers permitted more and more elaborate extensions of the procedures throughout the late 1970s and 1980s. Indeed, a clear line of such development is obvious in the arrangements for such set-piece affairs, from the 1977 Windscale inquiry onwards – including the Vale of Belvoir coal mine (1980), third London airport (1982), Sizewell (1982) and Hinkley C (1988) inquiries. Rationalized procedures for major inquiries – still controversial – were finally elaborated in a new DoE code of practice and inquiry procedure rules[29] in 1988.

These developments paralleled a continuing debate about the extent to which such inquiries should or should not be concerned with issues of 'policy'.[30] The fact is, whatever the formal position on the 'policy' issue – which tended to be framed, somewhat scholastically, in terms of constitutional proprieties – the inquiry system could not be denied an important, if indirect, policy influence in the environmental sphere over this period. It became a key vehicle through which, in the context of Britain's particular political and administrative culture, an agenda of environmental issues – amongst them, nuclear power, motorways, urban development of rural land, and minerals extraction – was able to become explicit between 1975 and 1989.

The contribution the public inquiry system – and hence land use planning law – has made to the emergence of an environmental politics in Britain has thus been surprisingly significant. However, the earlier sections of this paper pointed to still more specific tensions arising in the 1980s within the town and country planning system itself. These too helped define the range of issues we now think of as unproblematically 'environmental' – as will be plain from the two examples following.

III

The first concerns the issue of housing and industrial development within the green belt. In 1983–84, the Council for the Protection for Rural England (CPRE) led a national campaign aimed at discouraging the then Environment Secretary, Patrick Jenkin, from permitting even modest changes to the boundaries of the green belts around many of the country's major conurbations.[31] The impact of this campaign produced significant shifts in Government attitudes, and helped erect green belts to a new position of symbolic prominence in the public's understanding of environmental issues.

On the face of it, the sequence of events was straightforward. Following the June 1983 general election, Patrick Jenkin succeeded Tom King as Secretary of State for the Environment. His department promptly published two draft circulars, one of them aimed at releasing more undeveloped land for house building, the other at tidying up the boundaries of established green belts.[32] CPRE drew together a coalition of local authority associations, farming bodies, and Tory backbenchers, co-ordinating local pressure to such effect that, within less than three months, the Secretary of State was forced publicly to withdraw his proposals. Subsequently, the House of Commons Select Committee on the Environment, under its new chairman Sir Hugh Rossi, launched an inquiry, the outcome of which was a further vindication of the conservationist position. It was an unsettling political outcome for the Government. From that point on, all of the various political parties vied for ascendency on the issue of 'soundness' on the green belt issue, as a touchstone of environmental good faith – a development which, prior to the controversy, would have seemed inconceivable.

So this had the appearance of a straightforward case of pressure group politics – in which a body (CPRE) with a clear-cut policy commitment (sanctity of green belt) brought together a successful coalition on a politically sensitive matter for the Government.

But the reality was more complex. In the first place CPRE's immediate objective was much more ambiguous than appeared. If anything, it was concerned less with the substance of the draft green belt circular than with that of the draft circular on housing land. Whatever CPRE's public rhetoric about 'violation' of the green belts, it was the housing land circular, with its new shifts of emphasis to favour putative developers over established local authority land-use policies, that had given rise to the greater anxiety by CPRE,

40

in the context of escalating central government disparagement of local authority planners initiated under Michael Heseltine's regime (1979–82). Indeed, it was their success in using the public controversy surrounding the green belt issue to force the associated withdrawal of the second draft circular, that on housing land availability, that seemed the more significant 'policy' victory amongst CPRE's policy staff.

Why then was the green belt issue turned into such a *cause célèbre*? The answer is to be discovered in the broader context of shire- and home-county discontent into which the draft circular was dropped, and the irresistible political opportunity presented by its insouciant publication by the Government, rather than in any truly dramatic crisis in green belt protection itself. After all, as was argued repeatedly at the time, there had been a major expansion of the land area of designated green belt during the four years preceding the dispute, and a Tory Government would have been unlikely deliberately to stir up the hornet's nest of green belt prejudices, affecting parliamentary constituencies almost all of which were Tory-held, in the coarse fashion implied by CPRE's campaign.

The reality was that, in the circumstances of the time, the green belt presented itself to CPRE as a potentially potent political symbol, rather than as an unambiguous threatened category of planning restraint. In response to the series of shifts since 1979 in planning law and policy, aimed at eroding local authority planning controls, and ever-more determined and conspicuous political lobbying aimed at breaching local policies of planning restraint by interest groups like the House Builders' Federation and its new cousin, Consortium Developments Ltd. (whose Chair, Tom Baron, had been Michael Heseltine's specialist adviser on housing policy), substantial tensions and resentments were accumulating in urban and rural areas alike. Arguments about the Government's abolition of the metropolitan counties and the Greater London Council, intense disputes about structure plan reviews in growth areas like central Berkshire and north-east Hampshire, and growing debates about the connections between the decline of the main conurbations and the growth in the rural or quasi-rural population – all reflected a similar unease and anxiety about the implications of the Government's commitment to reduced planning bureaucracy in the name of increased efficiency and market individualism. CPRE's interest in these matters was well-established. It had voiced repeated concern to the Government about the implications for rural areas of the direction in which policy was heading. Moreover, CPRE also felt itself under intense internal pressure from other environmental groups, notably Friends of the Earth, who were seeking to take over its lead on rural conservation issues. Hence it needed to secure its position.

The green belt issue provided a golden opportunity. Erected as the focus for a forceful public campaign, the Government's intention to adjust the ground rules affecting green belt yielded, for the first time, a politically resonant symbol around which widespread local resentments and increasingly aggrieved and demoralized professional opinion could coalesce. Framed in 'environmental' terms, and touching sensitive points of tension between Home Counties' Tory backbenchers and their own ministers, it proved effective. Within a few weeks, CPRE, the Civic Trust and others had co-ordinated pressure from and within relevant constituencies and high-profile meetings with influential back-bench Parliamentary committees, as well as generating a succession of press 'revelations' and an Early Day Motion of more than sixty south-east Tory MPs. Most satisfactory of all, in terms of policy substance, the green belt *brouhaha* drew the more important housing land draft circular along in its wake. Within a few weeks, Patrick Jenkin was obliged to concede defeat and withdraw both of the offending proposals outright.

Truth to tell, the subsequent redraft of the green belt circular turned out to be only a modest advance on the initial draft that had caused so much political upheaval. But that was hardly the point. The true significance of the episode lay in the shock it had delivered to the Government about the political sensitivity of land-use planning issues when framed to echo within the newly emerging environmental discourse. Up till that point, debate about Government planning policies and the future of the planning system had lacked political bite. The green belt campaign altered that. Not only did the Select Committee on the Environment promptly enter the fray – a useful barometer of Parliamentary interest – but a succession of pamphlets from within the Conservative Party, highlighting back-bench anxiety at the Government's broader insensitivity on 'green' issues, also appeared for the first time not long after the controversy.[33] This boost to the embryonic 'greening' of the Tory Party was the true gain for environmental groups like CPRE.

In sum, what this brief saga suggests is that the elevation of green belt to its position of more central prominence in planning policy in the mid-1980s, and any difficulties this has since entailed (in terms of acute development pressures transferred wholesale to *non*-green belt areas, for example), were less a reflection of calculated new priorities of land use policy and practice than of political tensions generating the emergence of a new 'environmental' agenda within Britain's very distinctive political culture, on the back of opportunities presented by the planning system.

A second example of these same processes, equally vivid, arose sub-sequently, in the months (February-May) preceding the 1987 general election. The controversy focused on a pre-electoral package of measures (which became known by the acronym, ALURE – for 'alternative uses of agricultural land and sources of employment') developed principally by the Ministry of Agriculture (MAFF), aimed at assisting farmers to reduce food surpluses by moving away from established patterns of intensive production towards more diverse and, where appropriate, conservation-sensitive farm activities.[34] One ingredient of this package was a draft DoE circular to local planning authorities,[35] announcing the cancellation of the presumption in favour of the safeguarding of agricultural land from development, a presumption which had been in force since the 1947 Agriculture Act – not, on the face of it, an obvious matter for pre-electoral controversy.

This draft circular was seen by DoE and MAFF ministers and officials as an obviously sensible and timely adjustment of planning policy, to reflect new realities in the rural economy. However, environmental groups stood this strategy on its head and converted the issue into a politically volatile one, in the sensitive period in the run-up to the June general election.

As in the green belt case, a particular characterization and public dramatization of a draft circular was turned into a magnet for a volatile cluster of tensions and widely held suspicions concerning the Government's good faith – independently, as it were, of the technical merits of the instrument in question. CPRE and other environmental groups exploited the media and Parliament to advance a simple tactical proposition – that, by removing the formal principle of automatically protecting agricultural land from development, and not offering some equally strong alternative protectionist principle as a substitute, the Government was opening the flood-gates to the potential 'concreting' of large slabs of countryside.[36]

This became politically dangerous for the Government for several reasons. In the period since the 1983–84 green belt controversy, the political stakes on environmental issues had been rising steadily. The rise of the Alliance as a political force in the southern half of the country had contributed to this, and was now of especially acute concern in a number of Conservative constituencies.[37] Local environmental issues had become a particular fulcrum of controversy. The escalation in the numbers and rate of planning appeals upheld by the Secretary of State against local authority decisions – from 8,000 and 29 per cent respectively in 1980, to 13,000 and 40 per cent in 1987 – was a graphic indicator of change.[38] The continuing political sensitivity of planning issues in the south-east had been obvious too in rows during 1986 about the new 'village', Tillingham Hall, proposed unsuccessfully in the metropolitan green belt by Consortium Developments Ltd., and in disputes involving SERPLAN, the House-Builders' Federation and CPRE, about the implications of new population projections for rates of household formation (and hence new releases of housing land) in the south-east.

In these circumstances, and with Nicholas Ridley as Secretary of State, doubts in many rural and suburban constituencies potentially sympathetic to the Alliance about the Government's lack of commitment to sensitive planning were rife. Building on this, and profiting from information leaked in advance from within the Cabinet Committee dealing with the ALURE package, CPRE and other environmental groups launched a sharp and abrasive campaign aimed at the withdrawal and redrafting of the draft circular. The news media took the issue up with a vengeance.[39] After intense argument over ten weeks – including a tempestuous three-hour encounter inside 10 Downing Street at which senior DoE officials voiced acute resentment at CPRE's 'tendentious' campaign – the Government conceded, and negotiated a redraft of the circular, highlighting the new principle of 'protection of the countryside for its own sake', in terms adequate to the environmental groups.[40] Three days later, the general election date was announced. By its prompt climb-down, the Government ensured that a

43

'concreting the countryside' scare did not hand an electoral asset to the Alliance in south-east marginal constituencies.[41]

The conclusions to be drawn from this episode have echoes of those from the green belt saga treated above. In certain specific circumstances – in this case the intended modest recalibration of national land use strategy by means of a new DoE circular overturning previous long-standing advice to local authorities – the planning system again became an arena within which potent political symbols were conjured into being in a context of new environmental concerns – a context which subtly altered their significance. The pressure groups located an opportunity in the politically sensitive pre-election period to advance the importance of an environmental perspective in politically resonant terms. Seen in this light, the policy outcome – the vague new principle of 'protection of the countryside for its own sake' in the revised version of the circular – was actually less significant than the *fact* of a bruising, high-profile row with the Government, resulting in a further modest advance in the political resonance of the environmental agenda as a whole.

IV

In the light of this brief analysis of recent interactions between land use planning and 'the environment' as an emergent mainstream political issue in Britain, certain general points can be made.

In the first place, environmental politics have focused on *structural* tensions in contemporary industrialized societies. They touch on and reflect public anxieties about *long-term* trajectories of economic, social, and political commitment, embedded in our day-to-day patterns of existence.[42] Bodies seeking to modify such trajectories – notably, environmental groups like Friends of the Earth, Greenpeace, CPRE, and others – have had to be opportunistic and inventive in their ways of seeking purchase for their outlooks, within a political culture largely unreceptive to such novel perspectives. Grappling with these issues during the 1970s and 1980s, they gravitated towards those few elements of the polity which could give them leverage in this unpromising context – including the news media, the European Community's institutions, and the planning system. By adapting their concerns to fit most effectively within these frameworks, the groups helped generate a distinctive new 'environmental' agenda, to which, in the late 1980s, the main political parties felt obliged to begin responding seriously.[43]

It was no coincidence that in Britain rural and suburban land use issues played quite as significant a role in these processes as did more dramatic or conspicuous pollution and nature conservation issues. Throughout the decade, the country had a Conservative government. As land use tensions encouraged by Government policies built up in the Conservative home counties and beyond, it was through the planning system outside the metropolitan areas that the resulting frictions were best able to be expressed. Environmental groups found ways of sharpening the impact of these within the governing party, whilst pursuing their own purposes, with far-reaching implications.

It is easily forgotten, in the wake of the global environmental issues that have come to dominate more recent political discussion, that the embryonic 'greening' of the Tory Party in the late 1980s had an important land-use planning dimension. When Mrs. Thatcher made her historic speech to the Royal Society in September 1988,[44] just three weeks before the Conservative Party Conference, putting her imprimatur on the reality of the environmental problematic, she doubtless had many reasons.[45] But almost certainly one of them was the fact that her Government faced a record number of motions at the forthcoming party conference critical of her Environment Secretary Nicholas Ridley's handling of planning issues in Conservative rural and suburban England. Controversies of the kind described in this paper had contributed to this state of affairs, and these in turn had been made possible by the adaptability of the planning system as a potential arena of controversy.

It seems to us 'natural' that the green belt and the safeguarding of agricultural land from development should be seen as key environmental issues in Britain. But without the opportunities presented by the planning system, this would not have been so. They gained enhanced symbolic significance in the 1980s not only because of any significance they possessed as land-use issues, but because the planning system and the disputes that came alive within it thrust them upwards into the political light.

It is through cultural contingencies like these, quite as much as through the findings of science, that environmental agendas around the world are now being constructed.

NOTES AND REFERENCES

1 The paper follows McAuslan's use of the term 'land use planning', to embrace 'town and country planning, housing, road-building, compulsory purchase and community land' (P. McAuslan, *The Ideologies of Planning Law* (1980) 2).

2 R. Grove-White, 'Mysteries in the Global Laboratory' in *Times Higher Educational Supplement*, 26 October 1990.

3 For example, D. Bingham, *Law and Administration Relating to Protection of the Environment* (1973).

4 Compare Sir L. Scarman, *English Law – The New Dimension* (1975). Scarman, (now Lord Scarman) warned the British judiciary of the dangers of the legal system's continuing failure to respond imaginatively to novel public concern and dynamic new political realities such as the developing European Community. He pointed to the likelihood that, confronted with domestic legal institutions inadequately responsive to such changes, people would simply by-pass them and cast around for redress in other ways, with unpredictable social consequences.

5 *The Protection of the Environment* (1970; Cmnd. 4373).

6 The standing Royal Commission on Environmental Pollution was appointed on 20 February 1970.

7 The Department of the Environment was created on 12 November 1970, following the publication of the White Paper, *The Reorganization of Central Government* (1970; Cmnd. 4506) on 27 October.

8 A. Aldous, *The Battle for the Environment* (1972) 20.
9 *People and Planning* (The Skeffington Report) (1969).
10 Planning Advisory Group, *The Future of Development Plans* (1965).
11 P.H. Levin, 'Highway Inquiries: A Study in Governmental Responsiveness' (1979) 57 *Public Administration* 21–49.
12 id.
13 National Motorways Action Committee, *A Case Against the M16 Motorway* (1976); J.G.U. Adams, *Transport Planning: Vision and Practice* (1981); J. Tyme, *Motorways and Democracy* (1979).
14 This distaste was being reflected in 'doubts of principle' raised by DoE officials in evidence to a Parliamentary inquiry into EIA as late as 1980. See House of Lords Select Committee on the European Communities, Eleventh Report, *Environmental Assessment of Projects, Session 1980–81* (1981; H.L. 69) p. 2.
15 As in a succession of speeches by Mr. Heseltine and his deputy, Mr. Tom King, MP (Minister for Local Government) in 1979 and 1981 – see, for example, DoE Press Notices 576 (1979) and 39 (1980).
16 'Efficiency in Britain's Environmental Policy-Making; MINIS Reveal All' in *ENDS Report 107* (1983) 9–12.
17 D. E. Eversley, *Can Planners Keep Up if the Flight from the Cities Continues to Accelerate?* (paper to Royal Town Planning Institute, May 1982); 'Planners – Stand Up and be Counted' in *Countryside Campaigner*, September 1982.
18 For example, DoE circulars 22/80, *Development Control: Policy and Practice;* 9/86, *Land for Private Housebuilding*; 2/81, *Development Control Functions*; et al.
19 Central Berkshire and north-east Hampshire were particular arenas of land-use tension for the Government throughout the 1980s.
20 Crichel Down, a 725–acre piece of land in Dorset, was acquired compulsorily by the Air Ministry in 1937. The *brouhaha* surrounding its post-war fate – including a non-statutory inquiry – is regarded as a major landmark in the relations between the individual and the state in post-war Britain. See R. E. Wraith and B. Lamb, *Public Inquiries as an Instrument of Government* (1971) 202–5.
21 *Report of the Committee on Administrative Tribunals and Enquiries* (1957; Cmnd. 218).
22 J. Delafons, 'Working in Whitehall: Changes in Public Administration 1952–1982' (1982) 60 *Public Administration* 253–72. Also, McAuslan, op. cit., n. 1, ch. 2.
23 R. Gregory, *The Price of Amenity* (1971).
24 Formal rights of public involvement in water discharge consents did not exist until 1985 (when the Control of Pollution Act 1974 was implemented). Similar rights with respect to air pollution arose only with the Environmental Protection Act 1990.
25 I am especially grateful to Richard Macrory for some of the observations in this paragraph.
26 R. Grove-White, 'A Motorway Threat to Nuclear Democracy' in *New Scientist*, 13 March 1980; R. Grove-White, *Public Expectations and the Sizewell Inquiry*, paper to South Bank Polytechnic Conference, October 1982.
27 For example, R. Cowans, 'The Public Inquiries Fraud' in (1960) xxviii *Town and Country Planning*, 8–11; B. Wynne, *Rationality and Ritual* (1982) ch. 4.
28 Council for the Protection of Rural England, *Landscape, the Need for a Public Voice* (1975); M. Shoard, *The Theft of the Countryside* (1980); Friends of the Earth, *Proposals for a National Heritage Bill* (1982).
29 DoE circular 10/88, *Town and Country Planning (Inquiries Procedure) Rules 1988*, issued on 16 June 1988. The code of practice, *Preparing for Major Planning Inquiries in England and Wales* appears as Annex 1 to this circular.
30 D. Pearce et al., *Decision-Making for Energy Futures* (1979); Outer Circle Policy Unit and Council for Science and Society, *The Big Public Inquiry* (1979); B. Wynne, 'The Big Public Inquiry' in *New Scientist*, 28 June 1979; House of Commons Select Committee on the Environment, Fifth Report, *Planning Appeals, Call-In and Major Public Inquiries, Session 1985–86* (1986; H.L. 181).
31 M. J. Elson, *Green Belts* (1986); M. Davies, *Politics of Pressure* (1985). The present author

was involved personally in some of the events described, as CPRE's Director between 1981 and 1987.

32 The draft DoE circulars, *Memorandum on Structure and Local Plans and Green Belt* and *Land for Housing* were made available publicly in August 1983.

33 T. Paterson, *Conservation and the Conservatives* (1984); K. Carlisle, *Conserving the Countryside* (1984); A. Sullivan, *Greening the Tories* (1984).

34 HMSO, *Farming and Rural Enterprise* (1987).

35 Letter to MPs from Rt. Hon. Nicholas Ridley, MP, Secretary of State for the Environment, 13 February 1987.

36 Letter from CPRE's Director to William Waldegrave, MP, Minister for the Environment, Countryside and Planning, 11 February 1987.

37 The Green Alliance, *Electoral Study* (1987).

38 op. cit., n. 36.

39 'Thatcher Go-Ahead for Rural Revolution' *The Observer*, 8 February 1987. This was one of a welter of press, TV and radio reports on the issue.

40 DoE circular 16/87, *Development Involving Agricultural Land*, issued 8 May 1987, especially para. 3.

41 CPRE was planning to launch a major publicity campaign on the issue on the day before the anticipated election announcement, had the Government not conceded the point.

42 op. cit., n. 2.

43 *This Common Inheritance* (1990; Cm. 1200); The Labour Party, *An Earthly Chance* (1990); Liberal Democrats, *What Price Our Planet?* (1990).

44 Rt. Hon. Margaret Thatcher, MP, speech to the Royal Society, London, 22 September 1988.

45 T. Burke, 'The Turning Green Tide' in *Marxism Today*, April 1989.

Agriculture and Environment: The Integration of Policy?

MICHAEL WINTER*

THE DEMISE OF CUSTODIANSHIP

In the immediate post-war period a strong degree of consensus emerged over the appropriate means for protecting the countryside in Britain. Essentially it was assumed that protecting agricultural land from industrial and residential development and providing an appropriate framework of price support for farmers would combine to produce an attractive rural environment. At the heart of this thinking was the notion of custodianship, with farmers perceived as the natural custodians of the countryside.[1] Much of the subsequent history of the way in which the environment has been dealt with in agricultural policy has been to do with a gradual, and at times painful, acceptance that this model of custodianship was at best optimistic and at worst seriously misleading.

In many ways the custodianship model was a direct consequence of the preoccupation with the countryside displayed by the English upper and middle classes from late Victorian times.[2] It was a preoccupation with a culturally specific definition of countryside, in which landscape, buildings, and wildlife encapsulate environmental concerns. Many of the leaders of the environmental groups which emerged in the inter-war period or earlier perceived no conflict between their concern to preserve a picturesque countryside and the need for a healthy agriculture. Indeed, many of the leading members of, for example, the National Trust or the Council for the Preservation of Rural England were themselves landowners.

During the late 1940s and 1950s few voices were raised in protest at agricultural expansion. Food shortages were still real or very recent memories, and much urban development was concentrated in rebuilding cities damaged by bombing. Not until the 1960s did the custodianship role of agriculture come under any form of serious scrutiny. The removal of hedgerows was a cause of considerable concern at this time, and the 'Countryside in 1970' conferences held during the 1960s and presided over by the Duke of Edinburgh, focused, among other things, on this kind of landscape change.[3]

* *Centre for Rural Studies, Royal Agricultural College, Cirencester, Gloucestershire GL7 6JS, England*

I am grateful for comments on an earlier draft of this paper by my colleagues Drs. Susanne Seymour and Charles Watkins, although I remain solely responsible for the contents.

48

But the spirit of these meetings was positive and largely focussed on how planning and management could cater for competing demands upon land. A consensus between agricultural and conservation interests generally prevailed, with agreement over the inevitability of some changes. The emerging global concern over the misuse of pesticides scarcely dented this framework. True there were those in Britain working on the issue from the 1950s, but while Rachel Carson's *Silent Spring* did much to galvanize an emerging radical international environmentalism, local equivalents, such as Kenneth Mellanby's work, were too couched in the muted and careful tones of scientific enquiry to have a similar domestic impact.[4] It was characteristic of the English concern for visual landscape that the British equivalent to *Silent Spring* was a book focusing on the physical destruction of landscape features and wildlife habitats, Marion Shoard's *The Theft of the Countryside*, published as late as 1980.[5]

Thus, during the 1970s, agriculture's position remained relatively untarnished. The 1974-79 Labour Government was committed to continued agricultural expansion, and environmental considerations were relatively minor concerns both in government policy and the political processes directly surrounding agriculture. True, Labour's Countryside Bill, lost when the 1979 election was called, contained clauses with implications for rural land use, but these were relatively marginal to the main thrust of agricultural policy. The 1975 Government White Paper, *Food from Our Own Resources*[6] was firmly expansionist, and as late as 1979 another White Paper, *Farming and the Nation* affirmed that 'the productivity record of our agriculture and its potential for further growth in efficiency provide a sound base on which to promote expansion.'[7] That being so, the Government concluded that 'a sustained increase in agricultural net product is in the national interest and can be achieved without undue impact on the environment.'[8] The brief reference to the environment indicates an awareness of the issue, but nowhere in the report or its annexes is any analysis undertaken to support this assertion. Within one year of these productivist projections, the House of Lords Select Committee on the European Communities produced a report on the Common Agricultural Policy which concluded that 'the upward trend in production, unmatched by increases in demand, must be arrested because the resulting expansion of budgetary costs has become unsupportable'.[9] Once again the environment does not figure as an issue for concern in general agricultural policy discussions, but the contrast with *Farming and the Nation* on the desirability of future increases in production is quite remarkable.

The seeds for the demise of custodianship as an uncontested notion came with the 1981 Wildlife and Countryside Act. The passage of this legislation had a dramatic impact upon the perceived status of agriculture in relation to environmental concerns, because while it did not challenge the primary importance of agriculture in terms of both government policy and rural land use, it did bring into sharp focus some of the consequences of agricultural production both for the environment and, crucially, the public purse if the effects of policy were to be alleviated through compensation.[10] In policy terms

49

the separation of agricultural and environmental concerns at this time was clearly set out in the allocation of departmental responsibilities. The Wildlife and Countryside Bill was prepared by the Rural Directorate of the Department of the Environment (DoE) and the direct implications for agriculture, although debated strenuously at the time, were in retrospect quite minor with limited implications for the Ministry of Agriculture, Fisheries and Food (MAFF). The most important clauses referred to relatively small areas of land, sites of special scientific interest (SSSIs), affecting only about seven per cent of the land surface. The principles of the legislation to protect such special areas were derived from the Porchester Report on Exmoor and were based on the belief that agriculture would continue to be both profitable and expansive.[11] Hence there was a perceived need for compensation reflecting profits foregone to be embodied in management agreements. The Wildlife and Countryside Bill took this principle, developed to protect Exmoor moorland, and extended it to SSSIs, and key areas within national parks, throughout the country. It was a policy based on the identification and protection of key sites. Although it clearly had implications for those farmers concerned it did not represent the development of an environmental policy for agriculture, as members of the environmental lobby groups were only too well aware.

Thus, even before the bill had reached the statute book the tenor of the public debate had shifted to a focus on the wider countryside. Calls for the extension of planning controls and other forms of regulation became strident, and the Government was forced to look beyond the clauses of the 1981 Act and find other means of presenting a wider based policy for agriculture and the environment. This it did through championing the voluntary approach, in particular the work of Farming and Wildlife Advisory Groups, as the best means to secure environmental objectives throughout the farmed country-side.[12]

By the early 1980s it was quite clear that the consensus over agriculture's role in the countryside had broken down and the custodianship case could no longer be simply asserted by the farming lobby as a self-evident truth. It was now widely accepted that agricultural expansion had brought with it an enormous cost in lost wildlife habitats. Thus, reviewing the post-war period in the mid 1980s, Lowe et al. wrote as follows:

> the present generation is witnessing the most comprehensive and far-reaching change of the natural history and historical landscapes of Britain ever experienced in such a short period of time. What is so particularly alarming is that so little is understood about these changes – their magnitude and long-term consequences – yet what is known is simply appalling. The grim chronicle reads as follows: over the past 35 years, the nation has lost 95 per cent of lowland herb-rich grasslands, 80 per cent of chalk and limestone grasslands, 60 per cent of lowland heaths, 45 per cent of limestone pavements, 50 per cent of ancient woodlands, 50 per cent of lowland fens and marshes, over 60 per cent of lowland raised bogs, and a third of all upland grasslands, heaths and mires.[13]

However, these facts alone were not sufficient to prompt the kinds of political and policy changes that have subsequently come about. It was only the onset of a crisis in European Community agricultural policy which permitted policy changes which may yet have a direct and positive effect on the environmental destructiveness of so many contemporary agricultural practices.

THE AGRICULTURAL CRISIS AND CAP REFORM

The warnings of the House of Lords Select Committee on the European Communities in 1980, already referred to, proved to be of far greater prescience than the bullish approach adopted in *Farming and the Nation*. When their lordships returned to the theme of the Common Agricultural Policy in the 1984–85 session of Parliament, the crisis had already begun:

> All the evidence points to a situation in which surplus production of a range of products including milk, wine and cereals, of which the latter are in most serious surplus, will mount to the point where it becomes uncontrollable and the consequential cost unacceptable.[14]

Total gross *FEOGA*[15] expenditure within the EC rose from just over eleven million ECUs in 1980 to nearly twenty million in 1985, while the cost of storing and handling food surpluses within the United Kingdom nearly quadrupled in just four years between 1980 and 1984.[16] By 1984 69.8 per cent of the Community's entire budget was spent on agriculture.[17] On 31 March of that year the EC Council of Ministers approved the introduction of milk quotas. The legal basis for quotas lay in the existing regulations for the co-responsibility levy agreed in 1977, and quotas were first mooted publicly by the Commission in September 1978.[18] Nonetheless the move came as a profound shock to the agricultural industry and signalled that the period of agricultural expansion had come to an end in a far more definite manner than had the impact of environmental policy. Indeed for a while it seemed as though the crescendo of environmental concern in the aftermath of the 1981 Act would come to nothing, with the agricultural policy actors permitted to return to the familiar territory of supply questions.

The implementation of milk quotas became a central policy issue with much argument over the legality of quota trading.[19] In spite of the fears of farmers' groups that the economic consequences of quotas for farmers would be immediate and dramatic, producers proved able to make the necessary changes in farm management. In order to cope with quotas farmers were encouraged to limit their inputs of bought-in feedstuffs and to take a careful look at all their costs, including labour. Thus farm workers, the manufacturers of compound feed and milking machinery and, of course, workers in milk factories all suffered. The number of full-time hired farm workers on dairy farms declined by 27 per cent between 1983/84 and 1988/89, accounting for just over half of all hired job losses in agriculture during this period, although dairy farming accounts for just one in five of all farms.[20]

Some of these management changes had environmental implications. One of the consequences of quotas was a reduction in the use of purchased feedstuffs and a corresponding concentration on improving the utilization of grass. This led some farmers to destroy certain ecologically interesting

51

grasslands by 'reclaiming' them. Others switched from hay to silage. Before quotas a quarter of dairy farmers did not make silage, but by 1988/89 this figure had dropped to just eight per cent.[21] Pollution from silage effluent has become one of the major sources of agricultural pollution, but in 1984 the environmental consequences of quotas were scarcely considered. When the implementation of quotas came to be considered by the House of Commons Agriculture Committee, little evidence was received which might have caused the Committee to take a wider view of the issue.[22] But this was not the case with the House of Lords Select Committee on the European Communities, whose 1984/85 consideration of the Common Agricultural Policy drew general attention to the environmental aspects of CAP reform.[23] The committee had conducted an exhaustive survey of the environmental implications of proposed reforms to the CAP's structural policies in 1984, which clearly proved a turning point in its approach to the CAP and the means for achieving reform.[24]

Whereas the 1980 committee received evidence solely from farming and food organizations or individuals, in 1985 a small group of environmental groups provided written evidence on the intricacies of the CAP, although oral evidence continued to be the preserve of the actors in the agricultural policy community. These groups included the Council for the Protection of Rural England (CPRE), the Countryside Commission, and the Institute for European Environmental Policy. Whilst there may be considerable debate amongst political scientists over the influence of select committees on the content of government policy,[25] there can be little doubt that the list of expert witnesses and published evidence casts considerable light on shifts in policy debate and political agendas. It may be open to debate as to whether groups such as the CPRE can really claim to have achieved insider status within the agricultural policy community, but the Council certainly achieved in the mid 1980s a high profile as a commentator on farming issues rather than topics defined in a traditional manner as environmental issues. In a series of publications the CPRE has steadily attacked the CAP and offered its own recommendations for policy reform.[26] Of particular importance to its stance has been an acceptance that agriculture should continue to be supported but in ways which would encourage environmental protection rather than further increases in production. The CPRE is by no means a radical organization, neither in terms of green or leftist tendencies nor any commitment to the radical liberalism of market Conservatism. It is, moreover, firmly based in the shire counties with strong links with the farming community. Its critique of agricultural policies, therefore, firmly rests upon adapting traditional interventionist policies to support farming. As far as the House of Lords Select Committee on the European Communities was concerned the CPRE certainly seemed to be pushing at an open door. Whether their lordships' stance reflected a dissatisfaction with market Conservatism is open to conjecture, but certainly the 1984 report on *Agriculture and the Environment* roundly condemned the Ministry of Agriculture for its narrow interpretation of certain EC policies and its lukewarm commitment to conservation policies.[27]

Notwithstanding the conclusions of select committees and the pressure of environmental groups, a lead was needed from government. In 1985 this still seemed some way off with MAFF reluctant to expand its remit. At first sight this seems rather curious, for government departments might usually be expected to act in a proprietorial or even imperialist manner. In the case of MAFF, though, there had been concern for some time that it might be threatened. Its reluctance to press for new duties might be construed as a defensive posture in the light of threats to hive off other activities. Thus, in the late 1970s MAFF's jostling with the Department of the Environment over land drainage drew this observation from Richardson et al.:

> There was considerable sensitivity within MAFF that if land drainage was lost, the rot would set in and other functions would be lost to other departments, for example . . . health and safety, and education and training. . . . In theory a number of MAFF's functions could quite logically be transferred to other departments, thereby undermining the rationale for MAFF's existence.[28]

Additional concern within the Ministry on the implications of the series of Rayner reviews of civil service departments only served to reinforce the uncertainty within the Ministry. The National Farmers' Union (NFU), fearing the loss of its special relationship with a central government department with a seat at Cabinet, publicly pressed the Ministry to take a more positive role. In particular, the Union urged MAFF to assume the environmental mantle. This had less to do with farmers' commitment to environmental matters than with the NFU's determination to avoid ceding controls over agriculture to the DoE or any other conservation agency.[29] However, as late as 1985, the Government resisted attempts to insert changes in the 1985 Wildlife and Countryside (Amendment) Bill which would have given the Ministry a statutory responsibility to further conservation, a much stronger injunction than its existing duty to take conservation considerations into account in carrying out its duties. Yet just one year later the Ministry was given responsibilty to promote conservation under the terms of the 1986 Agriculture Act. This, of course, was a bill sponsored and promoted by the Ministry itself. The change of mood reflected a growing confidence within the Ministry that an integration of environmental concerns within its remit would serve to counter threats both to the Ministry and to agricultural support policies within the EEC. In its efforts to limit the cost of agricultural support, particularly the horrendous cost of storing surplus produce, the Government had turned to conservation as a politically acceptable policy for the support of agriculture.

The process had, in fact, begun as early as 1984 when in the autumn of that year the United Kingdom successfully moved amendments to article 19 of the new EC structures regulation, which had emerged from the ten-year review of the structures policies in 1983–84. These amendments would enable 'agricultural departments of Member States to designate areas where 'the maintenance or adoption of particular agricultural methods is likely to facilitate the conservation, enhancement or protection of the nature conservation, amenity or archaeological and historic interest of an area', and to give financial incentives to encourage appropriate farming practices in these environmentally sensitive areas (ESAs).'[30]

THE GREENING OF POLICY

Once under way the greening of the Ministry, at least as far as policy rhetoric was concerned, proceeded rapidly. ESAs provide the first case in point. ESAs are worth considering in some detail because their progress has been lauded by government and the farming lobby alike as offering an acceptable way forward for the integration of environmental and agricultural management.[31] In contrast to other protected areas, such as SSSIs and National Parks, ESAs are the responsibility of the Ministry of Agriculture (or Scottish and Welsh Office Agriculture departments) rather than the DoE and its agencies. The distinction between landscape protection and nature conservation so characteristic of the British approach to countryside management has been blurred by describing the new areas as 'of national environmental significance'.[32]

The broad criteria set by MAFF, the Welsh Office Agriculture Department and the Department of Agriculture and Fisheries for Scotland were that the ESAs should be areas:

(i) of national environmental significance;

(ii) whose conservation depends on the adoption, maintenance or extension of a particular form of farming practice;

(iii) in which there have occurred, or there is a likelihood of, changes in farming practices which pose a major threat to the environment;

(iv) which represent a discrete and coherent unit of environmental interest;

(v) which would permit the economical administration of appropriate conservation aids.

In return for a commitment to continue traditional farming where it was important environmentally, farmers would receive annual payments. The scheme began in six areas in 1987 and was welcomed as 'helpful' and 'imaginative' by the Country Landowners' Association (CLA) and the NFU which also commented favourably on the rates of payment which were seen as 'realistic' and 'likely to attract a good response'.[33] The organizations were also able to point to the positive aspects of ESAs which were seen as providing management payments rather than compensation.[34] In 1987 it was announced that a further six ESAs would be created in England and Wales, as well as new sites in Scotland and Northern Ireland, doubling the budget to £12 million.

The main characteristic of ESAs is their simplicity. Standard rates in each area are set, although in some areas the variety of landscape types and habitats necessitates a second or third tier of payment. The agreements vary according to the farming circumstances of each ESA. Most include restrictions on fertilizer use and stock densities, prohibitions on the use of herbicides and pesticides and on the installation of new drainage or fencing.[35] Farmers also

54

agree to maintain landscape features such as hedges, ditches, woods, walls, and barns. But the day-to-day details of their management procedures are not subject to scrutiny, nor do payments vary to reflect profit foregone. Indeed in very few cases has income been reduced. On the contrary, areas of traditional farming have been chosen and the payments reflect the need for these methods of farming to continue. By May 1989 2,700 farmers in England, covering some 103,640 hectares, had applied or were already participating in the scheme, representing 87 per cent of the expected uptake set by the Ministry, or 31 per cent of the total area covered by ESAs.[36]

If ESAs provide one of the main planks of the Government's new approach to environmental issues in agriculture, then new uses for land and buildings provide another. A characteristically Thatcherite set of policies – notwithstanding the former Prime Minister's much publicized 'green' speech to the Royal Society in 1988 – has been concerned with the encouragement of farmers to diversify their activities, either through new types of farming or through non-agricultural activities. The policy events which marked the development of these issues are relatively recent, and the earliest were not directly related to agriculture at all. A White Paper, *Lifting the Burden*, published in 1985, contained a chapter on the planning system which indicated a presumption in favour of allowing development unless 'that development would cause demonstrable harm to interests of acknowledged importance.'[37] This was followed in March 1986 with a circular, in which explicit encouragement was given for the conversion of redundant farm buildings.[38]

The full significance of these developments for agriculture became clear in February 1987 when, amidst a storm of controversy, the DoE and Agriculture Departments jointly issued a folder of documents under the general title *Farming and Rural Enterprise*. The documents became known as the ALURE (alternative land uses and the rural economy) package, and addressed the issues facing the agricultural industry whilst also speculating on some of the possibilties for land and income diversification. Most controversial of all were the rather imprecise proposals, given much media publicity, to ease restrictions on the industrial and residential development of agricultural land, primarily through a diminution of the Ministry of Agriculture's role in the planning process.

The proposals and policies, for the ALURE package was a combination of both, were the outcome of a policy group commissioned to produce proposals which would stem the tide of criticism of the Government's rural policies from within the shire counties:

> The establishment of the ALURE policy group had the highest priority within the most senior members of the Cabinet. The group consisted of three government ministers representing MAFF and the DoE, two Westminster backbenchers, one European MP, two members of the Upper House and a small group of party specialist advisers. The existence of the group and details of its membership and agenda were confidential, but its remit is known to have included agriculture, rural services and amenities as well as green and non-farm business issues. Above all, the need to keep in mind the Party's overall political objectives was a prime objective for the group.[39]

As Cloke and McLaughlin have also pointed out, the first known meeting of the group took place at the same time as the Conservative Party Conference in October 1986.[40] Within months of the launch of the ALURE package in the following February, the country went to the polls. Notwithstanding the political agenda, the launch of the package was far from successful. There appeared to be hostility between the DoE and MAFF, not least because the Ministry issued its statement twenty-four hours before the agreed date in an attempt to steal the limelight and appease critics at the annual general meeting of the National Farmers' Union, where a no-confidence motion in the Minister of Agriculture was under debate.[41] In so doing, though, the Ministry inevitably emphasized the benefits for farmers, not only from its own package of measures, which we turn to below, but also from the freeing up of agricultural land for development proposed by the DoE. The outcry from the Tory shires took some weeks to subside.

In reality both sets of measures were quite modest. As far as the Ministry was concerned, the proposals included a doubling of the number of ESAs, financial assistance for farm diversification schemes, and an increase in woodland planting promoted through a farm woodland scheme for farmers prepared to remove land from agricultural production. The farm woodland scheme was a particularly novel departure in that it introduced annual payments to compensate farmers for the loss of income from agriculture. Another land diversion scheme post-dating the ALURE developments was the set-aside scheme introduced by the EC in 1988 to pay farmers to take land out of arable production. It has accounted for some 110,000 hectares in the United Kingdom in the first two years, just 2.5 per cent of the eligible area.[42]

A NEW ISSUE: POLLUTION

In many ways it may seem rather curious to refer to agricultural pollution as a new issue for, as has been indicated earlier, it has been a cause of concern for many years. Certainly by the close of the 1970s official interest was growing and in 1979 the Royal Commission on Environmental Pollution issued a major report highlighting the complex issues surrounding the use of pesticides and fertilizers and the possible implications for environmental pollution.[43] The Commission pointed to the anomaly of the 1974 Control of Pollution Act which exempted farmers from prosecution if their actions were in accordance with good agricultural practice:

> In our view, it is important that pollution should be considered in the formulation of the codes of practice that define 'good agricultural practice'. Before embarking on our study, we explored this point among others in a preliminary discussion with MAFF. We were not persuaded that sufficient attention was being paid to the pollution that might be caused by agriculture. That problems might arise was recognized, but we were left with the impression that such problems were regarded as secondary in importance and as unavoidable concomitants of food supply. The approach appeared to us to beg the real question: whether the changes that have occurred, or are likely to occur, in agricultural

practices are such as to call for new attitudes in dealing with the consequential problems of pollution or even, perhaps, for some constraints on these practices.[44]

In truth the defence has only once or twice been successfully pressed in court.[45] Nonetheless, the anomaly assumed a symbolic significance and the House of Commons Select Committee on the Environment pressed for amendments, which were duly enacted under the 1989 Water Act.[46] In some ways it is probably the very complexity of the issues which have diminished their political salience until recently. Whereas the destruction of wildlife habitats and landscape features, such as hedgerows, woodland or wetland, is highly visible and immediate, many forms of pollution are less likely to be either noticeable or so easily traced to source. This is certainly the case for pollution caused by nitrogenous fertilizers entering aquifers or pesticide residues in food.

Pollution incidents which may have a greater immediate impact are associated with sudden and dramatic discharges of, for example, silage effluent or slurry particularly in water. In recent years such incidents in agriculture have increased and have received considerable publicity. In the south west, for example, the newly instituted National Rivers Authority (NRA) continued the intensive advisory campaign amongst farmers launched by the South West Water Authority in 1984, but this is being wound up in 1990 as the regulatory framework becomes tighter. MAFF grants for improving storage and handling facilities are available and were increased from thirty per cent to fifty per cent in 1989, and the NRA's maximum fines have been increased tenfold to £20,000.[47]

The slurry/silage problem, although likely to be persistent for many years to come, especially in adverse weather conditions, should be relatively easy to control compared to pollution caused by chemical fertilizers. The European Commission's 1980 drinking water directive became law in the UK in 1985, with a maximum admissible concentration of nitrate of 50 mg. per litre.[48] In a number of areas of the United Kingdom, especially the east, concentrations have been persistently above this level in ground water supplies. The problems for the authorities are manifold. In the first instance not all commentators are convinced that the standards are either desirable or attainable in the first place.[49] Even the extent and details of the 'problem' are contested. Moreover, the means for controlling levels are technically complex. It is difficult to implement the 'polluter-pays principle' (PPP) in a situation where the pollution may have occurred twenty, thirty or more years ago in a very different agricultural policy climate and where there is considerable dispute amongst agronomists and environmentalists over the precise causes of pollution:

> Wittgenstein reminded us that rules do not contain the rules for their own application and the PPP is surely a principle whose grounds of application are always likely to be both 'local' and keenly questioned. . . . What little evidence there is suggests that formal regulation of increasing farm pollution raises a range of particularly intractable administrative, compliance, and enforcement difficulties. More than any other, perhaps, the issue of nitrate pollution exemplifies these difficulties and shows why efforts to resolve

them are essentially contested. Anyone perversely wishing to present a challenging test for the applicability of the PPP would be hard pressed to devise anything more intractable than the question of nitrate pollution.[50]

It is scarcely surprising, therefore, that one analysis of the United Kingdom's response has criticised it for 'non-decision making'.[51] However, the 1989 Water Act substantially alters this picture with the prospect of tougher regulations in response to the proposed EC nitrate directive and a new code of good agricultural practice for the protection of water. At present, though, the main attempt to limit nitrate pollution rests with the establishment of ten nitrate sensitive areas, where farmers can benefit from financial inducements to limit their use of fertilizers, and nitrate advisory areas where intensive advisory campaigns are being conducted to reduce potential pollution.

THE CONTRADICTIONS OF POLICY: VOLUNTARISM VERSUS REGULATION

A major contradiction lies at the heart of many of these policies and, in particular, the manner in which they are implemented. While the current Government has been forced to adopt interventionist policies it has, nonetheless, retained its commitment to a non-directive policy style through its assertion of the rights of individuals, especially their property rights.[52] Thus the maximum freedom is given to owners and managers of land to interpret regulations, a philosophy of voluntarism. Examples of this are legion. Even a compulsory and highly regulatory scheme such as milk quotas was interpreted in the United Kingdom so as to allow the maximum degree of freedom of action for individual producers, particularly with regard to the legitimation of quota trading even if this was of doubtful legality *vis-à-vis* EC regulations.

Participation in the set-aside, the farm woodland scheme, and environmentally sensitive and nitrate sensitive areas schemes is voluntary in each case, in spite of the fact that the Government maintains that each provides an essential plank for the re-orientation of agricultural and environmental policies in the United Kingdom. In the case of set-aside, the Government has indicated its wish for the scheme to be used for positive environmental purposes and yet, with the exception of a premium scheme in the east of England which offers extra money for environmental management, this is left entirely to the managers of the land concerned. Similarly the MAFF farm woodland scheme and the Forestry Commission's woodland grant scheme, allow considerable freedom to recipients of grant to determine aims and objectives on a continuum from fully commercial hardwood planting to amenity planting. No attempt has been made to determine the appropriate balance between different types of planting at a national level. Moreover, insufficient account may be taken of the ecological implications of some planting on exisiting semi-natural habitats. It has to be said that the Forestry Commission is obliged to consult local authorities and, in certain instances other conservation agencies, on the desirability of the proposed planting schemes. This may allow modifications to some schemes according to environmental criteria but as each scheme is considered on its merits and no attempt is made to co-ordinate responses between authorities, no sense of overall planning for the public good emerges or, indeed, is intended.

A number of environmental groups and commentators are understandably concerned at the implications of voluntarism for the outcome of policies with supposedly environmental objectives. Exactly the same worries surround the encouragement given to farmers to find new uses for their buildings. The Government's intention is that this will provide stimulation to rural employment and housing, yet in reality many farmers eschew craft or industrial conversions and opt for lucrative residential conversions at the top end of the housing market. The impact of such conversions on both rural employment and rural housing need is minimal.

Alongside the constraints of voluntarism there remains a deep-rooted agricultural fundamentalism. Although the key symbols of the diversification debate – alternative land uses, diversification, value-added, agro-forestry, and so on – are very 'new', the style is reminiscent of the heady days of the 1940s and 1950s when the aim was to 'get agriculture moving'. The message that comes through is that land abundance presents new market opportunities, and that the role of government is merely to ease the transition for individual landholders and farmers. In reality such an approach is fundamentally misconstrued and detracts from the real need to consider land use in terms of national needs, environmental protection, and appropriate rural development.

In one area, however, fundamentalism and voluntarism are threatened. Water quality has become very much the preserve of the Department of the Environment and the National Rivers Authority, with MAFF seemingly marginalized, and EC directives have a major impact in defining pollution levels. Nonetheless, nitrate sensitive areas were set up and are being run by MAFF, very much according to the ESA model of voluntary involvement and compensatory payments. Indeed, this is the beauty of NSAs for the farming interests, for while their activities are causing what has been defined as pollution by the EC, the private water companies and MAFF are currently paying the cost of agriculture's nitrate pollution. However this is probably only a short-term arrangement, as the EC is planning a new directive requiring designation of nitrate vulnerable zones, in which farmers would be compelled to adopt nitrate conserving practices with only short-term compensation likely to be available.[53] Thus on the pollution issue, at least, farmers face a major departure from post-war norms on environmental controls in agriculture.

A NEW DEAL: SUPPLY CONTROL, REGULATION, AND ENVIRONMENTAL GOODS

The ESA programme, with its direct and tangible commitment to conservationist farming, marked a significant departure for agricultural policy, with farmers effectively paid by the agriculture departments to 'produce' environmental goods.[54] So far calls to extend the ESA approach more widely across the countryside have been ignored by MAFF and any expectation that the Ministry's farm and conservation grant scheme might extend ESA-style farming is misplaced. In terms of agricultural politics it is possible to argue that:

> ESAs have enabled a renovation of the 'permissive corporatism' which has, in the post-war period, been the approach to state involvement in the regulation of agriculture preferred by farming and landowning interests.[55]

However, in the light of the growth of regulatory policies regarding pollution and the increased commitment of the National Farmers' Union to supply control mechanisms rather than free-market solutions to agricultural surplus problems, it is scarcely surprising that some environmentalists have renewed calls for policies which combine the payment principles of ESAs with firm regulatory mechanisms for the achievement of the necessary goals. Divisions between the environmental bodies have emerged on this issue. The CPRE, for example, while pressing for stronger controls over farmers' actions with regard to pollution or the destruction of landscape features has developed the notion of environmental management payments (EMPs) as an extension of the ESA principle.[56] EMPs would be available to all farmers as an alternative to high-output agriculture, but the scheme would remain voluntary. In some ways this is close to the Ministry and EC's extensification scheme but what worries the Council is the lack of a direct environmental component to plans for extensification, which are essentially directed towards reducing production.[57] The Royal Society for the Protection of Birds, on the other hand, has declared itself in favour of a direct link between cutting surpluses and environmental payments, with farmers paid directly for farming in an environmentally favourable way and for reducing output.[58]

CONCLUSIONS

The focus of this paper has been on agricultural policy in the United Kingdom, particularly in England and Wales, but this has to be seen against the backcloth of European policies and economics. One of the reasons for the somewhat traumatic experience of the United Kingdom in the European Community is the nature of its agriculture. Although, at one level, the structure and economic efficiency of British farming has made it profoundly well suited to court economic success within the framework of the CAP, in other ways it has been ill-equipped to cope with the political and ideological framework of the CAP. Almost overnight United Kingdom agriculture found itself in very unfamiliar territory. Having been on the political margins of an urban-industrial polity for many years, it suddenly came to the centre-stage of politics and has remained there ever since. Despite the efforts to reform the CAP over the last decade, the underlying special legal status of agriculture remains unchanged within the framework of the Treaty of Rome. As Francis

Snyder has demonstrated, this has bedevilled Community law and political economy almost since its foundation.[59]

More recently, of course, agricultural problems lie at the root of the GATT's faltering progress in the Uruguay round of negotiations. Snyder points out that constitutionally the Rome Treaty can be interpreted as conferring upon 'agriculture a privileged legal, political and economic status which is equivalent to that of the European Community's *basic economic principles*'[60] (my emphasis). It is this, as well as the much vaunted strength of the European and national farm lobbies, which lies at the heart of the patchy progress towards CAP reform and the development of environmental policies for agriculture. It also means that the first Thatcher Government slowly came to realise that the reform of agricultural policy would demand more than merely the assertion of market principles. In the early 1980s, a combination of Thatcherite economics and the Rayner scrutiny of the civil service conspired to mute MAFF's voice both nationally and within the EC. As the problem of surpluses in Europe, and the environmentalist critique at home mounted, MAFF seemed devoid of ideas, direction or comment. This changed dramatically in the mid 1980s with MAFF almost assuming the mantle of a green ministry. However, its corporatist relations with the farming industry and competition with the DoE still pose severe limitations on the extent to which it can legitimately present itself as the harbinger of an environmental policy for agriculture. Despite the important advances that have been made in this direction, the Ministry's future is still far from clear and environmental policies for agriculture remain fragmented.

NOTES AND REFERENCES

1 For an account of the post-war developments in countryside planning and protection see A. Gilg, *Countryside Planning: The First Three Decades 1945–76* (1978).

2 On the development of British natural history and environmental concerns and their place in the cultural history of twentieth century Britain see D. E. Allen, *The Naturalist in Britain* (1976); P. Lowe and J. Goyder, *Environmental Groups in Politics* (1983); J. Sheail, *Nature in Trust: the History of Nature Conservation in Britain* (1976); M. J. Wiener, *English Culture and the Decline of the Industrial Spirit 1850–1980* (1981).

3 Conferences were held in 1963, 1965, and 1970. They resulted in some practical conservation work especially with regard to the creation of new landscape features, and in promoting this approach were something of a precursor to the Farming and Wildlife Advisory Groups which have become so significant in the 1980s. On these developments see: G. Cox, P. Lowe, and M. Winter, *The Voluntary Principle in Conservation: A Study of the Farming and Wildlife Advisory Group* (1990).

4 R. Carson, *Silent Spring* (1963); K. Mellanby, *Pesticides and Pollution* (1967). For an account of pesticides and conservation in the post-war period see N. W. Moore, *The Bird of Time: The Science and Politics of Nature Conservation* (1987); J. Sheail, *Pesticides and Conservation: The British Experience 1950–1975* (1985).

5 M. Shoard, *The Theft of the Countryside* (1980).

6 Ministry of Agriculture, Fisheries and Food, *Food from Our Own Resources* (1975; Cmnd. 6020).

7 Ministry of Agriculture, Fisheries and Food, *Farming and the Nation* (1979; Cmnd. 7458) para. 7.

8 id., para. 24.

9 Select Committee on the European Communities, Thirty Second Report, *The Common Agricultural Policy, Session 1979–80*; (1980; H.L. 156) para. 66.

10 On the politics of the Wildlife and Countryside Act see: P. Lowe, G. Cox, M. MacEwen, T. O'Riordan, and M. Winter, *Countryside Conflicts: The Politics of Farming, Forestry, and Conservation* (1986); G. Cox and P. Lowe, 'A battle not the war: the politics of the Wildlife and Countryside Act 1981' (1983) 4 *Countryside Planning Yearbook* 48; G. Cox and P. Lowe, 'Countryside politics: goodbye to goodwill?' (1983) 54 *Political Quarterly* 268.

11 Lord Porchester, *A Study of Exmoor* (1976).

12 G. Cox, P. Lowe, and M. Winter, op. cit., n. 3.

13 P. Lowe et al., op. cit., n. 10, p. 55.

14 Select Committee on the European Communities, Seventeenth Report, *The Reform of the Common Agricultural Policy, Session 1984–85* (1985; H.L. 237) para. 105.

15 *FEOGA* is the *Fonds Européen d'Orientation et de Garantie Agricole* or the European Agricultural Guidance and Guarantee Fund, established in 1962 under Regulation 25/62 using Article 40 (4) of the Treaty of Rome. It has a large guarantee section which finances the cost of subsidies, surpluses, and market control and a much smaller guidance section which attempts to influence the structure of the industry. See F. Snyder, *Law of the Common Agricultural Policy* (1985); F. Snyder, *New Directions in European Community Law* (1990).

16 op. cit., n. 14, para. 30.

17 id., para. 34.

18 M. Tsinisizelis, *The Politics of the Common Agricultural Policy: A Study of Interest Group Politics* (1985). Unpublished Ph.D. thesis, University of Manchester.

19 G. Cox, P. Lowe, and M. Winter, 'The Political Management of the Dairy Sector in England and Wales' in *Political, Social and Economic Perspectives on the International Food System*, eds. T. Marsden and J. Little (1990).

20 Milk Marketing Board, *Five Years of Milk Quotas* (1989).

21 id., p. 20.

22 House of Commons Agriculture Committee, First Report, *The Implementation of Dairy Quotas, Session 1984–85*, (1984; H.C. 14).

23 op. cit., n. 14.

24 Select Committee on the European Communities, Twentieth Report, *Agriculture and the Environment, Session 1983–84* (1984; H.L. 247).

25 G. Drewry (ed.), *The New Select Committees* (1985).

26 The main CPRE publications in this vein are as follows: D. Baldock and D. Conder (eds.), *Can the CAP Fit the Environment?* (1985); G. Sinclair, *How to Help Farmers and Keep England Beautiful: A Research Study on EEC Farm Funding* (1985); D. Baldock and D. Conder (eds.), *Removing Land from Agriculture: The Implications for Farming and the Environment* (1987); CPRE, *Paradise Destruction: How Europe's Farm Policies are Destroying the Countryside* (1990); T. N. Jenkins, *Future Harvests – The Economics of Farming and the Environment: Proposals for Action* (1990).

27 op. cit., n. 24.

28 J. J. Richardson, A. G. Jordan, and R. H. Kimber, 'Lobbying, administrative reform and policy styles' (1978) 26 *Political Studies* 54.

29 G. Cox, P. Lowe, and M. Winter, 'Agriculture and conservation in Britain: a policy community under siege' in *Agriculture: People and Policies*, eds. G. Cox, P. Lowe, and M. Winter (1986) ch. 11 at p. 181.

30 J. Blunden, N. Curry, et al., *A Future for our Countryside* (1988) 175.

31 This section of the paper draws on: D. Baldock, G. Cox, P. Lowe, and M. Winter, 'Environmentally sensitive areas: incrementalism or reform?' (1990) 6 *Journal of Rural Studies* 143. For another general account see C. Potter, 'Environmentally sensitive areas in England and Wales: an experiment in countryside management' (1988) 5 *Land Use Policy* 301.

32 D. Baldock, et al., op. cit., n. 31, p. 145.

33 id.

34 id.

35 id.

36 id., p. 147.

37 Department of the Environment, *Lifting the Burden* (1985; Cmnd. 9571) circular 14/85.

38 Department of the Environment, *Development by Small Businesses* (1986; circular 2/86).

39 P. Cloke and B. McLaughlin, 'Politics of the alternative land use and rural economy (ALURE) proposals in the UK' (1989) 6 *Land Use Policy* 235.

40 id., p. 237.

41 id., p. 238.

42 Jenkins, op. cit., n. 26, p. 26.

43 Royal Commission on Environmental Pollution, Seventh Report, *Agriculture and Pollution* (1979; Cmnd. 7644; chair: Sir Hans Kornberg) (1984; H.L. 247).

44 id., para. 1.8.

45 W. Howarth, 'Water pollution: improving the legal controls' (1989) 1 *Journal of Environmental Law* 25.

46 G. Cox and S. Seymour, 'Agricultural pollution and its regulation in the west country' (1990); paper presented at Franco-British Association for Rural Studies, Exeter.

47 id.

48 id.

49 B. T. Croll and C. R. Hayes, 'Nitrate and water supplies in the United Kingdom' (1988) 50 *Environmental Pollution* 163.

50 G. Cox and S. Seymour, 'Nitrates in water and the politics of the "polluter-pays-principle" ' (1990); paper presented at the 14th European Congress of Rural Sociology, Giessen.

51 M. Hill, S. Aaronvitch, and D. Baldock, 'Non-decision making in pollution control in Britain: nitrate pollution, the EEC Drinking Water Directive, and agriculture' (1989) 17 *Policy and Politics* 227.

52 G. Cox, P. Lowe, and M. Winter, 'Private rights and public responsibilities: the prospects for agricultural and environmental controls' 4 *Journal of Rural Studies* 323; M. Winter, 'Land use policy in the UK: the politics of control' 7 *Land Development Studies* 3.

53 Personal comment by S. Seymour.

54 D. Baldock, et al., op. cit., n. 31, p. 156.

55 id., p. 157.

56 Jenkins, op. cit., n. 26.

57 id.

58 Personal comment by C. Potter.

59 F. Snyder, op. cit. (1990), n. 15.

60 id., p. 107.

Conservation – a Secondary Environmental Consideration

LYNDA M. WARREN*

INTRODUCTION

During the late 1980s there was an upsurge of interest in the environment at all levels of society from the green consumer through to the Prime Minister. At government level, this interest culminated in 1990 in the publication of *This Common Inheritance: Britain's Environmental Strategy*,[1] a White Paper on environmental issues, and the enactment of the 'Green Bill', correctly entitled the Environmental Protection Act. Unfortunately, the Government's new-found enthusiasm has done little for the cause of conservation and may even prove to have been detrimental. The reasons for this are complex. One factor is that there is a fundamental misunderstanding of what environmental protection is all about and, in particular, a failure to appreciate the importance of conservation for its long-term success. This paper traces the evolution of the law relating to conservation and its social context in an attempt to explain the failure of government to pay adequate attention to such a crucial topic.

THE NATURE OF CONSERVATION

It is difficult to define the limits of conservation. The broadest meaning of the word encompasses the built environment and art treasures as well as the natural environment but the conservation of man-made things is beyond the scope of this paper. Within the natural world, conservation can include biological, geological and physiographical features. In the latter case there is considerable overlap with the maintenance of the amenity value of landscape features.

Conservation has no single purpose. In many cases the object of conservation will be the protection of a species for its own sake and for the pleasure that its existence brings to people. Most members of the Royal Society for the Protection of Birds (RSPB), for example, would probably justify their membership in similar terms. A less traditional view, but one that is of great importance, is that the purpose of conservation is to ensure sustainable use for future generations. This is the approach promoted in the World Conservation

* *Cardiff Law School, University of Wales College of Cardiff, P.O. Box 427, Cardiff, CF1 1XD, Wales*

Strategy, published by the International Union for Nature Conservation in 1980, and is central to the conservation policy of a number of voluntary organizations such as the World Wide Fund for Nature.[2] Conservation, in this context, is much more than the protection of a few interesting species or physical features and can be applied to all types of resources whether living or non-living, renewable or non-renewable. Whereas nature conservation can be categorized as a kind of activity and one in relation to land or water comparable to other uses such as farming, industrial development, or fishing, the conservation of resources is a philosophical approach of relevance to the management of all activities that consume resources. Nature conservation is then merely a management tool for achieving the much broader objective. Unfortunately, the narrower view of nature conservation is the one that is most widely held. This has led to confrontation from other user groups, notably farmers, fishermen and some recreational users, who adopt an anti-conservation stance in the face of what they see as threats to their livelihoods or interests.

A further reason for antagonism is the popular misconception that conservation means preservation. It is still not generally accepted that nature conservation does not mean an end to all other activities. Sites have to be managed in order to retain the quality of their habitats and this often involves practising traditional farming techniques. Only occasionally is the preservation of individual plants and animals warranted. Very rare species, such as the lady's slipper orchid, which, in the United Kingdom, is known only from a single specimen in Yorkshire, are under greatest threat from collectors. They can be protected by legislation prohibiting interference but this is very costly to enforce and can involve round-the-clock wardening. It is not, therefore, undertaken lightly and most nature conservation is far less artificial.

Two main factors have influenced the development of legislation for conservation in this country. The first is the undeniable inter-relationship between agricultural practice and the natural world. None of the vegetation in Great Britain is natural, but is all the result of human activities. The wilderness country in some of our National Parks owes its origin to centuries of woodland clearance and land management. Many upland heather moors are prime examples of artificially produced vegetation managed solely for game shooting. Animal distributions may not be completely natural either and one of our commonest animals, the rabbit, was introduced into Britain in historic times.

When Parliament first considered site conservation in the 1940s, therefore, it set it firmly against a farming background. The result is that conservation has been regarded as secondary to agriculture and there are inevitable conflicts of interest whenever it is suggested that conservation interests should be paramount. The farming context is also responsible for the lack of attention afforded the marine environment during the first thirty years of statutory site protection and partly explains why marine conservation has proved such a difficult objective to achieve.

The second factor is the strong voluntary involvement in conservation in

Great Britain. This started in the last century with organisations such as the National Trust[3] and includes national bodies with specialist interests, such as the RSPB and the Woodland Trust, together with those with a general conservation remit such as the Fauna and Flora Preservation Society[4] and the World Wide Fund for Nature.[5] Interestingly, both of these organisations were originally involved mainly in foreign projects, such as the conservation of African game, and only developed a domestic programme subsequently. There is also a network of county conservation trusts[6] which own nature reserves and play an important role in protecting local conservation interests.

The voluntary movement has been instrumental in procuring legislation for nature conservation.[7] While the results achieved have proved successful to a degree, the voluntary element has given rise to unforeseen consequences. The image that conservation has of being a trivial luxury is due, in no small part, to its association with bobble-hatted bird-watchers and the like. If the Government had taken the lead earlier, conservation might not be regarded as lightweight.

Voluntary organisations may also be partly responsible for the confrontation that is generated by conservation. Although Greenpeace and Friends of the Earth, which are the voluntary environmental organizations with the highest public profiles, are more concerned with pollution than nature conservation, their media-conscious approaches have ensured that their views strongly influence both public and political opinion about conservationists in general, leading to unnecessary alienation. Even when legislation has been enacted, there is an impression that this has been done as a concession to vociferous campaigners and lobbyists rather than as something central to government policy.[8] The lack of any real conservation measures in the Environmental Protection Act 1990 and in *This Common Inheritance* indicates that there has been no fundamental change in the Government's view since the passing of the Wildlife and Countryside Act 1981. The greening of the Thatcher Government appears only to extend to a belated recognition of the need to combat pollution and does not presage any broader acceptance of conservation philosophy.

CONSERVATION LAW

There is no discrete body of law that could be readily identified as conservation law. The most important legislation is included in Acts that also cover amenity and access such as the National Parks and Access to the Countryside Act 1949 and the Wildlife and Countryside Act 1981. Planning law also has an impact on conservation, albeit a far too limited one, and pollution law, which is scattered through several statutes, is obviously of great, but indirect, relevance.

There are three types of conservation law: species protection; habitat protection; and the protection of natural beauty. The earliest legislation was for the protection of birds.[9] This has been updated and modified on many occasions subsequently and is now contained in Part I of the Wildlife and Countryside Act 1981 but still retains a similar format.

Although the protection of sites of natural beauty is one of the objectives of the National Trust, which was founded in 1895, statutory protection for habitats and landscapes did not appear until 1949. During the early 1940s the Government set up a number of committees to report on various aspects of land use. These reports gave rise to major statutory changes in the immediate post-war years, of which the National Parks and Access to the Countryside Act 1949 was the final link. The Act dealt both with the protection and public enjoyment of the wider countryside and with habitat conservation. The former was made the responsibility of the National Parks Commission set up under the Act while the latter was entrusted to the newly created Nature Conservancy. This division of responsibility continues to this day in respect of England, despite drastic changes to both of the original organizations, but has been finally ended in Wales by the Environmental Protection Act 1990.

The most important legislation for nature conservation is the Wildlife and Countryside Act 1981 as amended by the Wildlife and Countryside (Amendment) Act 1985. Part I of the Act consolidates and amends previous species protection measures; Part II extends habitat protection to land other than nature reserves and to the sea; Part III amends the law on access to the countryside.

SPECIES PROTECTION

The main provisions[10] for the protection of individual species of plants and animals are to be found in Part I of the Wildlife and Countryside Act 1981. Birds are treated separately. It is an offence, punishable by a fine, to collect, injure or kill a wild bird, to collect or destroy its eggs or to collect, damage or destroy its nest.[11] In the case of species listed in Schedule 1, which are birds given special protection either at all times or just for the breeding season, higher fines may be imposed.[12] It is also an offence to disturb Schedule 1 species.[13] There are several defences of which the most important is that the act was carried out in accordance with the terms of a licence issued under s.16. Licences for scientific, educational or conservation purposes, or for bird-ringing or for photography may be issued by the Nature Conservancy Council (NCC). Licences for other purposes may be issued by the Secretary of State for the Environment or by the Agriculture Minister.

Although the provisions were drawn up after consultation with the RSPB and are based on the earlier Protection of Birds Acts 1954–1967, the conservation measures are tempered by other considerations. For example, not all birds are given the protection outlined above. It is not an offence for anyone to kill birds listed in Part I of Schedule 2 outside the close season,[14] so wildfowling can continue without hindrance during these times. Section 2(6), however, does empower the Secretary of State to make a Special Protection Order with respect to any of these birds which effectively creates an extra closed season of fourteen days. Special Protection Orders have been made during severe winter conditions. Before making such an order, though, the Secretary of State must consult with shooting interests.[15]

Furthermore, authorized persons, who are defined under s.27(1) as including the owner or occupier, or any person authorized by a variety of bodies including the local authority, are entitled by s.2(2) to kill the pest species listed in Part II of Schedule 2 at any time. A further, very important, defence provides that there is no offence if the otherwise unlawful act is the incidental result of a lawful operation and could not be reasonably avoided.[16]

For birds other than Schedule 1 species, s.4(3)(c) provides that the offences do not apply where an authorised person has acted out of necessity to prevent serious agricultural damage or damage to fisheries. This has become a let-out clause. A good example of its misuse is provided by the shooting of predatory birds by fish farmers. Although a licence could be issued for the purpose of preventing serious damage to fisheries under s.16(1)(k) fish farmers have had to rely on the defence of s.4(3)(c) because the appropriate Agriculture Minister has not issued licences. This is not satisfactory. The minister must consult with the NCC before issuing licences[17] which does provide an opportunity to influence the terms of the licence whereas s.4(3)(c) merely requires the defendant to show the necessity of the act.

Similar protective measures (and defences) are extended by ss 9–13 to wild animals listed in Schedule 5 and plants listed in Schedule 8.

Section 14 makes it an offence to introduce a non-native species into the wild, either by release or by allowing it to escape, unless the introduction complies with the terms of a licence. In the case of fish or shellfish the licence is issued by the Agriculture Minister.[18] Section 16(10) requires the minister to consult with the NCC as to the exercise of these functions and prohibits her or him from granting a licence unless advised by the Council as to the circumstances in which such licences should be given. Again the advantage lies with the Agriculture Minister who is not bound to act on the advice. A good example of this bias is provided by the practice regarding Manila clam farming.

The Manila clam is considered to be of great commercial potential. The Ministry of Agriculture, Fisheries and Food (MAFF) have issued licences to shellfish farmers under the Molluscan Shellfish (Control of Deposit) Order 1974.[19] It is a condition of the licences that the clams are covered by mesh in order to contain them. MAFF claim that, because of this condition, the clams are not being introduced into the wild and do not, therefore, come under the licensing requirements of the Act. Adult clams are not mobile animals, however, and the real danger of the species becoming established in the wild is from reproduction. Manila clams produce mobile larvae which could not be retained by the mesh. There is controversy, however, as to whether or not the species is able to reproduce in this country. MAFF think it cannot but the NCC think that it might. It is a warm water species and MAFF are of the opinion that seawater temperatures, even in the south, are never high enough for the larvae to be viable. The NCC have doubts, however, because it is known from experience in Canadian waters that Manila clams can adapt to colder conditions.[20] Nevertheless, the present position is that MAFF do not formally consult the NCC under the Act although they do seek their advice informally where proposed farms are on intertidal sites of special scientific interest.

Power to vary the schedules of protected species lies with the Secretary of State.[21] One of the functions of the NCC under s.24, however, is to review Schedules 5 and 8 every five years and to advise her or him of any changes that should be made. The advice given after the first quinquennial review in 1986 was not completely adhered to. For example, the NCC proposed that the basking shark and the freshwater pearl mussel should be added to Schedule 5[22] but this was not done.[23] Both species are of limited commercial importance and their inclusion was objected to by the fisheries ministers.

SITE PROTECTION

Species protection alone is insufficient. It is also necessary to conserve habitats through some form of site protection. There are three main legal mechanisms for protecting sites: national nature reserves (NNRs); sites of special scientific interest (SSSIs); and marine nature reserves (MNRs). NNRs were introduced in Part III of the National Parks and Access to the Countryside Act 1949, which empowers the NCC to enter into agreement with landowners for their establishment and management.[24] Where there is no possibility of concluding such an agreement, or where an agreement has broken down, it is possible for the NCC to acquire the land compulsorily under ss.17 and 18. Reserve management is to be for the purpose:

(a) of providing . . . opportunities for the study of . . . matters relating to the fauna and flora of Great Britain and the physical conditions in which they live, and for the study of geological and physiographical features of special interest in the area, or

(b) of preserving flora, fauna or geological or physiographical features of special interest in the area,

or for both these purposes.[25]

Section 20 empowers the NCC to make byelaws for the protection of NNRs. These may, for example, restrict access or prohibit interference with plants or animals in the reserve but may not interfere with the vested rights of owners or occupiers of land in a reserve.

The 1949 Act s.23 also imposed a duty on the NCC to notify the local planning authority of any areas of special interest by reason of their flora, fauna or geological or physiographical features but did not provide any statutory protection for these SSSIs. The Countryside Act 1968 s.15 improved matters somewhat by empowering the NCC to make agreements with owners and occupiers restricting their rights in return for payment but did not enable the NCC to take any action where no agreement could be reached. The Wildlife and Countryside Act 1981 sought to remedy this defect by

69

strengthening the notification system. Section 28 obliges the NCC to notify owners and occupiers of SSSIs of any potentially damaging operations. Four months notice to the NCC is required before these can be carried out during which time the NCC may seek a management agreement. Operations authorized by planning permission are excluded. In the case of so-called super SSSIs, section 29 enables the Secretary of State to make Nature Conservation Orders whereby potentially damaging operations are prohibited for a longer period for negotiation of a management agreement or to proceed with compulsory purchase. Compensation is payable by the NCC for certain losses incurred as a result of a section 29 order.[26]

The marine nature reserve provisions, which are also contained in the Wildlife and Countryside Act 1981[27], are based on the same format as the NNR legislation but the powers of the NCC are considerably restricted. Thus MNRs can only be designated by the Secretary of State upon application by the NCC, rather than by the NCC itself as is the case for NNRs. A long list of 'relevant authorities' is excluded from the effects of the byelaws with the result that an NCC byelaw to prohibit 'the killing, taking, molestation or disturbance of animals . . . in the reserve'[28] cannot, for example, apply to fish as these come under the remit of the local sea fisheries committees.

CONSERVING THE LIVING LANDSCAPE

The 1949 Act was concerned with the preservation of the natural beauty of the countryside and with facilitating public access to it as well as with nature conservation. The Act established a National Parks Commission with responsibility:

(a) for the preservation and enhancement of natural beauty in England and Wales, and particularly in the areas designated . . . as National Parks or as areas of outstanding natural beauty [AONBs];

(b) for encouraging the provision . . . of facilities for the enjoyment of [National Parks] and for the enjoyment of the opportunities for open air recreation and the study of nature afforded thereby.[29]

Despite these responsibilities the National Parks Commission had no real powers apart from the designation of National Parks and AONBs, administrative powers lying with local planning authorities.

National Parks are defined in s.5(2) as 'extensive tracts of country' of 'natural beauty' with opportunities for open-air recreation which is in accord with the recommendation of the Dower report[30] as endorsed by the Hobhouse Committee.[31] AONBs are based on 'conservation areas' proposed by Hobhouse.

ORGANIZATIONS

The Environmental Protection Act 1990 transforms the NCC into three national councils and a Joint Nature Conservation Committee. Reorganization has been a constant theme throughout the history of the NCC and its predecessor. The Nature Conservancy was created by royal charter in 1949 with three main functions: to provide scientific advice on the conservation and control of flora and fauna; to establish and manage nature reserves and to organize scientific services for conservation. Further details of its responsibilities were laid down in the 1949 Act. In 1964, the Nature Conservancy lost its independent status to become a committee of the newly constituted Natural Environment Research Council (NERC). Then, in 1973[32], scientific research into conservation was transferred to the Institute of Terrestrial Ecology of NERC and the conservation functions were separated off under a new statutory body, the Nature Conservancy Council.

The NCC retained responsibilities for nature reserves, for the provision of advice to government on policies for or affecting nature conservation, and for the provision of advice and information to the public, but its scientific functions were reduced to the commissioning or support of research relevant to its functions. In practice in-house research has been continued by the Chief Scientist Directorate.

Responsibility for preserving the living landscape has never been part of the NCC's role. It was originally given to the National Parks Commission by the 1949 Act. This was replaced with the Countryside Commission by the Countryside Act 1968 and its functions enlarged. Whereas the National Parks Commission had particular responsibility for natural beauty in National Parks and AONBs, the Countryside Commission had similar responsibilities for the whole countryside.[33]

The Environmental Protection Act 1990 merged the Countryside Commission's functions in respect of Wales with nature conservation functions in a new Countryside Council for Wales.[34] A similar merger is proposed in relation to Scotland by the Natural Heritage (Scotland) Bill which is currently before Parliament. In England, however, the two functions are to remain the responsibilities of separate agencies.

DEFECTS IN THE SYSTEM

The legislation for nature conservation outlined above, especially that in relation to site protection, has not been successful.[35] The fundamental reason is that nature conservation is not given a sufficiently high priority.[36] More powerful interests, especially agriculture, have thwarted any attempt at greater protection. From the very start, the legislation and administrative procedures have been characterized by two factors, a subservience to agriculture, and following from this, a voluntary approach. The whole structure of statutory nature conservation can be traced back to the conclusion of the committees set up in the 1940s to consider land use. Thus the Scott report on Land Utilization in Rural Areas[37] recommended that agriculture and forestry should not be subject to planning controls because, far from being a problem, they were instrumental in preserving rural

71

landscapes. This conclusion is a recognition of the important role of agriculture and forestry in creating and maintaining the countryside but fails to acknowledge that changes in farming practice might prove detrimental. Unfortunately, the belief that there would be no conflict between rural land use and natural beauty was taken up by the Dower report on National Parks[38] and endorsed by the National Parks Committee.[39]

The 1949 Act was the final piece of legislation based on the recommendation of these committees by which time there was little opportunity for manoeuvre. The Agriculture Act 1947 promoted farming production by giving security of tenure and guaranteed markets, and the Town and Country Planning Act 1947, by excluding agriculture from development controls, further protected the farmer. This left the 1949 Act to deal with conservation issues against an established rural-planning framework.

The separation off of nature conservation *per se* from wider aspects of countryside conservation began, unintentionally, with the Scott report. The terms of reference of the committee were:

> To consider the conditions which should govern building and other constructional development in country areas consistently with the maintenance of agriculture, and in particular the factors affecting the location of industry, having regard to economic operation, part-time and seasonal employment, the well-being of rural communities and the preservation of rural amenities.

The committee interpreted these terms of reference very widely. National Parks were advocated on recreational grounds, presumably as part of the rural amenities and as necessary for the public well-being. Nature reserves would have been much more difficult to justify in the remit, if they had not been tagged on after National Parks. The Dower committee, set up in response to the Scott report, was concerned with National Parks. It was not until after its report was published that the Wild Life Conservation Special Committee was set up, consisting of scientists.[40] Its recommendations[41] led to the creation of the Nature Conservancy, which was essentially a scientific body, and the inclusion of its nature reserve functions in the 1949 Act.

In retrospect, the cause of nature conservation was ill-served by the 1949 Act. The Scott report, and its successors, were well intentioned in seeking to broaden their review to include conservation issues but the legislation is still firmly seated in a land-use planning context. Because National Parks were essentially recreational, it was necessary to distance them from nature conservation, hence the separate administrative structure but, if there was to be any conservation legislation, it had to be in the 1949 Act and was thus caught by the agricultural immunities that percolated through the legislative package. The planning context is nowhere more clear than in the SSSI provisions which gave no protection at all to the sites but merely required local planning authorities to be notified of their existence. With a post-war presumption in favour of development it is not surprising that many SSSIs have been lost.[42] Even now, development on an SSSI can proceed if there is planning permission[43] which means that conservation interests may be overridden by pressure for development.

72

The case of *R. v. Poole Borough Council ex parte Beebee and others* (1990) (unreported) illustrates the inadequacies of the present system to protect conservation interests. The case concerns a grant of planning permission for housing development on heathland. The site is an SSSI because it supports a number of protected species including smooth snakes, sand lizards, Dartford warblers, nightjars, and hobbies, and is a potential Special Protection Area under the EEC birds directive.[44] Mr Justice Schiemann, in dismissing an application for judicial review of the decision to grant permission, said that the local planning authority had to strike a balance between the strong political/ historical arguments in favour of the development and strong conservation reasons against it. One particularly worrying aspect of this case is that the Secretary of State did not feel any need to call in the application despite a request to do so by the NCC.

Conservation also comes off second best where there are conflicts between agriculture and conservation. It is true that the Act gives the conservation bodies powers to establish NNRs but not without payment to the landowner either in connection with a management agreement or by compulsory purchase.[45] In the case of super SSSIs, section 30 of the Wildlife and Countryside Act provides for a landowner to be compensated for any depreciation in the value of his land brought about through a nature conservation order. This is surely a planning anomaly. Compensation for refusal of planning permission was more or less abolished in 1947.[46] Because agriculture continues to be, for the most part, outside of planning controls,[47] however, farmers are still given almost total freedom to use their lands as they wish.

The strength of the farming and forestry lobbies is so great, even now, that it has been claimed to be responsible for the break-up of the NCC. The afforestation of the Flow Country in Scotland was fiercely opposed by the NCC in a moment of uncharacteristic outspokenness. Although the site was saved, the cost was dear. The decision to split the NCC, which was announced[48] without warning and with no prior discussion with the Chairman, was made at Cabinet level and was widely rumoured to have been demanded by the Secretary of State for Scotland.[49] The country landowner is still very powerful in Scotland and conservation is intricately enmeshed with other rural uses. It was felt that a Scottish-run NCC would not have been so adamant in its opposition to the afforestation but would have balanced the economic advantages against the conservation losses.

The predominance of agricultural interests underlies the voluntary approach to conservation. The logic is simple. The countryside is created by farming and forestry; these should not be subjected to planning controls because to do so would deter production unnecessarily; therefore the farmer has freedom of action; therefore any measures restricting this freedom for conservation purposes should be with the agreement of farmers and should not be to their detriment. From the Government's point of view, the voluntary approach provides a useful excuse for not alienating those members of the electorate with other interests in the countryside and for not spending enough money.

73

There are numerous examples of the failure of the voluntary approach to protect conservation interests. Mr W. S. Morrison, speaking on SSSIs in the second reading debate on the 1949 Act, made a chillingly accurate prophecy:

> Commissioners and Conservancies can notify, inform and recommend, but if the notification, information or recommendation is disregarded, nothing happens ... As a broad administrative point ... there is no surer way of asking for trouble than providing for a conflict of opinion and failing to provide some means for resolving that conflict.[50]

On the other hand, Lord Bellwin, who introduced the Wildlife and Countryside Bill into the House of Lords, said that:

> the cause of nature conservation has been well served in the past, by the efforts of voluntary organisations and their parliamentary supporters, and by the willing co-operation of landowners and farmers. We intend that the Bill should promote and assist such activities ....[51]

The Wildlife and Countryside Act required the NCC to renotify every SSSI and inform the owners and occupiers of any potentially damaging operations that were to apply in future. The effectiveness of this new scheme is highly dependent on the co-operation of the landowner. The NCC do not have the resources to purchase every SSSI if no agreement can be reached, nor would it be desirable for them to do so. Achieving such co-operation requires an art of diplomacy beyond the skills of the average NCC field officer. Put simply, a landowner, probably a working farmer, is to be informed that certain activities are likely to be damaging and may not be undertaken until certain conditions are met. In other words, his freedom of action is being curtailed by strangers. As originally drafted, s.28 required the NCC to give notice of a proposed notification and allowed three months for objections to be made. As a result, many SSSIs were destroyed by farmers during the consultation period in order to avoid the possibility of restraints being imposed. It took four years for this disastrous provision to be rectified and even then it was done through a Private Member's Bill[52] albeit with government support.

The inadequacies of the voluntary approach have been even more in evidence in the implementation of the MNR legislation. The procedure outlined in the 1981 Act is for the NCC to submit applications for MNR designations to the Secretary of State. Draft orders must be advertised and there is provision for a public inquiry to be held if an order is opposed. In practice, the NCC must resolve all objections before making a submission to the Secretary of State and the inquiry procedure has not been used. Very many organizations, government bodies, and individuals are likely to have an interest in proposed MNRs which makes the task of the NCC onerous. Furthermore, an objector knows that, providing the objection is not totally trivial, the Secretary of State will not entertain a proposal in the face of such opposition. This amounts to a right of veto. The result has been a considerable delay in the designation of the first MNRs and compromises that weaken the byelaws. In the case of Loch Sween, which was to have been the first MNR in Scotland, the NCC have encountered such fierce local opposition that they have lost heart and now see no prospect of a statutory reserve. It is reserve. It is not that the locals are totally against conservation; indeed there is talk of establishing a voluntary marine reserve there. The real difficulty is a fear of controls being introduced from above. Similar problems arose in connection with the existing statutory MNRs at Lundy and Skomer, both of which already had voluntary status before negotiations began. The NCC blame the present antipathy on the bad feeling generated by the SSSI renotification in Scotland.

This brings into question the effectiveness of the NCC itself. As a statutory adviser to the Government it should be independent of the Government but this is not the case. At the same time, the Government will not take responsibility for the way it runs its affairs. Many of its difficulties stem from its inability to negotiate from a position of strength. Voluntary co-operation may be an ideal objective, but it is much easier to achieve with a little bit of pressure.

There is no doubt that conservationists have been critical of the NCC for a long time and a need for a change was recognised within the organization itself. Indeed, it had just completed an internal review when the break-up was announced. The split into three country councils is seen as divisive, however, and although a fresh start may bring some improvements, the restructuring has proved costly both in terms of money and time. After the Act was passed in November 1990, the NCC went into a state of limbo. Most efforts concentrated on getting the reorganizations worked out in time for the split in April 1991. At the time of writing (January 1991) it is impossible to say whether the new system will prove beneficial because, at the moment, no one, including staff of the NCC, knows how it will operate. Policies are for the new councils to decide and these do not formally exist as yet.

The merger of the NCC and the Countryside Commission in Wales and Scotland has been viewed with less hostility. There is such an obvious overlap in functions that unification appears sensible. Thus the NCC is responsible for the conservation of 'flora, fauna or geological or physiographical features'[53] and the Countryside Commission is responsible for preserving natural beauty which is defined as including the 'flora, fauna or geological or physiographical features'[54] of an area. Certainly the need to conserve the wider countryside, as well as its wildlife, has become more apparent since the 1949 Act so that the roles of the two agencies have, in theory at least, grown closer. In practice, however, the Countryside Commission has left nature conservation to the NCC and concentrated on landscape. Because it is essentially an advisory body, it has had no choice but to follow the voluntary approach. Advocates for the merger believe that a united agency would have greater powers and influence.[55] Nevertheless, the differences between the two organizations are fundamental. The NCC's central function is the conservation of nature for whatever purpose; the Countryside Commission's central role is to conserve natural beauty, including nature, for the benefit of public enjoyment. The two are not necessarily identical, neither do they require the same types of expertise. It is a matter of concern, therefore, that membership of the Joint Nature Conservation Committee, which is only responsible for nature conservation, is not restricted to persons appointed for their experience in or

75

scientific knowledge of nature conservation. The chairman of the Countryside Commission is included as are the chairmen of each of the new country councils, one of whom owes his appointment to his experience of countryside matters.[56]

Whatever the merits of a merger of functions may be, there must be disquiet over the motives of the Government in proposing it. Despite lengthy debates during the passage of the 1990 Act, the Government refused to commit itself to a future amalgamation between the new council for England and the Countryside Commission. Indeed, the main grounds for a merger in the other countries appears to be size. Having first claimed that a split of the NCC was justified on management grounds,[57] the Secretary of State decided that the new body for Wales would be too small to be viable,[58] hence the merger.

There is no doubt that a reorganization of the NCC was desirable and the creation of a unified body bringing together responsibilities for planning and management in the countryside and nature conservation might have been opportune. It is alarming, however, that so drastic a change could have been made on grounds of political and economic expediency with no public consultation, in contrast to other parts of the Environmental Protection Act which were drafted only after extensive consultation.

FUTURE PROSPECTS

If there is to be any significant progress using a voluntary approach to conservation it has to be through overwhelming public support. In the past this has been lacking and there have been insufficient resources for bringing about a change through education. The enormous public interest in the environment has changed all this. The conservation message has got through to people who could not see the merit in holding back production in order to save wildlife but are persuaded by the possibility of global catastrophe through uncontrolled development.[59] The voluntary environmental organizations have all seen a steady steep increase in membership and donations which have enabled them to lobby more effectively.

At the same time, the Government is under pressure from the European Community. Both the Wildlife and Countryside Act and the Environmental Protection Act owe their existence, in part at least, to the need to implement EC directives. The proposed directive on habitat protection will necessitate further changes if, and when, it is made.

Nevertheless, the Government is still firmly entrenched in its voluntary approach to nature conservation.[60] The usual justification, especially in relation to MNRs, is that the law would be impossible to enforce without local co-operation. This is not true, of course, although enforcement might be expensive. According to *This Common Inheritance*, the Government will designate more MNRs, yet the NCC are on the point of abandoning the latest proposal because of local opposition. Their experience has shown that persuasion is difficult, if not impossible. On a number of occasions in the past, Government ministers have said that time is running out for the voluntary approach.[61] It will be interesting to see whether the Loch Sween disaster marks its demise!

One positive step in the right direction would be if greater adherence were paid to s.11(1) of the Countryside Act which provides that:

> In the exercise of their functions relating to land under any enactment every Minister, government department and public body shall have regard to the desirability of conserving the natural beauty and amenity of the countryside.[62]

The Government have recently allocated environmental responsibilities to every ministry and department.[63] One useful function of these ministers could be to promote compliance with this provision. This would go some way towards redressing the balance between conservation and other interests. The Natural Heritage (Scotland) Bill appears to go even further. Clause 1 requires Scottish Natural Heritage (SNH), which is to replace the NCC and the Countryside Commission in Scotland, to 'have regard to the desirability of securing that anything done . . . in relation to the natural heritage of Scotland is undertaken in a manner which is sustainable'. Introducing the Bill, Lord Strathclyde said that its overriding purpose was to ensure that the natural environment in Scotland, and especially land and water resources, 'are managed in a sustainable way to secure the inheritance of succeeding generations'.[64]

While the emphasis on integrated management for conservation objectives is highly desirable, the Bill as worded, cannot achieve it. Neither is it likely that this is what is actually intended by the Government. Instead, integration is needed at a higher level so that the activities of different government departments are co-ordinated and there is no longer any need to balance conservation against other interests. The integrative measures in the Bill, however, are in the context of a nature conservation body and could prove retrograde by placing the emphasis on management rather than conservation. Integration is required in this area but it is the other interests that need to accommodate the needs of conservation not vice versa. In view of the attitude towards conservation in Scotland, however, the result is likely to be that the importance of conservation will be relegated even further.[65]

NOTES AND REFERENCES

1 *This Common Inheritance: Britain's Environmental Strategy* (1990; Cm. 1200).
2 It is important to distinguish sustainable use from sustainable development which is the term used by Mrs Thatcher in her speech to the Royal Society (27 September 1988).
3 The trust was made a statutory body under its full title, the National Trust for Places of Historic Interest or Natural Beauty, by the National Trust Act 1907.
4 Previously known as the Fauna Preservation Society, the organization was founded in 1903 as the Society for the Preservation of the Wild Fauna of the Empire and claims to be the oldest society in the world involved in international conservation.

5　Previously known as the World Wildlife Fund. The organization was set up as a fundraiser for other agencies involved in international conservation work but now takes an active role in projects.

6　These come under the umbrella of the Royal Society for Nature Conservation which was set up in 1912 as the Society for the Promotion of Nature Reserves with the aim of preparing an inventory of areas meriting reserve status.

7　The marine nature reserve provisions in the Wildlife and Countryside Act 1981 provide a recent example.

8　For example, although the Government were prepared to back Dr David Clark's Bill to amend the Wildlife and Countryside Act 1981, they were not prepared to find parliamentary time to present their own amending Bill.

9　There were Wild Bird Acts in 1880, 1881, 1894, 1896, 1902, 1904, and 1908.

10　Some species are protected by separate legislation either to control hunting or because their international conservation status dictates special protection. Examples include the Conservation of Seals Act 1970 and the Badgers Act 1973.

11　Wildlife and Countryside Act 1981 ss.1(1) and 21(1).

12　id., ss.1(4) and 21(1).

13　id., s.1(5).

14　id., s.2(1).

15　id., s.2(7).

16　id., s.4(2)(c).

17　id., s.16(10).

18　id., ss.16(4) and 16(9)(d).

19　S.I. No. 1555 as amended by S.I. 1983 No. 159.

20　Field surveys conducted by the NCC and MAFF in the Exe estuary revealed no sign of settlement of young although this is not conclusive evidence.

21　Wildlife and Countryside Act 1981 s.22.

22　See NCC 13th Report (1 April 1986 – 31 March 1987) Appendix 12.

23　The Government has just announced that these species are to be added to Schedule 5 together with the adder and the allis chad, which had also been suggested by the NCC (see report in *The Times*, 4 January 1991).

24　National Parks and Access to the Countryside Act 1949 ss.16 and 19.

25　id., s.15.

26　Wildlife and Countryside Act 1981 s.30.

27　id., ss.36 and 37 and Schedule 12.

28　id., s.37(2).

29　National Parks and Access to the Countryside Act 1949 s.1.

30　John Dower, *National Parks in England and Wales* (1945; Cmd. 6628).

31　*Report of the Committee on National Parks (England and Wales)* (March 1947; Cmd. 7121; Chair: Sir Arthur Hobhouse)

32　Under the Nature Conservancy Council Act 1973.

33　Compare the National Parks and Access to the Countryside Act 1949 s.8(1) with the Countryside Act 1968 s.1(2).

34　Environmental Protection Act 1990 ss.130 and 132.

35　In evidence to the House of Commons Environment Committee, Mr William Waldegrave, then Minister for the Environment, estimated that, in the previous 35 years, more than half of lowland heaths and fenlands, more than a third of ancient woodlands and a quarter of upland heaths and grasslands had been lost and blamed the Agriculture Act 1947. (H.C. Environment Committee, First Report, *The Operation and Effectiveness of Part II of the Wildlife and Countryside Act, Session 1984–85* (1984: H.C. 6–I) Q249.

36　Even the Chairman of the NCC, Sir William Wilkinson, seems to accept that conservation is not of overriding importance. In his review in the NCC's 16th Report (1 April 1989 – 31 March 1990) he says 'I believe the Act stems from a commendable attempt to be fair'. If conservation is as important as conservationists would have us believe, fairness should not be relevant.

37 1942; Cmd. 6378.
38 op. cit., n. 30.
39 op. cit., n. 31.
40 At the time, the power and influence of scientists was considered to be much greater than it actually was. There was a belief that scientific endeavour would provide answers to all sorts of intractable problems of the past. For further discussion see Sir Dudley Stamp, *Nature Conservation in Britain* (1969) which gives a historical account, and Sir William Wilkinson's review in the latest NCC Report, op. cit., n. 36.
41 Wild Life Conservation Special Committee, *Conservation of Nature in England and Wales* (1947; Cmd. 7122; Chair: Dr J.F. Huxley)
42 Sites continue to be lost or damaged as indicated by statistics in the annual reports of the NCC. In the year ending 31st March 1989, 39 sites suffered long-term damage or were lost and a further 261 sites suffered short-term damage (NCC, op. cit., n. 36).
43 Wildlife and Countryside Act 1981 s.28(8) Under the Town and Country Planning General Development Order 1988, S.I. No. 1813, article 18, the local planning authority must consult with the NCC before granting permission.
44 Directive 79/409/EEC, OJ 25.4.79 L 103.
45 Annual payments for management agreements amounted to £4,289,000 in 1989/90 and it is predicted that this figure will rise to £9 million over the next two or three years if agreements currently under negotiation are successfully concluded (op. cit., n. 36).
46 Town and Country Planning Act 1947 s.20 and Schedules 3 and 4.
47 The Town and Country Planning Act 1990 s.55(2)(e) excludes the use of land for agricultural or forestry purposes from the definition of development. Operational development on agricultural land is not excluded but may be permitted development under the Town and Country Planning General Development Order 1988, S.I. No. 1813.
48 Mr Ridley, 156 *H.C. Debs.*, col. 484 (11 July 1989).
49 See, for example, comments by Mr Bryan Gould, 165 *H.C. Debs.*, col. 56 (15 January 1990).
50 463 *H.C. Debs.*, col. 1493 (31 March 1949).
51 415 *H.L. Debs.*, col. 983 (16 December 1980).
52 Subsequently enacted as the Wildlife and Countryside (Amendment) Act 1985.
53 Nature Conservancy Council Act 1973 s.1.
54 Countryside Act 1968 s.21(7).
55 See, for example, A. and E. MacEwen, *Greenprints for the Countryside. The Story of Britain's National Parks* (1987).
56 It should be noted, however, that Sir John Burnett, Deputy Chairman of the NCC, was of the opinion that the failure to merge the NCC and the Countryside Commission in England was illogical and wanted the Chairman to be on the Joint Nature Conservation Committee. (H. L. Select Committee on Science and Technology, Second Report, *Nature Conservancy Council, Session 1989–90* (1990; H.C. 33–I) Q110.)
57 165 *H.C. Debs.*, col. 43 (15 January 1990).
58 165 *H.C. Debs.*, col. 44 (15 January 1990).
59 The hostile response to the Government's proposals to give special protection to the adder (see letters to *The Times*, 12 January 1991) suggests that the wider public's appreciation of green issues may, like Mrs Thatcher's, be essentially egocentric.
60 The Government was strongly supported by the H.C. Environment Committee in their Report, op. cit., n. 35. Although critical of the Act, especially ss.28 and 29, the Committee were convinced that the voluntary approach was the right one.
61 In the third reading debate on the Wildlife and Countryside Act, Mr Tom King, then Minister for the Environment, said 'We still have our fears about whether the voluntary system will work . . . this is the last opportunity for us to ensure [it does]'. He went on to say that there was 'determination on both sides of the House that if the voluntary system fails we shall deal with the matter more rigorously'. 9 *H.C. Debs.*, col. 1309 (30 July 1981).
62 A more precise commitment is contained in the Water Act 1989, s.8(4) of which requires the National Rivers Authority to promote conservation to such an extent as it considers desirable, although attempts to include similar provisions in the Electricity Act 1989 failed.

In any event, this slight concession in favour of conservation is counter-balanced by the requirement of the NCC to have due regard to the needs of agriculture and forestry and to the economic and social interests of rural areas (Countryside Act 1968 s.37). Note that in this case the duty is not tempered by desire. Furthermore, the Agriculture Act 1986 s.17(1) requires the Agriculture Minister to endeavour to achieve a reasonable balance between the agricultural industry, the economic and social interests of rural areas, conservation, and public enjoyment of the countryside. The position of conservation is further weakened by a proviso that such endeavours must be consistent with the Minister's agricultural functions. And this is supposed to be a conservation measure!

63   Department of the Environment Press Release 515 (25 September 1990).

64   523 *H.C. Debs.*, col. 575 (19 November 1990).

65   Sir William Wilkinson expressed the opinion that no amount of devolution would alter the impact of the Wildlife and Countryside Act (op. cit., n. 36). He was writing before the publication of this Bill, however, and might think differently now.

Law and the Regulatory Environment of Waste Management

NEIL HAWKE*

THE DEVELOPING ENVIRONMENT

The management of waste, along with a variety of other issues impacting on the environment, has now arrived centre stage in a fast-developing agenda for the environment. In contemporary terms, the critical time-scale for any meaningful examination of the law's policy and technique stretches from the Control of Pollution Act 1974, enacted just after British accession to the European Economic Community, to the present when, at the time of writing, the Environmental Protection Bill is about to be enacted and the Government's promised White Paper on the environment has been published. From this cross-roads there is a very interesting view of progress in the task of managing waste through the law's facilities. It is the task of this case study to map the unfolding of what, hitherto, has been a very traditional 'axis' for the law's approach to waste management. In crude terms that axis has emphasised the (statutory) regulatory environment under Part I of the Control of Pollution Act 1974 and the available common law techniques for the distribution of liabilities. The central question to be asked here is whether this axis can be developed adequately for the purpose of coping with increasing anxieties about the treatment and management of waste.

This central question begs a variety of other questions, all of which have to be addressed in this attempt to evaluate the law as an instrument (and perhaps *the* most important instrument) for the imposition and proper enforcement of responsibilities in the present context. To what extent should economic instruments seek to replace or complement traditional legal regulation here? To what extent should a private law contractual approach seek to supplement traditional public law-based regulatory techniques, where the powers of the regulator are often closely confined by the relevant statutory authority? Is there an effective collaboration between these public law-based regulatory techniques and the private (common) law rules of tort, ensuring a rather more automatic distribution of 'real' liability in the wake of failures to follow the regulatory code? Underlying many of these questions are further questions about the limits of law enforcement in the field of waste management as well as the status and influence of EEC law.

* *Professor of Law, Leicester Polytechnic, P.O. Box 143, Leicester LE1 9BH, England.*

The regulatory model takes us to the very heart of the law's preoccupation with environmental control in recent times. That regulatory model is characterized by a licensing facility which, in turn, is enforced (predominantly) by strict liability criminal offences. The axis previously referred to emphasises the fundamental differences between this statutory regulatory model and the common law heads of tortious liability, operating as they often do retrospectively for the purpose of distributing liabilities. The crude logic underlying this axis should show that the more efficient the anticipatory regulatory regime, the less likely it is that the common law heads of tortious liability will come into play. In other words, the more thorough the licensing process for a land-fill site, the less likelihood of actions in tort for nuisance, trespass, and so on when waste or leachate from waste escape from the subject site, even though a licence from a regulatory agency does not signal automatic immunity from common law tortious liabilities. The theme that is taken up in the following section deals with the development of the regulatory model, beyond the somewhat limited licensing facilities that first appeared as Part I of the Control of Pollution Act 1974. That development, which has emerged from a lengthy debate[1], proceeds in two directions. One of those directions involves a widening and deepening of the whole licensing framework while the other draws on common law concepts from contract and tort as a means of strengthening the traditional regulatory model.

DEVELOPING THE REGULATORY MODEL

At the very heart of the emerging environmental protection legislation is the idea that the waste disposal authorities – often the county councils – should not continue as site operators in their own right and as regulators. This situation has dominated debate about law and policy in the area since the Control of Pollution Act first appeared on the statute book. Henceforth the licensors and regulators will be the waste regulation authorities and the operational arm of local authorities' land-fill activities will be conferred on 'arm's length' companies whose creation is a requirement of the legislation. Also built into the legislation is the further requirement that these 'arm's length' companies operate in a truly competitive environment with companies from the private sector. A notable model for the uncompromised regulatory authority is the National Rivers Authority charged with the licensing and enforcement of discharges to the aquatic environment under the Water Act 1989[2].

Control by public law licensing will be a central feature of the new waste regulation authorities' functions as it was of their predecessor waste disposal authorities. The use of the contract and its bed of rules from private rather than public law may well represent a very effective reinforcement for the traditional regulatory model in the present context, relying as it does on the licence backed by criminal sanctions for non-compliance. There is evidence suggesting that those subject to regulation, in the context of grants of planning permission at least, are far more deferential to a planning agreement founded in contract as opposed to a licence or (in this case), a planning permission.[3] Indeed, it may be argued that the law's policy at present is preoccupied more with fixing liability on the licensee and those with whom she or he deals in contract than with any liability of the waste regulation authority in negligence arising from licensing. This policy direction suggests that the law of tort and (in particular) negligence may not necessarily facilitate a widespread distribution of liability for loss, damage or injury: the liability may not travel beyond the immediate contracting parties[4]. It is not intended to enter into a lengthy analysis of developments in the law of negligence, except to say that the statutory regulatory agency may often be seen to be immune from liability in negligence where any failure on its part in the discharge of the regulatory function is defined as economic loss rather than some more tangible damage or injury.[5] Assuming that the waste regulation authority's licensing powers are aimed at avoiding damage or injury to individuals and/or property, the apparent logic of the law at present is that the authority may be subject to an enforceable duty to take reasonable care in the exercise of its licensing function. A much more difficult question is whether this duty not to be negligent extends to environmental damage where, for example, some natural feature is damaged or destroyed (say) by leaching from a 'badly' licensed land-fill site. In these realms of speculation it is easy to foresee that the courts would want to limit the regulators' legal liability if only on the rather nebulous ground of 'public policy'.

The (arguable) development of the law's policy away from fixing negligence liability on the regulatory agency should not disguise the very significant introduction of a statutory duty of care in the new environmental protection legislation. This development was foreshadowed by the (standing) Royal Commission on Environmental Pollution[6] and now appears in the legislation as a fusion of techniques from the law of tort and the criminal law. Essentially the legislation provides that it shall be an offence for a person to act in breach of the statutory duty of care, by failing to prevent the escape of waste in her or his control, for example. However, the legislation does not stop here because the Secretary of State is empowered to prepare and issue a code of practice providing practical guidance on the discharge of the duty. Any such code will be admissible in evidence and, furthermore, if any part of the code appears to a court to be relevant to any question arising in proceedings it shall be taken into account in determining that question. The code is likely to deal with security at sites and in transport. If therefore the defendant in criminal proceedings here is found to have failed to make (say) a container secure from vandals where it is left outside the gates of the site, resort to the detailed guidance of the code is likely to lead to a conviction on the foundation of common law negligence principles.

Thus far, a picture of the developing regulatory model has shown how contractual and related legal principles have the potential to widen perspectives in the waste management licensing process, along with the release of operational activities from the newly christened waste regulation authorities. These fundamental developments may well go hand-in-hand with the possible extension of the regulatory authority's immunity from liability in tort (negligence in particular) in respect of any loss caused thereby in so far as that loss can be characterised as economic loss. These two developments (one statutory, the other common law) are matched by the third development just referred to. In this case statute is borrowing common law standards in relation to negligence, crystallising those standards in a quasi-legal code and making them enforceable under the criminal law where the defendant is found to have acted in breach of that statutory duty of care.

Despite these modifications to the status and powers of the regulatory authority, the licensing process still lies at the very heart of statutory control. The environmental protection legislation widens quite considerably the licensing discretion available. Notable features of the new discretion include the power to refuse a licence if the applicant is not considered to be a 'fit and proper person'. Even if the applicant is considered to be a fit and proper person for present purposes, the authority may reject the application if this is necessary for the purpose of preventing pollution of the environment, harm to human health or serious detriment to the amenities of the locality.[7] The widening of this licensing discretion is accompanied by a renewal of the previous requirement in Part I of the Control of Pollution Act for a licence application to be accompanied by any necessary planning permission. The issue of dual control under this and the town and country planning legislation is dealt with later. For the moment, though, it is worth emphasising that the contract may play an important regulatory role in so far as a planning agreement might be employed by the collaborating planning authority for the purpose of revoking an outdated, inappropriate planning permission.[8] In this way a replacement consent can be in place which is relevant to the apparent demands of the land filling and related activities contained in the licence application to be considered by the waste regulation authority. The agreement will often contain a covenant by which the planning authority agrees to grant a fresh planning consent in return for an agreement to forego compensation entitlement under the Town and Country Planning Act 1990.

A potentially important dimension in this waste regulation process is the translation of the so-called 'polluter-pays principle'.[9] Provision is made in the environmental protection legislation for the imposition of charges as part of the licensing process, by means of detailed schemes to be made by the Secretary of State. At the time of writing the scope of such schemes is unknown. Nevertheless, interest in the development of the regulatory model must also excite interest in the purpose and effectiveness of the charging mechanism. Here we have an important convergence of legal and economic regulation, posing a fundamental question about the purposes of any charging regime in the present context. It has been observed that 'charges may have several impacts that are relevant from a policy perspective: an incentive impact and a redistributive impact'.[10] The fundamental question to be addressed in relation to any scheme developed under the legislation is whether the charges are capable of having an incentive impact. The likelihood is that the charging scheme will seek only to have a redistributive impact through a 'claw-back' of administrative costs incurred by the regulatory authorities. The related (policy) question is whether charges could be justified at a high level or, rather, a *sufficiently high* level for the purpose of acting as incentives in favour of more efficient land-filling operations, for example. Such a policy question is difficult by virtue of the need to articulate the meaning and requirements of 'efficiency' in this context.

Interestingly the legislation empowers the regulatory authority to revoke a licence if it appears that a licence holder has failed to pay any charge due. This power of revocation is in addition to a more general power of licence revocation (and suspension) detailed elsewhere in the legislation. A prominent example of revocation is likely to occur where the regulatory authority considers that the licensee is no longer a 'fit and proper person' to hold a licence. This power is closely related to powers that permit enforced transfer of licences at the instance of the regulatory authority. Significantly, there is no reference in the legislation to compensation entitlement on revocation, although there is an appeal against the authority's actions here to the Secretary of State. If an appeal against revocation is pursued, the revocation decision is ineffective pending the appeal decision unless the authority is of the opinion that revocation is necessary for the purpose of preventing or (where that is not practicable) minimizing pollution of the environment or harm to human health. Any unreasonable reliance on these reasons by the authority creates an entitlement to compensation.

The hub of the law's control in the present context is the definition of the term 'controlled waste'. Such waste means household, industrial, or commercial waste. The perspective is found in the prohibition of the unauthorized deposit, treatment or disposal of controlled waste: a criminal offence unless covered by an appropriate licence. Reference is made elsewhere to the fact that deposition of waste may also require planning permission, and the fact that failure to obtain a necessary planning permission could also trigger sanctions under the Town and Country Planning Act. The regulatory framework also takes account of controlled waste that may be difficult or dangerous.[11] In this case a complex system of consignment notes is required as the waste travels from cradle to grave. As the waste goes from producer to carrier to disposer so the law expects close monitoring, backed again by criminal sanctions for failure. The very detailed provisions here are at the time of writing under debate with a view to amendment.[12] One particular concern is the need to strengthen the chain of responsibility referred to above. That need could well be satisfied by the creation of distinct contractual obligations binding the parties to their respective obligations. If legislated, such a requirement would add to the catalogue of statute's 'borrowings' from private law in aid of the enforcement effort.

Finally in this context, Parliament has addressed the problems of 'fly-tipping' through the Control of Pollution (Amendment) Act 1989. This legislation attacks the problem by requiring carriers of controlled waste to be registered, it being assumed that the act of 'fly-tipping' is unlawful under the environmental protection legislation and its predecessor Control of Pollution Act. Subject to some exemptions[13] and defences, it is now an offence for any person who is not a registered carrier of controlled waste, in the course of any business of his or otherwise with a view to profit, to transport any controlled waste to or from any place in Great Britain[14].

CONSOLIDATING THE REGULATORY MODEL

A wealth of debate in recent years has culminated in the new range of statutory provisions to be found in the environmental protection legislation. The fundamental change has been referred to already, namely, the separation of local authority regulatory from operational functions, together with a widening of the licensing discretion. However, many parts of the system of control have been maintained: in particular the system of licensing itself, backed up in turn by a range of criminal sanctions. The legislation has also maintained other pre-existing features such as the need for an appropriate planning permission, as well as the core definition of 'controlled waste'. However, the important background of EC requirements means that issues such as the definition of 'controlled waste' are open to change. This is certainly the case at present as the two central directives are recast.[15] A new directive is likely to contain a more comprehensive definition of subject wastes which will be defined with greater precision.

Subject to specific EC requirements, consolidation of many of the so-called fundamental features of the system are not without controversy. An important example crops up in the foregoing area of wastes definition where the environmental protection legislation continues with an exclusion of agricultural and mine and quarry waste from the statutory definition of 'commercial waste'. Although the policy arguments are difficult, the usual view in favour of an exclusion of mine and quarry waste from control under the control of pollution and the new environmental protection legislation is that wastes here can be and are dealt with under the terms of any planning permission through which the operation is established. The same argument cannot extend to agricultural waste, bearing in mind that planning controls under the town and country planning legislation do not generally extend to agricultural operations and uses. That apart, a strong policy argument against the inclusion of agricultural waste in the statutory definition is the simple impracticability of an extension of controls over such a comprehensive area. Despite this great limitation, one of the great pollution by-products of agricultural waste – water pollution – is addressed in fairly comprehensive terms under the Water Act 1989. This legislation addresses in considerable detail the need for greater and more effective security measures in relation to slurry, for example.

Although the policy indicators suggest that some types of waste are to remain outside the control framework, the law in its consolidation phase seems to adopt an ambivalent attitude to the question of recycling. The environmental protection legislation contains various incentives to encourage the waste collection and disposal authorities to undertake recycling activities. On the other hand, the law, as interpreted by the courts, continues to emphasize the need to regard the status of a substance by reference to its origin, whatever may happen to it subsequently.[16] Again, the policy of the law appears to be heavily slanted in favour of ensuring that there is no room for abuse of control while seeking to tackle recycling through initiatives from the statutory regulatory agencies. On a more general level, the current Collection and Disposal of Waste Regulations 1988[17] display a complex web of policy priorities in so far as they stipulate that various activities fall outside the licensing framework. An example that always creates difficulty in practice relates to various substances deposited for the purposes of 'construction currently being undertaken on the land'. A related provision in the regulations permits a deposit on land for a period not exceeding three months for the purposes of future construction on the subject land. In both cases the regulations indicate that a disposal licence is not required.

While the environmental protection legislation introduces a variety of innovation in the present context, it seems unlikely that the prescribed offences underpinning the enforcement process will go much beyond the familiar confines of strict liability. The legislation is notable for its prescription of an offence in failing to comply with a duty of care. The 'principal offences' associated with unauthorized deposition do stretch to include any person who knowingly causes or knowingly permits the unauthorized deposition of waste. Evidence from the prosecution of water pollution offences indicates a preference for the prosecution of the offence of 'causing' rather than the offence of 'knowingly permitting' the polluting activity.[18] This is explained by two primary factors : the absence of *mens rea* requirements in strict liability offences and the helpful reversal of the onus of proof requiring the defence to disprove the allegation.[19] This second factor arises from the practical difficulty of actually catching the polluter 'red-handed'. Although the issue of enforcement is returned to later, it is necessary in this section on consolidation to point to another potentially helpful provision that is duplicated from Part I of the Control of Pollution Act.[20] The legislation takes, as a starting point, the principal offence of unauthorized deposition and goes on to add that (subject to certain exceptions) the person responsible is also liable for damage caused by the waste. This, potentially, is an enormous aid to proceedings for civil enforcement although the writer is unaware of any occasion when these statutory facilities have been used. Interestingly the legislation goes on to add that the provision is without prejudice to any liability arising otherwise than under the subject subsection.

ENFORCEMENT

Some reference has just been made to the question of enforcement where the central pre-occupation must be with the extent to which the environmental protection legislation permits the exercise of a wider set of powers. The key to this issue is the narrow licensing discretion previously available to the waste disposal authorities under the Control of Pollution Act. The classic anecdote is that which often occurred when criminal enforcement was available only if the prescribed act was associated with the act of deposition. Consequently, infractions associated with insecure site fencing, for example, could not be pursued by prosecution. Recent litigation[21] also indicated very strict limits for the licensing process, an attitude driven by a need (apparently) to avoid a duplication of controls available under other legislation such as the Public Health Act 1936.

When they were first introduced under the water pollution provisions in Part II of the Control of Pollution Act 1974, public registers were regarded as an important development in public accountability for pollution control. Despite some criticism, that view is largely sustainable and was probably the spur for the introduction of public registers in the provisions governing waste management in the environmental protection legislation. There is a clear utility in the introduction of registers so that, in particular, the licences and their conditions issued by the waste regulation authorities become public property. If the content of these registers is free of the technical complexity affecting similar registers now provided for under the Water Act 1989 then there is every chance that there will be a realistic opportunity for a widening of enforcement opportunities to the larger community. Any such development can only be regarded as crucial in extending the reach of the law's enforcement, particularly in aid of individuals' efforts at enforcement.

The final matter to be addressed under this heading concerns another issue that impacts on the question of accountability. However, in this context the matter of insurance and bonding concentrates on attempts to raise environmental standards – and accountability – through financial strategies. Although there is now clear statutory authority in the environmental protection legislation justifying the imposition of conditions on a licence requiring insurance and bonding in respect of a land-fill operation, for example, the position was not always as clear under the predecessor provisions of the Control of Pollution Act.[22] Even if the insurance and bonding regime was better developed in this country, startling evidence can be found in the United States of America showing that the courts may sometimes be tempted to give the clauses of some insurance policies an arguably eccentric interpretation.[23] Much hangs on the interpretation of phrases such as 'sudden and accidental occurrences' where land-fills have started to leach. In one famous instance the insurers sought to rely on an exclusion in respect of any sudden and accidental occurrence and succeeded when the land-fill site started to leach.[24] In other proceedings it has been observed that ' . . . pollution exclusion was solely meant to deprive active polluters of cover'.[25] In this country the Royal Commission on Environmental Pollution has examined the options in the present context.[26] However, both insurance and bonding, although they have great potential in ensuring ever better standards of waste management, are very slow starters as aids to the regulatory machine. On the one hand there is evidence that bonds are difficult to come by from the financial institutions, particularly in the case of smaller companies.[27] On the other hand insurance provision is weak largely (so it seems) because the insurance industry does not yet understand the nature of the technical risks involved. One possibility is that such a lack of understanding will reduce as environmental audits become part of well-accepted practice by companies in the waste management industry. This trend will again re-inforce the influence of contractual techniques for standard setting and enforcement.

A CONFUSION OF REGULATORS

At an earlier point in this work reference was made to the enforcement process and the so-called 'principal' offence of unauthorized deposition of waste under the environmental protection legislation. However, the deposition of waste may also amount to 'development' requiring planning permission under the town and country planning legislation. If that deposition is undertaken without a planning permission, the local planning authority is empowered to issue and serve an enforcement notice under the same legislation. Both areas of law – under the environmental protection and town and country planning legislation – are beset by very technical rules for the purpose of determining whether a disposal licence is or is not required and for the purpose of determining whether or not a planning permission is required. Some of the technicality was hinted at earlier in the brief reference to the Collection and Disposal of Waste Regulations. Equal measures of technicality percolate the town and country planning legislation: examples abound. One of the most controversial examples emerges from the fact that if activities, such as dumping, occur on agricultural land the normal exclusion of agricultural activities from many planning controls may apply. However, to attract the available immunity it is necessary to establish that the dumping is requisite for the use of the subject land for agricultural purposes. Not surprisingly the phrase 'requisite for agricultural purposes' has attracted a lot of technical legal argument.[28] A lot may hang on whether the farmer is providing a convenient, commercial dumping ground for somebody else's waste.

In practice a number of variables will determine whether one agency or another – the waste regulation authority or the local planning authority – takes the enforcement action. In some instances a policy on enforcement may anticipate the problems arising and determine the distribution of enforcement action. In other instances enforcement may simply depend on whether the incident came to the attention of one agency but not the other. If the incident comes to the attention of both agencies the legal and factual complexity may lead to an agreement that one agency will act, if only because the facts suggest an 'easier' enforcement option. Since the planning authority and the waste regulation authority will often be one and the same county council the mechanics for such organisational agreements will be relatively straightforward in many cases. This state of affairs is underpinned by the requirement, adverted to earlier, that the environmental protection legislation visits on an applicant for a disposal licence, namely a requirement that there shall be an appropriate planning permission in force as a pre-requisite to the application.

The planning authority and the waste regulation authority have the further responsibility of deciding on enforcement action if there is an alleged infraction of the terms of any licence actually granted. The relation between the two agencies at this point is governed very largely by their respective interests and 'ambitions' in relation to the licensed activities. Two areas of possible tension in practice are final elevations for completed land-fills and the problem of methane gas. In the first case the respective agencies may disagree, the one (a planning authority) preferring modest elevations, the other (the waste regulation authority) being amenable to much steeper elevations. In the second case a requirement to abstract methane gas may be seen by the planning authority to delay or even prejudice restoration of the subject land.

The so-called 'confusion' of regulators does not end here because other legislation, as well as the environmental protection legislation, provides various agencies with opportunities to regulate the waste management process. The Water Act 1989, for example, empowers the National Rivers Authority to enter land for the purpose of remedying the source of water pollution which could well be a leaching land-fill site.[29] Equally, the integrated pollution control provisions of the environmental protection legislation introduce extended regulation of so-called 'scheduled' industrial processes with a considerable polluting potential. In so far as waste management is part of the process, this will come under the regulatory powers of Her Majesty's Inspectorate of Pollution.

THE DISTRIBUTION OF LIABILITIES

The emphasis so far has been on the law's regulatory framework, governed essentially by the rules of public administrative law. However, it has been seen that rules of private law in relation to contract and tort have been encouraged to enter the picture, either by the courts (particularly in relation to an apparent policy in favour of greater immunity in the law of tort for the licensing agency, the waste regulation authority) or through the statutory provisions in the environmental protection legislation through which a duty of care is enforceable both through the criminal law and through the medium of the law of tort.

The common law tradition depends on a distribution of liabilities through the accidents of litigation. The environmental protection legislation may yet prove to be a very significant vehicle in the process of distributing liabilities after the event as well as providing a range of anticipatory powers to counter polluting activities. Whether these processes of distribution and anticipation are seen to operate effectively will depend on enforcement preferences shown by the regulatory agencies and (to a lesser extent) private individuals. The reference here to 'regulatory agencies' in the plural is deliberate in view of previous comments about the duplication of enforcing agencies in some sectors of pollution control. The plurality of enforcers, though, is nothing very new. By way of an example, the local authorities have for many years had – and still have – quite flexible powers which enable measures to be taken in relation to land that may be contaminated by unlawful dumping, for example. These powers in the Public Health Act 1936 have an impressive pedigree and allow not only anticipatory action in relation to land considered to be a 'statutory nuisance' in these circumstances but also a distribution of liabilities in so far as those responsible may be subject to an order of the magistrates' court directing an appropriate clean up.[30]

Whether there is a statutory nuisance depends on common law perceptions of a nuisance.[31] However, and more significantly, the Public Health Act provisions are not a normally recognized avenue for the treatment of problems arising from contaminated land. This fact does focus on the important distinction between regulatory action (aimed usually at remedial measures involving some requirement to cease the offending actions) and the distribution of liabilities after the event. If only by virtue of resource starvation of the regulatory agencies, their enforcement function may be patchy, on past evidence. In these circumstances infractions will be judged rather more frequently by reference to common law standards in areas like the law of trespass and nuisance. Typically the owner of land affected by leaching (for example) from an adjacent land-fill may be able to pursue proceedings for an injunction and damages. These circumstances would suggest that the waste regulation authority also could act in order to enforce the terms of the licence in question. If the above claim of patchy enforcement action can be sustained on the evidence it seems likely that fewer complaints will be forthcoming here if the Secretary of State is minded to exercise her or his wide default powers against the waste regulation authorities under the provisions of the environmental protection legislation. No doubt the continuing development of charging will dispel complaints about regulatory enforcement based on resource starvation. Furthermore, reference has been made to the development of links between the regulatory function (and its enforcement) and the availability of compensatory remedies in favour of any individual adversely affected by licence infraction. This, though, is not the end of the story.

The individual affected by leaching, for example, may pursue common law remedies of the sort adverted to already. One such remedy is nuisance and the related head of strict liability arising from the principle in *Rylands* v. *Fletcher*.[32] This area of strict liability has particular merit in so far as no proof of fault is required. Unfortunately the passage of time has seen this head of strict liability reduce in significance because of doubts about its scope. New hope for this head of strict liability now emerges from a proposed EC directive on civil liability for damage caused by waste.[33] The focus for the strict liability regime is likely to be the producer of the waste in question. The motivation behind the directive includes the desire to encourage the adoption of clean technologies as

91

well as control of the amount of waste arising. If the fault lies with some other individual such as a carrier the directive will undoubtedly facilitate legal action by the producer, to enable the payment of an indemnity, for example. Nevertheless, in some circumstances the producer's liability will be excluded where she or he can rely on defences such as contributory negligence or where she or he can prove that the waste was transferred lawfully to a disposal site. The directive will benefit the individual making a claim through a need to establish a causal link only by reference to the highest probability: that of a link between the producer's waste and damage to the environment.

ECONOMIC INSTRUMENTS

A further motivation behind the proposed directive on strict liability for waste is the so-called 'polluter-pays principle'. This principle underlies much of the rationale for the use of so-called economic instruments as means by which better environmental standards can be achieved in waste management and elsewhere. Reference has been made to charging in the operation of waste management licensing: this process is directly related and begs the question about how extensive charging should be, as well as the accompanying question about the essential purpose of charging, as well as other economic instruments.[34]

Economic instruments are almost always complementary to statutory regulatory powers and are often seen as 'internalizing' environmental behaviour. This is seen when charges or tax incentives, for example, operate to speed innovation in industrial production processes. Simultaneously though, direct regulation is maintained to enable a continuing 'grip on the actors'. Although economic instruments have a complementary status, the environmental protection legislation as it governs waste management in particular brings a closer relationship with economic instruments in two important respects, first through licensing powers that can provide for insurance and bonding on the part of the licensed land-filler and, second, through the facilities for charging which (as was seen above) may well facilitate a better funded enforcement process.

CONCLUSIONS

The recent publication of the Government's White Paper on the environment[35] and related work by Professor David Pearce for the Department of the Environment provide a significant if sometimes cautious backdrop to the Environmental Protection legislation. The significance of that back drop emphasises just how much has been achieved through the law in developing and refining the regulatory framework over the last two decades. What we see in the environmental protection legislation is a new chapter in waste management law, with the White Paper and related debates pushing the focus forward to a realization of the potential of the new legislation and some of its equally new ideas as discussed previously. The critical message is found in three objectives: the need for an effective regulatory model, the availability of a system (related in part to the new regulatory framework) that allows distribution of liabilities and recognition of concepts of 'sustainable' development such as the 'polluter-pays principle'. The arrival of a vehicle in the form of the environmental protection legislation that can foster these objectives emphasises that the vehicle still needs encouragement if the development of effective standards and their implementation is to continue. In large part this can be achieved through variety in the law's techniques for the purpose of regulation and the distribution of liabilities. Some of those techniques are more subtle than others, as where licence conditions requiring insurance of waste management activities force a gradual improvement of land-fill standards. If this and other techniques developed from public and private law are to work, the challenge goes beyond the regulatory agencies. Implementation and enforcement of the new law and emerging techniques for dealing with waste management will depend on lively, imaginative perceptions of a growing list of options for action, allied with a far more dynamic appreciation of responsibilities and liabilities.

NOTES AND REFERENCES

1 See, for example, Department of the Environment/Welsh Office, *The Role and Functions of Waste Disposal Authorities, A Consultation Paper* (1989).
2 Water Act 1989, ss. 1–4.
3 N. Hawke, 'Planning Agreements in Practice' (1981) *Journal of Planning and Environment Law* 5, 86.
4 *Murphy* v. *Brentwood District Council* [1990] 2 All E.R. 908; [1990] 3 W.L.R. 414, H.L.
5 id.
6 *Eleventh Report of the Royal Commission on Environmental Pollution* (1985; Cmnd. 9675).
7 *Attorney-General's Reference (No. 2 of 1988)* [1989] 3 W.L.R. 397.
8 op. cit., n. 3.
9 For a commentary on this principle, see House of Lords Select Committee on the European Communities, Tenth Report, *The Polluter Pays Principle, Session 1982–83* (1983; H.L. 131).
10 OECD, *Economic Instruments for Environmental Protection*, (1989) 14.
11 Control of Pollution (Special Waste) Regulations 1980, S.I. 1980 No. 1709.
12 Department of the Environment/Welsh Office, *Special Waste and the Control of its Disposal, A Consultation Paper* (1990).
13 Control of Pollution (Amendment) Act 1989, s.1(2)(4).
14 id., s. 1(1).
15 Directives 75/442, OJ 25.7.75 L194 and 78/319, OJ 31.3.78 L84.
16 See, for example, *Long* v. *Brooke* [1980] Crim. L.R. 109; *R.* v. *Rotherham M.B.C., ex parte Rankin*, *The Times*, 6 November 1989.
17 S.I. 1988 No. 819.
18 See N. Hawke, 'Crimes against the Environment,' (1987) 16 *Anglo-American Law Review* 93–4.
19 *Alphacell* v. *Woodward* [1972] 2 All E.R. 475.
20 Control of Pollution Act 1974, ss.3 and 88.
21 op. cit., n. 7.

22 But see now *R. v. Secretary of State for the Environment, ex. parte Shropshire County Council*, January 26 1987 (unreported).

23 N. Hawke and S. Nudds, 'Insurance and the Enforcement of Waste Disposal Laws' (1988) 17 *Anglo-Am. Law Rev.* 239.

24 *Jackson Township* v. *Hartford Accident and Indemnity Co.* 186 N.J. Super 156 (Law Division, Ocean County).

25 *Niagara City* v. *Utica Mutual Insurance Co.* 427 NYS 2d 171 (NY Sup. Ct. 1980).

26 op. cit., n. 6.

27 op. cit., n. 3.

28 *North Avon District Council* v. *Secretary of State for the Environment* (1980) 40 P. & C.R. 33 is a prominent example.

29 s. 115.

30 Public Health Act 1936, ss. 92–99. See now similar powers in Part III of the Environmental Protection Act.

31 *National Coal Board* v. *Thorne* [1976] 1 W.L.R. 543.

32 (1866) L.R. 1 Exch. 265.

33 COM (89) 282.

34 op. cit., n. 10.

35 *This Common Inheritance* (1990; Cm. 1200).

Crimes against the Aquatic Environment

WILLIAM HOWARTH*

BACKGROUND

The Water Act 1989 provided the legal vehicle for the Government's privatization of the water industry.[1] The original plan for privatization had been that the ten regional water authorities, which had comprehensive responsibilities for the management of water within their areas, would be sold off into private ownership allowing new private bodies to undertake the same responsibilities as had previously been discharged by public sector bodies. However, this plan for water privatization soon encountered difficulties. A central problem[2] was that the former regional water authorities had possessed integrated management functions relating to all aspects of the hydrological cycle,[3] as then provided for under the Water Act 1973. Essentially this meant responsibility for water, from the time that it fell upon land to the point when it became part of the sea, was entrusted to the same body. Matters such as water resources, water supply, sewerage and sewage treatment, pollution control, and land drainage were all entrusted to the regional water authority for the area concerned.[4] Whilst integrated control allowed for the co-ordinated exercise of water management responsibilities, it also gave rise to certain conflicts of interest within the regional water authorities. Most notably, it had the consequence that the body with responsibility for pollution control also had responsibility for the treatment of sewage, a function which was a serious and persistent cause of river pollution. Hence, the body with the key policing role in relation to the aquatic environment was frequently found to be the most significant criminal in relation to that environment. This state of affairs was less than satisfactory whilst sewage treatment was a public sector activity; it would become quite intolerable if privatization provided a commercial motive for ineffective policing. In a familiar rural metaphor the Secretary of State for the Environment, Mr Ridley,

* *Director, Centre for Law in Rural Areas, and Senior Lecturer in Law, University College of Wales, Aberystwyth SY23 3DZ, Wales*

An earlier version of this paper was delivered at the University of Wales Staff-Student Conference at Gregynog on 15 November 1990, and the author is grateful to those who expressed comments about it on that occasion.

95

recognized the unacceptability in principle of private water companies becoming both 'poachers' and 'gamekeepers' in relation to the aquatic environment.[5]

The compromise which was reached between the policy objective of privatization and the need to safeguard the aquatic environment was to draw a division between the 'utility 'and 'regulatory' functions of water management. The utility functions of water supply and sewage treatment, which constituted the most attractive commercial features of the industry, were privatized and allocated to the Water Services Companies, referred to in the Water Act 1989 as 'water and sewerage undertakers'. The regulatory functions involving such matters as discharge licensing, water quality monitoring and bringing legal proceedings passed to a new public body, the National Rivers Authority. It is this Authority that is now entrusted with responsibility for the control of water pollution in England and Wales.

The National Rivers Authority came into being on 1 September 1989 at a time when concern about the quality of watercourses was greater than ever before. The most recent survey of the quality of waters in rivers and estuaries conducted by the Department of the Environment[6] had shown that the quality of rivers and estuaries had declined by two per cent in aggregate during the preceding five years, and that certain lengths of water were in an especially poor state, for example, the estuary of the Mersey which was thought to be the worst polluted estuary in Europe.[7] The House of Commons Environment Committee had recently published a report recommending that significant changes were needed in the law and administrative practices concerning water pollution control.[8] Some of these recommendations were given effect through the provisions of the Water Act 1989. The 1989 Act re-enacted the former legislation on water pollution, contained in Part II of the Control of Pollution Act 1974,[9] along with a number of changes designed to give effect to the policy objectives of the new authority.

Over the first year of the existence of the National Rivers Authority the use of legal proceedings has featured significantly in the armoury of measures employed by the authority in protecting the aquatic environment. This chapter seeks to outline the legal powers of the authority in relation to water pollution, to illustrate the use which has so far been made of those powers, and to indicate some developments in the law which are required for better protection of the aquatic environment in the future.

THE GENERAL DUTY TO PROTECT THE AQUATIC ENVIRONMENT

The general regulatory responsibility of the National Rivers Authority for non-utility water functions leads the way into a range of particular powers and duties.[10] Broadly, the authority is allocated specific responsibilities in the following areas: control of pollution;[11] water resources;[12] flood defence;[13] salmon and freshwater fisheries;[14] and navigation, conservancy and harbour authority functions.[15] As an umbrella over these particular functions, the authority is subject to a general environmental duty.

The general environmental duty requires the authority,[16] in formulating or considering any proposals, so far as is consistent with its functions, to exercise any power conferred on it with respect to those proposals so as to further the conservation and enhancement of natural beauty and the conservation of flora, fauna, and geological or physiographical features of special interest.[17] Without prejudice to these obligations, the authority is also placed under a duty, to such an extent as it considers desirable, generally to promote the conservation and enhancement of the natural beauty and amenity of inland and coastal waters, and of land associated with such waters, and the conservation of flora and fauna which are dependent on the aquatic environment.[18]

In order to give practical guidance to the authority with respect to the general environmental duty, and to promote desirable practice, the relevant minister[19] may approve a code of practice relating to these matters.[20] In exercise of this power the *Code of Practice on Conservation, Access and Recreation* has received ministerial approval[21], and provides guidance to the authority on a range of matters including the exercise of its function in relation to the control of pollution.[22] Although a breach of the code does not of itself constitute a contravention of the general environmental duty, or give rise to any criminal or civil liability, the relevant minister is placed under a duty to take into account whether there has been or is likely to be a contravention in determining how she or he should exercise her or his powers by virtue of the Act[23] in relation to the authority.[24]

THE FUNCTION OF THE AUTHORITY IN RELATION TO CONTROL OF POLLUTION

Subject to the requirements of the general environmental duty, the specific powers and duties of the authority in relation to the control of pollution are provided for under chapter I of part III of the Act. Broadly, the most important features of this chapter are, first, the strategic approach towards the control of water pollution for which it provides and, secondly, the particular offences relating to pollution which it specifies. In both instances, however, the powers and duties concerned arise in relation to waters referred to as 'controlled waters', a term incorporating four sub-categories: relevant territorial waters, coastal waters, inland waters, and ground waters.[25]

The strategic duty of the authority in relation to the control of pollution in controlled waters is formulated in three parts: first, the classification of water quality; second, the specification of water quality objectives; and, third, the duty to achieve and maintain these objectives. The mechanism for the classification of the quality of waters enables the Secretary of State to make regulations prescribing a system of classifying the quality of waters according to criteria specified in the regulations.[26] Classification of waters is to consist of general requirements as to the purposes for which waters are suitable, specific requirements as to substances that are required to be present in, or absent from, water, and specific requirements as to other characteristics of water.[27] In accordance with these powers the Surface Waters (Classification) Regulations 1989[28] have been made, classifying waters by reference to their suitability for abstraction for supply, after treatment, as drinking water. Discussions are presently under way as to the system of classification which is to be applied in relation to non-potable waters.[29]

The second part of the strategic duty in relation to water quality allows the Secretary of State, for the purpose of maintaining and improving the quality of controlled waters, to serve a notice on the authority specifying a classification in relation to water quality, and a date, and thereby establish a water quality objective for any waters by reference to the water quality classification system.[30] The water quality objective for any waters which are the subject of a notice of this kind is the satisfaction, after the date specified in the notice, of the requirements of the classification specified in relation to the particular waters concerned.[31] Hence water quality objectives are met where the standard under the water quality classification scheme which has been specified by the Secretary of State is achieved in relation to the particular waters concerned.

The final part of the strategic duty in relation to water quality is the statement that it is to be the duty of the authority[32] to exercise the powers conferred upon it in relation to the control of water pollution in such a manner as to ensure, so far as is practicable, that the water quality objectives specified by the Secretary of State for any waters are achieved at all times.[33] The overall import of the provisions is that a range of particular powers and duties in relation to pollution offences, discharge licensing powers and matters concerning information about water quality are to be used with a particular purpose in mind. That is, that the authority is to ensure, *so far as practicable*, that specified water quality objectives are achieved at all times.

REACTIVE OFFENCES CONCERNING WATER POLLUTION

The individual powers which may be exercised by the authority, as a means of achieving the strategic objective of maintaining water quality objectives, include a range of particular criminal offences in relation to which the authority acts as the principal enforcing authority. The main offences concerning water pollution provided for under the Act may be considered under the two headings of reactive and proactive offences, depending upon whether an offence involves actual pollution of water or whether it relates to an act which is unlawful because it constitutes a pollution hazard regardless of whether any pollution has actually occurred.[34] The key offence in the reactive category is that of 'causing or knowingly permitting' poisonous, noxious or polluting matter to enter any controlled waters.[35] Although slightly differently formulated offences are provided for in relation to trade effluent and sewage

98

effluent, in practical and legal terms the key to establishing a prosecution for pollution of waters under the Act lies in showing that the accused either caused or knowingly permitted pollution of the waters concerned.

The requirement of showing that the entry of polluting matter into waters is 'caused or knowingly permitted' is not new to this area of law, and the same wording can be found in a series of previous enactments providing for essentially the same offence.[36] Likewise a sizeable body of case law provides guidance as to the meaning of the phrase.[37] In the most general terms the following principles may be distilled from past decisions.[38] First, the disjunctive form of the phrase envisages two distinct matters, causing pollution *or* knowingly permitting it. A person *knowingly permits* pollution where she or he fails to prevent pollution where that failure is accompanied by knowledge.[39] Second, the offence of *causing* pollution is an offence of strict liability for which there is no requirement that the accused acted intentionally or negligently: it is enough that a positive and deliberate act leads to pollution for it to have been 'caused' within the meaning of the provision.[40] Third, as a counterpart of this, a passive looking on will not amount to causing pollution, though it may amount to knowingly permitting pollution in some circumstances. For this reason it is vitally important that prosecutions are pursued under the correct limb of the disjunction.[41] Fourth, it is possible that the chain of causation may be broken by the act of a third party, or an act of God, such that the accused may properly be said not to have *caused* the pollution.[42] Finally, there may be situations where collaborative activities involving more than one party give rise to pollution. In such circumstances it is vital that the correctly formulated offence is pursued *against the appropriate party*.[43]

Despite the legal principles surrounding the offence of causing or knowingly permitting pollution being reasonably well established, it is evident that the offence fails to provide adequately for all the circumstances which contribute to the overall problem of deteriorating water quality. The reason for this is that the offence conceives of water pollution as the result of an identifiable entry of polluting matter into a watercourse, usually, as a result of a discrete pollution incident. In practice a great deal of pollution occurs otherwise than as a result of dramatic escapes of polluting matter arising from incidents of the kind that form the case law surrounding the interpretation of the 'cause or knowingly permit' requirement. The more serious, pervasive, and intractable problems of water pollution arise through the gradual transmission of diffuse pollutants into watercourses through rainwater run-off from land or percolation of contaminating substances through soil. These kinds of problem can only be tackled proactively as difficulties arising from potentially polluting land use.

PROACTIVE OFFENCES CONCERNING WATER POLLUTION

Although enabling powers to regulate land use to prevent water pollution were available under previous legislation,[44] no regulations of this kind had ever been made. A renewed urgency for preventative water pollution legislation was given by incidents such as the disastrous fire at the Sandoz chemical factory in Basle in Switzerland in which 30 tonnes of agricultural chemicals, including powerful biocides, and 150 kg of mercury were washed into the Rhine by fire-fighting water.[45] Likewise, the recognition of difficulties such as the contamination of drinking water by nitrate has made it clear that only a proactive approach will be effective in stemming pollution by diffuse pollutants. Accordingly, the Water Act 1989 contains three provisions dealing with the prevention of water pollution along with firm policy commitments by the Government to the use of these powers.[46]

The first proactive measure allows for regulations to be made requiring precautions against pollution to be taken by those with possession of potentially polluting substances. Hence, the Secretary of State is empowered to make regulations prohibiting persons having or gaining custody of poisonous, noxious or polluting matter unless prescribed precautions have been taken for the purpose of preventing or controlling entry of the matter into controlled waters.[47] The exercise of this power is imminent in the sphere of agricultural pollution with the Department of the Environment having published a consultation paper on *Regulations to control silage, slurry and agricultural fuel oil installations.*[48] The proposals indicate that farmers will in future be required to construct facilities for the storage of silage, slurry and fuel oil in accordance with specifications set out in appendices to the regulations and that failure to do so will be an offence punishable to the same extent as the principal water pollution offences.[49] In addition to the prevention of water pollution from farms, the Government has recently stated that it intends to introduce similar regulations in relation to chemical and industrial fuel stores.[50]

The second proactive measure provides for the Secretary of State, after consultation,[51] to make an order designating an area a *water protection zone* and prohibit or restrict the carrying on in that area of specified activities where she or he considers it appropriate to do so to prevent or control the entry of poisonous, noxious or polluting matter into controlled waters.[52] In contrast to the previous provision, the emphasis here is not so much upon the substance concerned as the area in which the activity takes place. Accordingly, the powers may be exercised either where an area is in need of special protection for conservational reasons or where water drawn from the area is used as a source of supply and so required to be free from particular kinds of contamination.[53] As yet, no orders have been made in accordance with this power.

The third power in relation to proactive regulation concerns the particular problem of contamination of drinking water supplies through nitrates applied to land as fertilizer. The degree of contamination in some areas is such that drinking water fails to meet requirements provided for in European Community directives relating to drinking water.[54] A special provision directed at this problem allows the relevant minister to make an order designating land as a *nitrate sensitive area* where she or he considers it

100

appropriate to do so with a view to preventing or controlling the entry of nitrate into controlled waters as a result of anything done in connection with the use of any land for agricultural purposes.[55] Following the designation of such an area the minister may enter into agreements with owners of land in the area whereby, in consideration of payments made by the minister, the owner accepts obligations imposed to prevent or control the entry of nitrate into controlled waters.[56] Agreements of this kind have been entered into in relation to ten areas in England designated under the Nitrate Sensitive Areas (Designation) Order 1990.[57] This order enables agreements to be entered into whereby farmers limit application of nitrogen fertilizer to specified maximum amounts and take other measures intended to reduce nitrate contamination of watercourses. Although the schemes so far provided for seek to reduce nitrate contamination through voluntary agreements with farmers in specified areas, the minister is empowered to impose further requirements, prohibitions or restrictions, the contravention of which amounts to a criminal offence.[58] The problem of nitrate pollution of water supplies is a serious one in certain parts of the country and the areas that have so far been designated are relatively small by comparison to the total area affected. It is not improbable that more extensive measures will be required in the near future if drinking water quality objectives are to be comprehensively realized.

LAW ENFORCEMENT EXPERIENCES: THE *SHELL* CASE

Moving from the legal powers of the National Rivers Authority in relation to the protection of the aquatic environment to the use which has been made of those powers, some important trends in the enforcement of the law are to be discerned. Amongst the most notable water pollution prosecutions brought by the National Rivers Authority in the first year of its existence was that of *Shell UK* brought before Liverpool Crown Court on 23 February 1990.[59] Although the case arose from an incident which took place before the authority came into being, and was brought under previous legislation,[60] it was widely regarded as an indication of the new authority's embarking upon a more litigious attitude to pollution problems than its predecessors, and a court taking a more serious view of the nature of the offence involved than previously. The facts were simply that some 30,000 gallons of heavy black Venezuelan crude oil escaped into the River Mersey through a fracture in a pipeline owned by the defendants due to substantial corrosion of the pipe by reason of contact with sea water. As a result of the incident a ten-mile oil slick was created on the river, between 200 and 300 birds were killed and another 2,000 were oiled and at risk from the after-effects of ingestion and the loss of insulation. Although the precise cause of the fracture was not ascertained, Mars-Jones J. observed that the defendants had failed to discharge the high duty of care which they owed to the community. The strict liability associated with the offence of causing pollution was recognized,[61] and the defendants pleaded guilty to the offence.

The National Rivers Authority v. *Shell UK* is of greatest importance in relation to the sentencing aspects of the case. It was noted that the defendants had already paid some £1.4 million to local authorities and volunteers who had been involved in the cleaning up operation and to settle third party claims arising out of the incident. The company had also funded a scientific enquiry to monitor the long-term effects of the incident. Mars-Jones J. noted, however, that the defendants had enormous resources and could pay a fine of several million pounds without being unduly affected thereby. Despite the vast financial resources of the company, he gave full credit for the fact that they had an outstanding record in the field of conservation, and in particular of the protection of amenities of the area, and noted that were it not for these matters the fine that he would impose would have been 'substantially greater'. Taking careful attention of all aspects of the case the judge held that the appropriate penalty was a fine of £1 million with costs awarded against the defendant.

The decision is, by a considerable margin, the heaviest fine imposed upon a polluter under the legislation dealing with freshwater or coastal pollution and so provides a clear indication that courts are prepared to take a sterner line in relation to this kind of crime. In addition it raises some substantial general issues concerning the appropriate punishment for environmental offences. In the first place, it is significant that the past record of the defendants on the environment appeared to be a weighty consideration in determining the amount of the fine. On the one hand the previous expenditure of the company on conservation and other worthwhile causes could be seen as the purchase of an environmental 'insurance policy' to be claimed upon in the event of future mishap of this kind.[62] To be fair to the company, however, the fine imposed may have represented a relatively small amount by comparison to the harm done to their corporate environmental image and the corresponding investment costs which they had put into projection of their company as an environmentally caring concern. It may well have been that the expenses arising directly from the incident were the tip of the iceberg compared with the expenditure required to restore the company's environmental reputation to its former state.

More generally, the imposition of large fines upon corporate bodies raises considerable difficulties as to the effectiveness of this sanction in this sort of context. The transcript of the case reveals that Mars-Jones J. was especially concerned with the overall profitability of the company, and, in particular, with the Tranmere Oil Terminal and the Stanlow Refinery between which the fractured pipeline ran, and took particular note of the fact that this small part of the company's operations made an annual profit of almost £5 million. The difficulty noted by the judge remains, however, that a big company with a substantial turnover can absorb a financial penalty of several million pounds without being unduly affected thereby. It may well be that the ultimate payers of the fine and costs are the consumers of the company's products in a similar manner to that in which any other kind of production overhead is met.

Serious difficulties arise in relation to the imposition of fines upon large corporate water polluters and bring into question the suitability of financial penalties as a punishment for environmental offences by corporations.[63] Mars-Jones J. had said in the *Shell* case, 'the only penalty I can impose is a fine'.[64] Given the form in which the proceedings had been brought this was strictly correct. However, it is clear that powers were available to the courts to impose custodial sentences against individuals in respect of a water pollution offence. Specifically, on summary conviction a term not exceeding three months could be imposed in addition to a fine not exceeding the statutory maximum of £2,000, and on indictment a term not exceeding two years could be imposed in addition to a fine of unlimited amount.[65] Although the use of the powers to impose a custodial sentence is obviously dependent upon there being an individual rather than a corporate body against whom to bring proceedings, the identification of an individual against whom to proceed is the subject of a specific statutory provision. This provides that:

> Where a body corporate is guilty of an offence under [the Water Act 1989] and that offence is proved to have been committed with the consent or connivance of, or to be attributable to any neglect on the part of, any director, manager, secretary or other officer of the body corporate or any person who was purporting to act in any such capacity, he, as well as the body corporate, shall be guilty of that offence and shall be liable to be proceeded against and punished accordingly.[66]

Moreover:

> Where the affairs of a body corporate are managed by its members [the above provision] shall apply in relation to the acts and defaults of a member in connection with his functions of management as if he were a director of the body corporate.[67]

Although there is as yet no instance known where these powers have been used as a basis for bringing proceedings against an individual in a company which has caused water pollution, the potential which they hold for action against officers of a company, possibly brought in conjunction with an action against the company, is considerable. In a suitable case, such proceedings would provide a more appropriate mechanism for the punishment of water pollution than a prosecution of the company concerned. In addition, the apprehension of this form of proceedings might provide a more effective deterrent against water pollution than presently exists for those individuals who are able to shelter behind the anonymity of a large corporation and so avoid becoming a party to criminal proceedings.

The capacity to pierce the corporate veil provided for in relation to the water pollution offence, though penologically more appropriate to certain kinds of case, may give rise to difficulties in respect of establishing culpability. Case law from other contexts has established that the reference to a 'manager' refers to someone who manages the company rather than a particular branch of its operations.[68] Likewise it is established that showing that a duty has been neglected on the part of an officer of the company is a question of fact to be answered by looking at the circumstances of the case.[69] In the last resort, however, showing that a particular pollution offence is committed with the 'consent or connivance' or 'attributable to any neglect' of a company official will depend upon the extent to which the courts will allow officials to abdicate personal environmental responsibilities.

The recent acquittal of defendants charged with manslaughter in the *P&O case*,[70] arising out of the sinking of the *Herald of Free Enterprise* in 1987, illustrated the difficulties which may arise in seeking to establish that a director or company official knew that there was an 'obvious and serious risk' of a crime being committed. The same difficulty for the prosecution would probably not exist in relation to an offence of strict liability such as the *causing* of water pollution.[71] Moreover, increasingly high expectations of corporate environmental management policies in the future may mean that the circumstances in which an offence is committed by an official of the company by *neglect* of a duty to take environmental precautions may become increasingly easy to establish. Certainly the path of individual as well as corporate liability for environmental crimes has been followed in the United States of America where it has been suggested that 'being a Director of a company which harms the environment is not a position to take up lightly. Personal liability is the norm.'[72] The scope for personal actions against an official of a company committing an environmental offence is increasingly coming to be recognized in this country. Water pollution offences could provide a particularly appropriate context in which to pursue such proceedings.

WATER POLLUTION FINES

Moving from the broader difficulties arising from the *Shell* case to the more general picture in respect of fines for water pollution, a clearer overall view can be drawn from a scan of the other cases which have been brought during the first year of the National Rivers Authority. A survey of the most serious pollution incidents, in terms of the amounts of fines imposed, of those reported in *Water Guardians*, the newspaper of the National Rivers Authority, revealed the following notable decisions.

(i)   Proceedings brought by the Anglian region of the Authority resulted in a fine of £10,000 imposed by the Crown Court, along with an award of an estimated £40,000 costs, against a farmer who allowed some three million gallons of pig slurry to pour into the River Sapiston killing some 10,000 adult fish. In addition, the Authority sought compensation of £27,000 for the cost of restocking the river with fish.[73]

(ii)   Fines totalling £4,000 and costs were imposed by Gowerton Magistrates for pollution of the River Lliw by Max Recovery (Holdings) Ltd., operators of the Gwenlais Fawr waste tip. Licence conditions relating to the tip required several anti-pollution precautions to be taken but these had not been observed before tipping began and as a consequence of seepage the river became overgrown with sewage fungus.[74]

(iii)   Using computer analysis of downstream water tests, National Rivers Authority scientists identified the source of two pollution incidents on the River Dee as chipboard manufacturers Kronospan Ltd. of Chirk. Llangollen magistrates imposed fines of £4,000 in relation to the incidents, one of which involved formaldehyde and the other soluble oil, and ordered the company to pay another £4,000 by way of costs.[75]

(iv)   Yorkshire Water Services was fined a total of £4,000 for pollution of the River Worth, near Harworth, with ferric sulphate. The company pleaded guilty before Keighley Magistrates Court, but were nonetheless fined the maximum on the two counts and had costs awarded against them after magistrates had heard that the spillage from the Oldfield Sewage Treatment Works had caused the river's acidity to increase by up to 100,000 times and to have killed over 250 trout and a large number of smaller fish.[76]

(v)   A Leicestershire pig farmer was fined £10,000 for polluting a tributary of the River Soar with slurry and causing extensive fish mortality. Leicester Crown Court was informed that a pollution control officer had found the brook grey and with an oxygen level 80 per cent lower than it should have been as a result of a land drain taking slurry from 4,000 pigs through an irrigation ditch and directly into the watercourse.[77]

(vi)   A.Hughes and Son (Skellingthorpe) Ltd, a firm which processed dead animals, was found guilty on two charges of polluting the Skellingthorpe catchwater drain and fined a total of £30,000. Lincoln Crown Court noted the 'apparently cavalier attitude' of the company, which had not bothered to consult the Authority for advice on action which could have prevented or minimized the effect of the incidents, and ordered the firm to pay a further £15,000 in costs.[78]

(vii)   The Mid-Sussex Water Company were fined £20,000, with £5,000 costs, for pollution of underground water reserves after about 1,000 gallons of diesel fuel leaked from a corroded pipe into a borehole. In imposing the sentence at Lewes Crown Court, Gower J. expressed the strong opinion that the shareholders of the company should pay the fine and that it would be unfair if it was left to be paid by the water company's consumers.[79]

Although these decisions represent the most severe penalties that have been imposed for water-pollution offences brought by the authority,[80] the levels of fine imposed show spectacular increases above previous penalties that would have been imposed for this offence.

In terms of its general prosecution policy, the authority has brought more cases to the Crown Courts, which can impose unlimited fines upon polluters, than previously.[81] This may have contributed to the general increase in the levels of fines awarded.[82] The published data presently available[83] only extends to the end of the financial year 1989/90 including the period from 1 April 1989 to 1 September 1989 during which statistics were provided by the shadow Regional Units of the National Rivers Authority. Nonetheless, this data indicates a total of 25,563 pollution incidents for the year (the corresponding figure was 24,560 in 1988/89) with 292 prosecutions pursued (254 in 1988/98).

278 prosecutions were successful, and total fines of £1,272,505 were imposed (£124,695 in 1988/89). This averages out at a fine of over £4,500 per conviction overall, but when the atypical outcome of the *Shell* case is removed from the calculation the average is brought down to slightly under £1,000.

Although present levels of fines for water pollution offences represent a considerable advance upon those imposed in previous years, it has been suggested that in relation to certain kinds of incident they are still not adequate. Hence, in respect of the serious problem of agricultural pollution of watercourses,[84] it has recently been stated by the House of Commons Public Accounts Committee that prosecutions are too infrequent, fines are too low and do not generally reflect the severity of the pollution caused. More specifically the MPs were disturbed that the 'polluter-pays' strategy was not being effectively applied in relation to agricultural pollution, and were openly critical that the courts were not playing their full part, and urged the Ministry of Agriculture, Fisheries and Food and the National Rivers Authority to take a firm line on prosecutions.[85] Perhaps with the same concern as to the relative levels of fines and the degree of harm done to the aquatic environment by pollution incidents in mind, the Government has recently announced its intention to increase the levels of fines which magistrates' courts can impose for water pollution offences to £20,000.[86]

CONCLUSION

This brief survey of the administration and law relating to the protection of the aquatic environment has highlighted both the progress which has been made over the first year of the National Rivers Authority and the progress which remains to be made. Overall the new administrative machinery for the regulation of the aquatic environment must be an improvement upon previous arrangements if only by the removal of the conflict of interests which beset the former regional water authorities. Further improvements will lie in the new authority asserting its independence in pursuit of environmental improvement, however unpopular with polluters the measures may be, and the Government, where necessary, ensuring that the authority is not prevented from doing so by being starved of central funding.

In relation to the substantive law the need for prevention rather than cure is such an obvious one that there is no real excuse for preventative regulations not having been made long ago. Nonetheless, better later than never is the unavoidable response to the moves towards proactivism in water pollution control regulation. Beyond the substantive law, the use which has been made of it by the new authority is to be commended, as is the awakening of the courts to the sentencing powers which are available to them. Individual as well as corporate liability is certainly a preferable option in certain kinds of case and this should be considered more carefully by prosecutors. The signal for higher levels of fines from the Government will hopefully impress upon all concerned that crimes against the aquatic environment will in future be taken very much more seriously than in the past. Only by taking these kinds of measure can there be any hope of bringing about an end to the continuing decline in the state of our watercourses.

NOTES AND REFERENCES

1 Generally see: *Privatization of the Water Authorities in England and Wales* (1986; Cmnd. 9734); Department of the Environment, *The Water Environment: the Next Steps* (1986); Department of the Environment (Consultation and Policy Documents), *The National Rivers Authority: the Government's Proposals for a Public Regulatory Body in a Privatized Water Industry* (1987);D. Kinnersley, *Water: Rivers, Politics and Pollution* (1988); and R. Macrory, 'The Privatization and Regulation of the Water Industry' (1990) 53 *Modern Law Rev.* 78.
2 Another difficulty which arose in discussion was the question of whether privately owned bodies were legally capable of acting as *competent authorities* for the purposes of overseeing the implementation of European Community water directives.
3 Generally see: R. A. Okun, *Regionalization of Water Management* (1973).
4 Although, by way of exceptions to this, independent water supply companies existed and sewage treatment functions could be subcontracted to local authorities.
5 Speech by the Rt. Hon. Nicholas Ridley, Secretary of State for the Environment, 22 May 1987, included as Annex A to Department of the Environment, *The National Rivers Authority: the Government's Proposals for a Public Regulatory Body in a Privatized Water Industry* (1987).
6 Department of the Environment, *Water Quality in England and Wales 1985* (1986).
7 House of Commons Environment Committee, Third Report, *Pollution of Rivers and Estuaries, Session 1986–87* (1987; H.C. 183)
8 id.
9 Re-enacted in Part III, ch. I of the Water Act 1989 (*The Protection and Management of Rivers and Other Waters: Control of Pollution*).
10 Generally see W. Howarth, *The Law of the National Rivers Authority* (1990).
11 Ch. I, Part III, Water Act 1989.
12 id., ch. II.
13 id., ch. III.
14 id., ch. IV.
15 id., ch. V.
16 The same duty is imposed upon the Secretary of State, the Minister of Agriculture, Fisheries and Food, the Director General of Water Services, water undertakers, sewerage undertakers, and internal drainage boards (ss.8(1) and (7) Water Act 1989).
17 id., s.8(1).
18 id., s.8(4). Special environmental duties are also provided for in relation to sites of special scientific interest (id., s.9).
19 The 'relevant Minister' means the Secretary of State or the Minister of Agriculture, Fisheries and Food (id., s.10(5)(a)).
20 id., s.10(1).
21 The code was approved under the Water and Sewerage (Conservation, Access, and Recreation) (Code of Practice) Order 1989, S.I. No. 1152.
22 See, in particular, s.11(iii).
23 Specifically the Secretary of State and the Minister of Agriculture, Fisheries and Food have the power to issue directions to the Authority under the Water Act 1989, s.146.
24 id., s.10(2).
25 The sub-categories of *controlled waters* are defined in s.103 Water Act 1989.
26 id., s.104(1).
27 id., s.104(2).
28 S.I. 1989 No. 1148.

29 See *This Common Inheritance* (1990; Cm. 1200) para. 12.6; National Rivers Authority, *Annual Report and Accounts 1989/90* (1990) 20; and National Rivers Authority, *Corporate Plan 1990/91* (1990) 29.

30 s.105(1) Water Act 1989.

31 id., s.105(2).

32 The same duty is imposed upon the Secretary of State (id., s.106(1)).

33 id., s.106(1).

34 Although the terminology of 'reactive' and 'proactive' has previously been used in relation to matters of law enforcement, it serves equally to distinguish between those regulatory offences which are committed by involvement in the undesired activity and the criminalization of activities which are preparatory to that activity. Generally see B. M. Hutter, 'An Inspector Calls' (1986) 26 *Brit. J. Criminol.* 114.

35 s.107(1) Water Act 1989.

36 See ss.2 to 5 Rivers Pollution Prevention Act 1876; s.2(1) Rivers (Prevention of Pollution) Act 1951; and ss.31(1) and 32(1) Control of Pollution Act 1974.

37 Generally see W. Howarth, 'Causing, Knowingly Permitting and Preventing Pollution' (1990) *Utilities Law Review* 105.

38 Generally see W. Howarth, *Water Pollution Law* (1988).

39 *Alphacell Ltd.* v. *Woodward* [1972] 2 All E.R. 475, at p. 479.

40 id. and *Wrothwell Ltd.* v. *Yorkshire Water Authority* [1984] Crim. L.R. 43.

41 *Price* v. *Cromack* [1975] 2 All E.R. 113.

42 *Impress (Worcester) Ltd.* v. *Rees* [1971] 2 All E.R. 357.

43 *Price* v. *Cromack* [1975] 2 All E.R. 113; and *Welsh Water Authority* v. *Williams Motors (Cymdu) Ltd.* (1988) Unreported CO/1080/88.

44 Under ss.31(4) and (5) Control of Pollution Act 1974.

45 op. cit., n. 7, para. 89.

46 Department of the Environment, *The Water Environment: the Next Steps* (1986) S.5; and *This Common Inheritance* (1990; Cm. 1200) paras. 12.16 and 13.18.

47 s.110(1) Water Act 1989.

48 Published in January 1990.

49 That is, the offences under s.107 Water Act 1989.

50 *This Common Inheritance* (1990; Cm. 1200) para. 12.18.

51 Consultation is to take place with the Minister of Agriculture, Fisheries and Food in an area wholly or partly within England (s.111(1) Water Act 1989).

52 id., s.111(1).

53 *The Water Environment: the Next Steps* (1986) S.5; and *Pollution of Rivers and Estuaries* (Observations by the Government on the Third Report of the Environment Committee in Session 1986–7) (1988) para. 4.12.

54 See Directive 80/778/EEC relating to the quality of water intended for human consumption (OJ 30.8.80 L229); and Case 337/89, *Commission* v. *United Kingdom*, discussed [1990] *Water Law* 6.

55 s.112(1) Water Act 1989.

56 id., s.112(2).

57 S.I. 1990 No. 1013; and note amendment by Nitrate Sensitive Areas (Designation) (Amendment) Order 1990, S.I. No. 1187.

58 ss.112(4) and (5) Water Act 1989.

59 Reported in [1990] *Water Law* 40.

60 s.31(1)(a) Control of Pollution Act 1974, which corresponds with s.107(1)(a) Water Act 1989.

61 Discussed above.

62 In the context of the judge's remark that the penalty would have been substantially greater if Shell had not had an outstanding record for conservation, a letter to the *Guardian* by Bilsborough quipped, 'In the unhappy event of my being found guilty of a crime could I record, for the benefit of any judge who may be reading, that I am a member of Greenpeace, Friends of the Earth, the Soil Association and the RSPB . . . . I trust that my future fine will now be substantially less than it would otherwise be' (*Guardian*, 28 February 1990).

63 Similar difficulties can arise in relation to fines imposed upon nationalized industries with no shareholders, where fines are ultimately paid by the consumers of the product who have no power to appoint or dismiss the officials concerned. Generally, see J. C. Smith and B. Hogan, *Criminal Law* (6th ed. 1988) 170–6. Hence there was an outcry in 1951 when the Yorkshire Electricity Board was fined £20,000 for contravening a defence regulation (see id., p. 175 n. 8).

64 [1990] *Water Law* 41.

65 s.107(6) Water Act 1989, formerly s.31(7) Control of Pollution Act 1974; and see n. 86 below.

66 s.177(1) Water Act 1989, formerly s.87(1) Control of Pollution Act 1974: see also s.25 Forgery and Counterfeiting Act 1981, but contrast s.18 Theft Act 1968.

67 s.177(2) Water Act 1989, formerly s.87(1) Control of Pollution Act 1974.

68 *Tesco Supermarkets Ltd.* v. *Nattrass* [1972] A.C. 153, at p. 178.

69 *Huckerby* v. *Elliot* [1970] 1 All E.R. 189.

70 Discussed by D. Bergman, 'Recklessness in the Boardroom' (1990) *New Law J.* 1496; and see also W. J. Maakestad, 'Corporate Homicide' (1990) *New Law J.* 356.

71 See above.

72 Quotations from P. A. Smith, 'Criminal and Civil Liability of Company Directors and Senior Mangers' p. E5, a paper delivered at the conference, *Environmental Law and Practice*, London, 7 November 1990.

73 (1990) 1 *Water Guardians* 2.

74 (1990) 4 *Water Guardians* 2.

75 (1990) 6 *Water Guardians* 2.

76 (1990) 8 *Water Guardians* 2.

77 (1990) 9 *Water Guardians* 2.

78 (1990) 10 *Water Guardians* 3.

79 (1990) 10 *Water Guardians* 1.

80 Other than the *Shell* case, discussed above.

81 *This Common Inheritance* (1990; Cm.1200) para. 12.24.

82 National Rivers Authority, *Annual Report and Accounts 1989/90* (1990) 18.

83 id., p. 79.

84 Generally, see National Rivers Authority/Ministry of Agriculture, Fisheries and Food. *Water Pollution from Farm Waste 1989* (1990)

85 House of Commons Public Accounts Committee, *Grants to Aid the Structure of Agriculture in Britain, Session 1989–90* (1990; H. C. 150) para. 28.

86 *This Common Inheritance* (1990; Cm.1200) para. 12.24. The increase in summary fines for water pollution offences is provided for in s.145(1) Environmental Protection Act 1990 which came into effect on 1 January 1991.

Environmental Awareness and United Kingdom Energy Policy

JOHN WOODLIFFE*

The production, conversion, transportation, and end-uses of energy in the economy of an industrialized state have significant impacts on the local, regional and, increasingly, global environment. Scientific understanding and public awareness of the linkage between energy and the environment have grown steadily over the past two decades, resulting in the demand for a framework of policy-making that seeks to balance and integrate both energy and environment objectives.[1] Political acceptability is, however, likely to prove the ultimate determinant of action to protect the environment. A recent study by the Organization for Economic Co-operation and Development (OECD) identifies eleven major areas of environmental concern where energy-related activities play a role in some degree.[2] The areas are: (i) major life-threatening environmental accidents or perceived risks thereof caused, for example, by unplanned releases of radioactivity in the course of the production of nuclear energy or of the transport or storage of radioactive materials; (ii) groundwater pollution which is the result, for example, of an oil leak from underground storage tanks;[3] (iii) maritime pollution occasioned by the discharge of oil by ships at sea and by tanker accidents; (iv) land use and siting impact associated with the development of mines or construction of power stations and refineries; (v) radiation and radioactive releases attributable to the front and back ends of the nuclear fuel cycle; (vi) solid waste disposal of sludge and fly ash produced by air-pollution abatement measures such as flue gas desulphurization;[4] (vii) hazardous air pollutants such as lead that are emitted by petrol-driven vehicles; (viii) ambient air quality, which is especially affected by discharges of SO_2 and NO_x from stationary combustion facilities and by CO emisssions from mobile sources; (ix) acid deposition – again, related principally to emissions of SO_2 and NO_x – that produces deleterious effects, both locally and much further afield upon, among other things, lakes, forests, and buildings; (x) stratospheric ozone depletion (this is tentatively linked to harm to human health occasioned by increased levels of ultraviolet radiation. In this area, the responsibility of fossil fuel and biomass combustion appears to be secondary to that of chlorofluorocarbons.); (xi) global climate change or global warming as it is commonly known, that is

* *Faculty of Law, Leicester University, Leicester LE1 7RH, England*

produced by the build-up of so-called 'greenhouse gases'. Increases in world temperature could trigger rises in sea level, changes in rainfall and weather patterns, and shifts in food-growing regions. CO_2 emisssions are responsible for more than half of global warming, and fossil-fuel burning contributes nearly three quarters of all CO_2 emissions.

This inventory is far from immutable. The capacity of science to identify and measure new hazards and pollutants puts continuing pressure on political decision-making to accede to public demands for action.[5] Moreover, there are substantial variations in the impact that each of the areas listed has on the environment. Several of these areas are specifically addressed by other contributors. This paper adopts a narrower brief; it focuses on the incorporation of environmental goals in the formulation and implementation of United Kingdom law and policy over the past twenty years appertaining to the production and use of energy. For this purpose, the conceptual model of energy and environment decision-making employed in the above-mentioned OECD study is adopted: this involves, first, identification of potential policy responses to the environmental impacts of energy production and use. A pre-requisite of each response is that it 'provide[s] the energy needed for an activity with the lowest environmental impact, at the least cost, and the maximum of energy security possible.'[6] Other constraints to be taken into account are the political and institutional barriers to action at the level of industry, consumers, and governments. The next stage in the process is a review of the policy measures (such as information, regulation, and economic instruments) available for implementing chosen policy response. The review must include an assessment of each policy instrument according to its effectivemess in changing consumer behaviour and its effects at a micro- and macro-economic level.[7]

ENVIRONMENTAL FACTORS IN THE DEVELOPMENT OF UNITED KINGDOM ENERGY POLICY

Over the past two decades United Kingdom policies on energy and the environment, in common with those of other industrialized countries, have developed from 'either the need to respond to an identified national or regional problem or from the need to meet a policy objective as set out in an international agreement.'[8] These trends are a reflection of the widespread recognition of the transboundary and often global nature of many environmental problems. This in turn results in scrutiny of and the shaping of national energy policies within regional and international fora. For member states of the European Community, this collaborative approach has assumed an even closer form since the Single European Act 1986, where it is stipulated that 'environmental protection requirements shall be a component of the Community's other policies.'[9] In addition to participating in the application and development of the 1979 Convention on Long-range Transboundary Air Pollution,[10] drawn up by the United Nations Economic Commission for

Europe, the United Kingdom is a participating country in the International Energy Agency (IEA) of the OECD and the Intergovernmental Panel on Climate Change set up under the auspices of the United Nations Environment Programme and the World Meteorological Organization.[11] There is thus considerable force in the argument that in energy affairs today there is 'no longer such a thing as a coherent national policy'; coherence is attainable only by means of a global energy policy that takes into account 'the environmental issues raised by the global energy system and fuel mix.'[12]

In retrospect, the turning-point may be seen to have been the energy policy review conducted by the Labour Government in 1977.[13] It acknowledged that the traditional approach of United Kingdom governments to energy policy was 'rather insular' and called for greater attention to be paid to international considerations and the European Community (para. 8). The goal of energy policy was 'to secure that the nation's needs for energy are met at the lowest cost in resources, consistently with security and with environmental, social and other objectives.' (para. 4). The main source of environmental anxiety was nuclear power (paras. 7, 41).[14] The review singled out 'transfrontier pollution, with pressure particularly from Scandinavia for a reduction in emissions of sulphur oxides' (para. 40), but added:

> there is a danger of improved standards being set up as an absolute objective, not related to evidence of environmental impact and with little regard to costs.

The review re-affirmed support for the principle of 'best practicable means' (BPM) and foresaw major investment in the coal industry as part of the United Kingdom's long-term energy strategy (para. 45 *et seq.*). The review did purport to put down some markers for the future including: the development of coal conversion research; encouragement of energy conservation (para. 15); and the establishment of viable renewable energy sources (para. 48 *et seq.*).

A shift in the priorities of United Kingdom energy policy is evident from a speech in 1982 by the then Secretary of State for Energy, Nigel Lawson.[15] While detecting a growing public interest in the forms of renewable sources of energy and in the importance of conservation as levers on the demand side, he stressed that nuclear power remained a vital part of Unite Kingdom policy. He outlined the task of Government thus:

> ... to set a framework which will ensure that the market operates with a minimum of distortion and that energy is produced and consumed efficiently.

This market ideology provided the touchstone for a programme of privatization of state-owned industries in the energy sector, culminating in 1990 in the first instalment of the sale of the electricity industry. During the 1980s the United Kingdom became a net exporter of oil (produced from fields in its North Sea Continental Shelf) and coal. The United Kingdom also continued the expansion of a significant nuclear programme. Two of the major goals of national energy policy were thereby satisfied; diversification and security of supply. Towards the end of the decade, both the EC Commission and the International Energy Agency expressed concern about the Government's articulation of energy policy on a case-by-case basis; this absence of a comprehensive policy statement explaining the reliance on market forces and defining the proper role of government complicated attempts to plan a mid- to long-term strategy.[16] A parliamentary statement in December 1989 by the Secretary of State, John Wakeham, set out the ingredients of the Government's current approach to policy: it is to ensure that the United Kingdom:

> has adequate, diverse, and secure supplies of energy in the forms that people want at the lowest realistic prices. It aims to achieve this wherever possible by ensuring that energy prices reflect their true economic costs and by subjecting as much of energy supply as is practicable to the operation of market forces, bearing in mind the State's strategic responsibilities for health and safety, the protection of the environment, and the elimination of energy waste.[17]

While the policy mix is much as before, a higher profile is accorded to protection of the environment. The Government has indicated that in shaping domestic policies it will take into account the threat of global warming – 'one of the most important issues facing the world today.'[18] The political commitment to the protection of the global environment was forcefully underlined by the former Prime Minister, Margaret Thatcher, in speeches to the Royal Society[19] and the United Nations.[20]

In assessing which of the changes in United Kingdom energy policy during the 1980s have had most impact on environmental goals, two events stand out. First, the Government succumbed to considerable international pressure and overturned the long-standing position of the Central Electricity Generating Board (CEGB) that no substantial expenditure should be incurred in the installation of flue gas desulphurization (FGD) plant at existing coal-burning power stations until the causes of the acid deposition ('acid rain') affecting soil and surface waters in Scandinavia were scientifically proven.[21] The CEGB announced in July 1986 that it proposed to retrofit 6000 MW of coal-fired generating capacity with FGD equipment over the period 1988–1997.[22] These measures would reduce the annual current emissions of SO_2 from what is by far the largest single source of such emissions in the United Kingdom[23]

The second dramatic reversal of policy occurred in November 1989 – three and a half months after the 1989 Electricity Act received the Royal Assent – with the Government's announcement of the removal of the nuclear power industry from the planned electricity privatization.[24] It thus remains in the public sector. This volte-face was prompted to a large extent by the revelation during the planning of the privatization of new information about the real costs of nuclear power; this showed 'a systematic bias in CEGB costings in favour of nuclear power.'[25] Accordingly, nuclear power was less economic than electricity generated from fossil-fuel stations at current prices. At the same time, the Government abandoned its plans for three more pressurized water reactors (PWRs) to follow on from Sizewell B, pending a full-scale review of the prospects for nuclear power in 1994 when Sizewell B nears completion. The decade had started with the announcement of a massive £15 billion ten-year rolling programme of 15 GW of PWR capacity starting in 1982.[26] The Government recognizes the part that nuclear power can play in

113

reducing acid rain and combating global warming and thus 'wishes to maintain the nuclear option'; but it is conditional on nuclear power becoming 'more economic' and on the industry demonstrating it can 'maintain high standards of safety and environmental protection'.[27]

The singular position of nuclear power described above is taken account of in the Electricity Act 1989. Section 21 stipulates that licensed public electricity suppliers in England and Wales[28] must contract for a certain minimum level of electricity from non-fossil sources (predominantly nuclear) until 1998.[28a] The purpose of this requirement, known as the non-fossil fuel obligation (NFFO), is to secure diversity and security of supply. To spead the cost of purchasing the higher priced nuclear-generated electricity, suppliers will pay a fossil fuel levy (FFL) of 10.6 per cent on sales of electricity that are gained from fossil fuel sources.[29] The levy, in essence a subsidy to nuclear power, is estimated to run initially at £900 million a year, after which it should slowly decline.[30] The environmental implications of the non-fossil fuel obligation are considered further below.

In September 1990, the Government published a major policy document, *This Common Inheritance: Britain's Environmental Strategy*,[31] the first comprehensive White Paper on the environment. This sets out the philosophy behind the government's approach to environmental problems affecting Britain, Europe, and the world. It also includes a series of measures on energy designed to contribute to a reduction in global warming;[32] these are considered below.

ENVIRONMENTAL PRIORITIES IN THE ENERGY SECTOR: CURRENT TRENDS

The centre-piece of the United Kingdom's strategy for combating its own greenhouse gas emissions is directed at emissions of CO_2 that result from the use of fossil fuels. The aim is to keep such emissions to 1990 levels by the year 2005. As mentioned above, earlier projections of new nuclear generating capacity have been drastically revised downwards. This has in turn reduced the projected savings in CO_2, SO_2 and NO_x emissions that an expansion of the nuclear power programme would otherwise have produced. Implementation of the main elements of United Kingdom strategy is already under way on two main fronts: energy efficiency and renewables.

ENERGY EFFICIENCY

The House of Commons Energy Committee report on the greenhouse effect observed that 'the most obvious and most effective response to the problem of global warming' lies with 'improvements in energy efficiency',[33] a view with which the Government agreed.[34] The European Community likewise regards energy efficiency and energy conservation as 'the corner-stone of integration of the environmental dimension into energy policy'.[35]

114

Three major current initiatives on energy efficiency are outlined in the 1990 White Paper.

1. *Electricity generation and supply under the Electricity Act 1989*

It is the Government's belief that the privatization of the electricity industry 'will lead to very substantial reductions in CO_2 emissions'.[36] Three examples are given in support of this claim. First, the introduction of competition among electricity generators will provide them with a strong incentive to produce electricity more efficiently. Already, the two main non-nuclear generators, PowerGen and National Power, have indicated that gas will be their first choice of fuel for power generation.[37] In comparison with coal-fired plant, combined-cycle gas-turbine plants are able to cut emissions of carbon dioxide and sulphur dioxide by 59 per cent and almost 100 per cent respectively, and achieve a 45 per cent rate of efficiency as opposed to 35 per cent for coal.[38]

The second example is the non-fossil fuel obligation referred to earlier; this is intended to encourage electricity generation from non-fossil fuels such as nuclear power and renewable sources of energy.

Lastly, the Electricity Act 1989 imposes duties on public electricity suppliers 'to develop and maintain an efficient, co-ordinated and economical system of electricity supply';[39] in addition, the terms of their licences require them to provide information and advice to their customers on the efficient use of electricity.[40] The Act also establishes the post of Director-General of Electricity Supply (DGES) whose duties include monitoring the performance of licence holders and taking account of the physical environment of activities connected with the generation, supply, or distribution of electricity.[41]

2. *Industry and Commerce*

Industry and commerce, which includes housing and the public sector, account for around 30 per cent of national CO_2 emissions. Energy efficiency in this sector is promoted by a government body, the Energy Efficiency Office (EEO). Since April 1989, this body, through its best practice programme, has provided information and guidance on energy efficiency technologies and management techniques. It also assists the energy efficiency industry with developing marketing opportunities for equipment and consultancy services. In this respect, one of the most promising technologies for reducing CO_2 emissions is combined heat and power (CHP).[42] This highly fuel-efficient technology, which can operate with any fuel, using plant of any size, is already widely used and is likely to prove an attractive option for the soon-to-be-privatized generating companies.[43]

3. *Buildings*

Heating, lighting, and electrical appliances in buildings account for nearly half of all energy use in the United Kingdom. A significant part of the EEO's best practice programmme is aimed at this sector. New building regulations prescribing higher thermal insulation standards for new houses came into force on 1 April 1990.[44] Also under consideration for inclusion in future building regulations is a system of energy 'labelling' of buildings.[45] The EEO is also proposing to introduce a home energy efficiency scheme, to provide advice and grants for lower-income households in both public and private sector housing.[46]

Finally, it should be noted that energy efficiency and fossil fuel CHP schemes can form part of the non-fossil fuel obligation since both satisfy the twin aims of security of supply through diversity of fuel inputs.[47]

RENEWABLE SOURCES OF ENERGY

At present, virtually all of the 1.5 per cent of electricity generated from renewable sources (renewables) derives from hydro power.[48] The most comprehensive survey of the potential of United Kingdom renewable energy technologies is in Energy Paper 55.[49] This suggests that renewables 'could make a useful and economic contribution to the UK economy from the late 1990s' and possibly account for one quarter of current electricity supply by 2025.[50] The treatment of renewables in the 1990 White Paper is cautiously optimistic. It recognizes that some technologies such as the use of methane from land-fill sites are already commercially viable; the majority,[51] however, will require more research, not least into their environmental impacts. The Government has earmarked £50 million for expenditure on renewables research and development, demonstration, and promotion over the period 1990–1992, and significantly, has allocated a tranche of the non-fossil fuel obligation to renewables.[52] As described earlier, the higher cost to public electricity suppliers that the obligatory purchase of non-fossil fuel electricity capacity entails is met by the imposition of a levy on all sales of electricity produced from fossil fuels. From 1 September 1990, suppliers are required to contract for a total of some 102 MW of renewable capacity by 1998.[53] Contracts have been concluded for some seventy-five projects that are to be supported by the levy; they include, in descending order of contribution : waste incineration, gas from land-fill, hydroelectric, and wind.[54] Further orders will be laid before Parliament for up to 600 MW of renewable capacity and will cover projects that were not ready for contracting when the 1990 order was laid.[55] The Government intends to institute a fundamental review of its renewables programme in 1991.

INSTRUMENTS[55a]

The Government shares the view expressed in the Energy Committee's report on the greenhouse effect[56] that there are 'market imperfections in the energy efficiency field;'[57] it rejects, however, the 'mixture of regulation, penalties, and

116

incentives' recommended by the Energy Committee[58] to combat those imperfections. The way forward is through the free market 'lubricated by information and advice.'[59] On the broader issue of the best instruments for tackling environmental consequences of global warming, the Government likewise dismissed the committee's strong reservations on the operation of market mechanisms.[60]

The 1990 White Paper acknowledges the vital role of the 'polluter-pays' principle as a means of influencing potential polluters.[61] It dismisses, however, the widely held view that regulation is the best instrument of control, arguing that it is unresponsive to technical change and inaccurately gauges the precise level of control at which the most cost-effective balance between environmental benefits and compliance costs is reached.[62] The Government's stated preference is for market-based approaches that integrate economic and environmental concerns and which influence the behaviour of consumers and producers in ways that benefit the environment.[63] While this approach regards the price mechanism as the key to tackling the environmental consequences of the consumption of energy, it discounts the introduction (other than in the transport sector) in the 'next few years' of energy taxation or other measures directly raising the relative price of energy.[64] This will only change when competitor countries are prepared to take similar action.[65]

No form of energy production is environmentally benign; there will always be some impact on the environment. For example, the flue gas desulphurization system involves limestone as a feedstock and produces as a by-product either gypsum or sulphur.[66] A further unanticipated by-product of FGD plant is chloride which poses a threat to water supplies.[67] Similarly, a tidal barrage may produce emission-free electricity yet flood important wildlife habitats.

These examples point up a central problem in establishing the precise synergy between environmental and energy goals. On the one hand, low energy prices are a disincentive to investment in energy efficiency; on the other hand, reliance on free market forces requires clear proof that energy prices reflect their true social and environmental costs. Whether there is a system that can accurately assess and allocate these 'external costs' is still a matter of considerable controversy.[68] The need for more research into the development of a methodology for quantifying the environmental costs and benefits of each energy technology is recognized by the Government.[69]

Under the auspices of the National Advisory Group on Eco-Labelling, the United Kingdom is contributing at a European level to what is called 'ecobalance research' or 'life-cycle analysis'. This seeks to measure the environmental impacts of such products as washing machines or motor vehicles throughout their life cycle, from the extraction of raw materials for their manufacture to the dumping of the product in a land-fill.[70]

IS PRIVATIZATION OF THE ELECTRICITY INDUSTRY ENVIRONMENTALLY FRIENDLY?

Prima facie, the environmentally desirable objectives of energy efficiency and energy conservation co-exist uneasily with the goals of the privatized electricity industry which 'will make their profits from selling electricity, and the more electricity they can sell, the higher will be everyone's profits'.[71] There are several indications that environmental concerns have been put second to commercial profitability.

The first indication is the Government decision announced in April 1990,[72] to modify the £26 million FGD programme launched in 1986 to reduce pollution emissions from 12,000 MW of plant in compliance with the EC directive on large combustion installations.[73] The directive requires cuts of 40 per cent in sulphur emissions by 1998 and 60 per cent by 2003, using 1980 as the base year. The revised FGD programme envisages the retrofitting of 8000 MW of plant only.[74] The Government response to critics of its decision is that the directive does not stipulate any specific form of abatement technique; its aims can be met by means other than retrofitting, such as switching to gas-fired stations and imported low-sulphur coal.[75] The desire to reduce the pre-privatization investment commitments of PowerGen and National Power is probably nearer the mark.

The second significant development is the treatment accorded to energy efficiency objectives in the Electricity Act 1989. This proved to be one of the most contentious issues during the passage of the bill through Parliament. The House of Lords inserted into the bill a new clause on the efficient use of electricity. The new clause would have empowered the Secretary of State, in consultation with the Director-General of Electricity Supply, to require each distribution company to produce evidence to the Director showing that it 'has made such arrangements as will promote the efficient use of electricity.' The Secretary of State would also be authorized to direct any distribution company 'to take specific action in this area and if appropriate . . . refuse or amend any application for tariff increases or major capital projects.'[76] The House of Commons Energy Committee felt sufficient sympathy for the principle of the Lords' amendment to publish a separate report on the matter. The report does, however, find the amendment technically deficient, not least for its failure to recognize that major capital investment would normally be made by generators and not suppliers of electricity. The committee called upon the Government to introduce amendments to strengthen the obligation to provide energy efficiency.[77]

Attempts by the opposition parties to write this obligation into the legislation along with several new clauses on energy conservation and protection of the environment failed in both Houses. The main thrust of these amendments was to require the DGES to promote efficiency and conservation of energy by (i) ensuring that suppliers take such steps as are reasonable to maximize energy efficiency and conservation, and (ii) setting annual targets for improvement in energy efficiency for suppliers.[78]

Other amendments sought to achieve annual target reductions in pollution and to introduce the radical concept of least-cost planning.

Least-cost planning (LCP): a missed opportunity

The essential idea behind LCP is that no new plant can be built unless it can be demonstrated that the required capacity cannot be met by additional measures of efficiency or conservation. In effect, every pound invested in energy conservation measures will yield more saved units of electricity than that same pound spent on investing in new generating capacity.[79] This policy has had a measure of success in Norway and the United States of America.

Underlying LCP is the radical notion that the consumer does not buy electricity as such, but services such as heat, light, and motive power. These end-uses are only minimally secured by market mechanisms. If electricity and other fuel suppliers view themselves as providers of services rather than of kilowatt hours, then the issue is simply one of how that demand is best met. LCP places the choice squarely between investment in more power-plant construction or in raising end-use efficiency.

Thus, in the United States of America, customers are offered low-cost energy audits from the electricity supplier who will offer low-interest loans to enable the customer to buy, for example, high-efficiency lighting, heating, and other appliances. Everyone gains: the company gets a more rapid return on its investment; the customer gets lower bills; and the impact on the environment is lower. In this way, LCP balances supply and demand-side resources in order to meet the needs of energy users at the least cost.[80]

Despite widespread all-party support for the concept, LCP was given a hostile reception by the then Secretary of State for Energy, Cecil Parkinson, who described its operation in the United States as 'a disaster.'[81] Without regulatory pressure it is unlikely that the electricity industry will adopt LCP, thus confirming the view of one expert that 'privatization and environmental accountability cannot be separated from a strong and independent public interest regulation.'[82]

THE UNITED KINGDOM RECORD ASSESSED

1. *Energy policy or energy politics?*

As the environment moves rapidly up the scale of political priorities of both Government and electorate, there are signs that the 1990s may herald a breakdown of the ceasefire in the United Kingdom energy policy debate that was a mark of the late 1980s.[83] First, the privatization of the gas and electricity industries will accelerate the inter-fuel substitution and market interpenetration already taking place within those industries and take the battle for primary energy markets into the remaining public sector energy industries, namely nuclear and coal. National Power has begun to loosen its dependence on British coal, by announcing plans for new gas-fired power stations, for coal-mining joint ventures overseas and for gaining access to long-term gas supplies from the North Sea.[84] The nuclear industry is vigorously pressing what it regards as its environmental advantages over fossil fuel.[85] The British coal industry is on the defensive and its economic prospects after its contracts with the power-generating companies terminate in 1993 look bleak. In the autumn of 1990, the gas industry sponsored a series of newspaper advertisements and position papers by independent experts on key environmental issues, designed to show the industry's 'green' credentials. Indeed, campaigning is increasingly conducted along acrimonious lines. Nuclear Electric is proposing that, in return for industry's role in combating global warming, nuclear power should be accorded 'environmental credits' set at £8 for every tonne in reduction of CO_2, to replace the fossil fuel levy when this ends in 1998.[86] However, nuclear power's long-term prospects in the United Kingdom are highly problematic: when the NFFO and FFL end in 1998 nuclear power will be even less economically attractive to the electrical distribution companies. The economic, safety, and environmental preconditions for a revival of nuclear power as a 'realistic option for energy policy during the next twenty years' are increasingly unlikely to be met.[87]

Conversely, proponents of renewable energy projects argue that the limited lifespan of the FFL gives an unfair advantage to nuclear power since nuclear stations are already built and have only to cover their running costs.[88] The Government's projected expenditure of £22 million on research and development of renewables in 1992 is in real terms no higher than it was ten years previously.[89] The House of Commons Energy Committee has recently called for a radical review of the Department of Energy's research and development programme which continues to lean heavily towards nuclear research; in particular it calls for an examination of how mistakes were made in costing a pioneering programme of research into deep-sea wave power (Salter's Duck) which was wound up in 1983.[90] The critical issue remains whether the development of renewables is best left to the private sector or to state planning and investment.[91]

Lastly, the Labour Party's environmental programme, *An Earthly Chance*, published in October 1990, is further evidence of a breakdown of consensus on energy policy. While the programme rules out any new nuclear power station, it opposes the switch to gas-fired plants which is the favoured policy of the Government as well as PowerGen and National Power; Labour's preference is for clean-burn coal-fired stations.[92]

2. *The Tortoise of Europe*

On the European front, the United Kingdom lags behind its Community partners in cutting down CO_2 emissions. At the meeting of EC environment ministers in October 1990, a compromise agreement was reached that committed the Community *as a whole* to stabilizing CO_2 emissions at 1990 levels by the year 2000, while allowing the United Kingdom to proceed at a slower pace towards its target of stabilizing emissions by 2005.[93] Despite the isolation of the United Kingdom, the compromise enabled the Community to present a united front at the Second World Climate Conference in November 1990.[94] This is yet another reason which makes the early removal of the label the 'dirty man of Europe' less likely.[95] When measured against the achievements of its major competitors, the United Kingdom is again at the back of the field in the area of energy efficiency. Thus, current building insulation standards are on a par with those introduced in Sweden fifty years ago. Denmark operates a scheme for mandatory energy audits whenever dwelling houses are bought and sold. When a similar proposal was mooted as an EC draft directive in 1987, it was vetoed by the United Kingdom. Several voluntary schemes have recently appeared, such as the national home energy rating scheme launched by the National Energy Foundation. The United States of America already bans the sale of appliances that are unacceptably inefficient;[96] in contrast, the 1990 White Paper only contemplates a voluntary system of energy labelling of domestic appliances. But the British Government intends to seek agreement within the European Community on (i) a common scheme for energy efficiency labelling of electrical appliances, and (ii) minimum efficiency standards for such equipment as well as for central heating boilers and industrial heating equipment.[97]

United Kingdom expenditure on energy efficiency per head of the population lags substantially behind many European states. In 1988–89, there was a twelve per cent decline in investment in energy-saving materials[98] and the budget for the Energy Efficiency Office had, in real terms, halved in value from its peak three years previously.[99] Whereas, between 1973 and the mid-1980s, the United Kingdom had improved its energy efficiency at a rate twice the European Community average, it has now fallen behind other EC states.[100]

These developments are now out of kilter with policy trends in the rest of the European Community. The EC Directorates-General responsible for energy and the environment have put mandatory least-cost planning among the priorities for action in promoting energy efficiency.[101] There is also a potential clash looming between the United Kingdom and the Community over the introduction of a carbon tax on fossil fuels which Carlo Ripa de Meana, the Environment Commissioner, is reported to favour strongly.[102] The United Kingdom remains hostile to the introduction of such a tax in the foreseeable future.[103] The rise in Community GDP that completion of the single market is expected to generate will lead to a significant rise in SO_2 and NO_x emissions above the levels that would prevail in the absence of the single market.[104] This will accentuate the need for an integrated Community policy on energy and the environment grounded in the concept of sustainable development. It is also imperative that co-ordination between different sectors of the economy is strengthened so that reductions in emissions in the energy sector are not wiped out by corresponding increases in the transport sector.

The United Kingdom has been slow to accept that the key to effective action is international co-operation. It deserves credit, however, for taking the initiative to secure a framework convention on climate change; it now accepts there is a responsibility to provide technological and economic assistance to help developing countries tackle the root causes of global warming; and it is a belated convert to the principle of precautionary action.[105] For the foreseeable future the environmental dimension of United Kingdom energy policy is likely to be driven by market-based approaches but within a policy framework that, increasingly, will be defined and controlled by the European Community.

NOTES AND REFERENCES

1 See generally OECD/IEA, *Energy and the Environment: Policy Overview* (1989).
2 id., ch. III.
3 Energy-related activities are no longer regarded as having a major impact upon surface water quality: id., p. 27.
4 See further under the development of UK energy policy, below.
5 op. cit., p. 10.
6 id., p. 4.
7 id., p. 6.
8 id., p. 23.
9 Article 130R.
10 Cmnd. 9034.
11 Of particular influence in setting the terms of the debate is the notion of sustainable development set out in the report of the World Commission on Environment and Development, *Our Common Future* (1987) ch. 7.
12 Remarks of Sir Ian Lloyd, Chair, House of Commons Energy Committee at a seminar on 'Environmentalism's Changing Climate', reported in *Atom*, May 1990, p. 19.
13 Department of Energy, Energy Paper no. 22 (1977).
14 See also report of the Royal Commission on Environmental Pollution, *Nuclear Power and the Environment* (1976; Cmnd. 6618; chair, Lord Flowers).
15 Department of Energy, Energy Paper no. 51 (1982).
16 COM (88) 174/11 final, para. 390; OECD/IEA, *Energy Policies and Programmes of IEA Countries: 1988 Review* (1989) 541, at 556, 559.
17 162 *H.C. Debs.*, col. 447 (1 December 1989).
18 Government Observations on the Sixth Report from the Committee (Session 1988–89) on the Energy Policy Implications of the Greenhouse Effect (1989; H.C. 611) para. 1.
19 27 September 1988.
20 *The Guardian*, 9 November 1989.
21 *Acid Rain: The Government's Reply to the Fourth Report from the Environment Committee (Session 1983–84)* (1984; Cmnd. 9397) para. 1.3.
22 Memorandum of Department of the Environment submitted to the Environment Committee, First Report, *Air Pollution, Session 1987–88*, (1988; H.C. 270–II).
23 Energy Committee, Sixth Report, *Energy Policy Implications of the Greenhouse Effect, Session 1988–89* (1989; H.C. 192-I). Table 6, para. 50.
24 159 *H.C. Debs.*, col. 117 (9 November 1989). This decision had been foreshadowed by the withdrawal in July 1989 of the Magnox stations from the privatization.
25 Energy Committee, Fourth Report, *The Cost of Nuclear Power, Session 1989–90* (1990; H.C. 205) para. 46.
26 David Howell, Secretary of State for Energy, 976 *H.C. Debs.*, col. 287 (18 December 1979).
27 In September 1990, the Government granted planning permission for a new nuclear power station, Hinkley Point C, but postponed a decision on funding the cost of the project until 1994: 177 *H.C. Debs.*, col. 604 (6 September 1990).
28 This paper does not address the position of the electricity industry in Scotland.

28a See the Electricity (Non-Fossil Fuel Sources) (England and Wales) (No. 2) Order 1990, S.I. No. 1859 (in force 29 September 1990).

29 John Wakeham, 167 *H.C. Debs.*, col. 28 (12 February 1990). See also the Fossil Fuel Levy Regulations 1990, S.I. No. 266.

30 *This Common Inheritance: Britain's Environmental Strategy* (1990; Cm. 1200) para. 15.36. The EC Commission has approved the levy, which constitutes a state aid under the Treaty of Rome, until 1998: op. cit., n. 25, para. 113.

31 id. (hereinafter referred to as the 1990 White Paper).

32 id., pp. 19, 64 ff. Pressure on space prevents consideration of other aspects of energy use and production raised in the White Paper that have significant environmental impacts, including transport, air pollution, and radioactive waste disposal. See 1990 White Paper pp. 72, 142, and 200.

33 op. cit., n. 23, para. 102.

34 *Government Observations on the Sixth Report from the Committee (Session 1988–89) on the Energy Policy Implications of the Greenhouse Effect* (1989; H.C. 611) para. 4.1.

35 Communication from the Commisssion to the Council on *Energy and the Environment* COM (89) 369 final, para. 51.

36 op. cit., n. 30, Annex C.4

37 'National power moves into gas exploration' *The Guardian*, 17 October 1990. PowerGen and National Power are the successors to the CEGB.

38 op. cit., n. 23, para. 65.

39 s.9 (1).

40 167 *H.C. Debs.*, col. 28 (12 February 1990).

41 s.3.

42 op. cit., n. 23, para. 125 ff. The DGES is enjoined to keep CHP under review.

43 PowerGen is reported to be carrying out a feasibility study for a CHP station on the site of Shotton Paper Mills, North Wales: *Financial Times*, 9 October 1990.

44 The Building Regulations (Amendment) Regulations 1989, S.I. No. 1119.

45 op. cit., n. 30, Annex C.16.

46 id., Annex C.22.

47 op. cit., n. 34, para. 5.4.

48 op. cit., n. 23, para 85.

49 Department of Energy, *Renewable Energy in the UK: The Way Forward* (1988).

50 id., p. 2.

51 Examples are: small-scale hydropower; wind energy; tidal power; biofuels; passive solar design; and the burning of dry wastes. Annex C, Part B

52 op. cit., n. 34, para. 3.7.

53 *Financial Times*, 1 October 1990. The total of renewable capacity is less than the output of a small conventional power plant.

54 *Financial Times*, 4 October 1990.

55 op. cit., n. 30, para. c.43. By 1992, the largest renewable energy project in the UK, a £136 million plant in Wolverhampton, that will generate energy from discarded rubber tyres, should be operational: *Financial Times*, 26 October 1990.

55a See generally, *Energy and the Environment*, op. cit., n. 1, Part IV.

56 op. cit., n. 23, para. 107.

57 op. cit., n. 34, para. 4.5.

58 op. cit., n. 23, para. 113.

59 op. cit., n. 34, para. 4.7.

60 id., para. 5.1

61 op. cit., n. 30, para. 1.34.

62 id., para. 1.27.

63 id., para. 1.28.

64 id., para. 1.31.

65 id., para. 5.26.

66 The Environment Committee, First Report, *Air Pollution, Session 1987–99* (1988; H.C. 270–I)

para. 69 ff. An 1800 MW station requires 300,000 tonnes of limestone and produces nearly half a million tonnes of sulphur: 502 *H.C. Debs.*, col. 1091 (16 May 1989).

67 'Power plants clean-up may pollute rivers' *The Guardian*, 1 November 1990.

68 op. cit., n. 23, para. 135. See further, O. Hoymeyer, *Social Costs of Energy Consumption* (1988) Commission of the European Communities, EUR 11519; Jones, 'Social Costs of Energy' *Atom*, May 1990, p. 23.

69 op. cit., n. 30, para. 15.37.

70 J. Elkington in *The Guardian*, 10 November 1990.

71 Evidence of the Energy and Power Systems Group submitted to the Energy Committee, Third Report, *The Structure, Regulation, and Economic Consequences of Electricity Supply in the Domestic Sector, Session 1987–88* (1988; H.C. 307–II) p. 319; See also, 'Energy use threatens electricity profits' *Financial Times*, 25 October 1990.

72 170 *H.C. Debs.*, col. 629 (4 April 1990).

73 Directive 88/609 EEC, OJ 7.12.88 L336.

74 Contracts for retrofitting the 4000 MW Drax power station have been concluded and final tenders have been invited for building FGD plant for the 2000 MW power stations at Ferrybridge and Radcliffe: *Financial Times*, 7 August 1990.

75. Mr Trippier, 167 *H.C. Debs.*, col. 918 (21 February 1990).

76 House of Lords Select Commitee on the European Communities, Eighth Report, *Efficiency of Electricity Use, Session 1988–89* (1988; H.L. 37).

77 Energy Committee, Fifth Report, *Electricity Bill: Lords Amendment on Efficient Use of Electricity, Session 1988–89* (1989; H.C. 478).

78 150 *H.C. Debs.*, col. 347 ff. (6 April 1989); 502 *H.L. Debs.*, col. 1087 ff. (16 May 1989).

79 150 *H.C. Debs.*, col. 382 (6 April 1989).

80 See W. Patterson, *The Energy Alternative* (1990); 'Environmentalism's changing climate' *Atom*, May 1990, at p. 22.

81 157 *H.C. Debs.* col. 556 (20 July 1989).

82 T. O'Riordan, 'Electricity privatisation and environmental accountability' 17 *Energy Policy* (1989) 143.

83 M. Jones, 'The UK energy debate in 1980s : ceasefire or new consensus?' 18 *Energy Policy* (1990) 381.

84 op. cit., n. 37. In 1988, the Monopolies and Mergers Commission recommended that ten per cent of gas produced from fields in the UK North Sea continental shelf should be sold to a customer other than British Gas: Cm. 500.

85 See P. Jones, *Energy and the Need for Nuclear Power* (1989); D. Donaldson & H. Tolland, *Nuclear Power and the Greenhouse Effect* (1990).

86 'Nuclear revival plan will go to government' *Financial Times*, 3 October 1990.

87 See J. Surry, *Nuclear Power: Phoenix or Dodo?* (1990) Key Environmental Issues: No. 10., p. 11.

88 'Renewable energy plan falls below expectation' *Financial Times*, 18 September 1990.

89 Mr. Spicer, 162 *H.C. Debs.*, col. 34.

90 Energy Committee, Seventh Report, *The Department of Energy's spending plans 1990–91, Session 1989–90* (1990; H.C. 462). For 1990–91, renewables account for 11.3 per cent of the Department of Energy's total research and development budget.

91 D. Elliot, *Renewable Energy* (1990) Key Environmental Issues: No. 13., p. 12.

92 Advanced technologies, such as pressurized fluidized bed decombustion are still at the research stage: op. cit., n. 23, para. 96.

93 op. cit., n. 30., para. 5.1.

94 'EC deal agreed over gas emissions' *Financial Times*, 30 October 1990.

95 Greenpeace UK, *Why Britain Remains the Dirty Man of Europe* (1990).

96 op. cit., n. 23, para. 115.

97 op. cit., n. 30, para. 5.31; Annex C.IV.

98 University of Sussex, *Case study of potential for reducing UK CO_2 emissions* (1990) Science Policy Research Unit.

99 op. cit., n. 23, para. 102; A. Warren, 'Blowing too hot and cold' *Environment Guardian*, 30 August 1990.

100 op. cit., n. 23, para. 106.
101 op. cit., n. 35, para. 55.
102 Boodle Hatfield, *European Business Brief* (October 1990) 3; 'Carbon emissions tax for EC environment package' *Financial Times*, 19 November 1990.
103 op. cit., n. 30, para. 5.26.
104 H. Folmer, *Environmental Impacts of the Single European Market* (1990) Key Environmental Issues: No. 2, p. 8.
105 op. cit., n. 30, paras. 4.17, 1.18.

Traffic Growth: The Problems and the Solutions

STEPHEN JOSEPH*

Transport is fast shaping as one of the big environmental issues of the next decade. Road traffic is the fastest growing source of greenhouse gases; road building is one of the biggest single causes of wildlife habitat destruction, and both traffic and new roads account for growing general intrusion and problems in the local environment. But the policies which are behind these problems are not working in their own terms either, but are producing road congestion and poor public transport services. Transport directly affects people's lives, and pressures for policy changes are growing because of public perceptions of a 'transport crisis'; this gives an opportunity to propose transport policies which are more environmentally sustainable as well as solving transport problems. Resort to law is one tool increasingly used by those campaigning for transport policy change, though with limited success. In seeking for solutions to transport and environment problems, new laws are not seen as an important element, since the main changes needed are (with exceptions) administrative and financial rather than legal. But new laws and enforcement of existing laws on the speeds, use, and parking of road traffic and the condition of vehicles may in fact be a useful element in an alternative transport policy.

THE POLICY BACKGROUND

Transport policies throughout the developed world were for many years based on motor vehicles, and on satisfying predicted demand for road space. There has been a belief that it is possible to provide congestion-free roads, and indeed to follow the experience of the United States of America in planning a whole society around the car. In pursuit of this, other road users – pedestrians, cyclists, bus users – were simply forgotten, and are still too often ignored in traffic counts. The United Kingdom, like the United States but unlike most European countries, added to this policy a determination to minimize public spending on public transport, with reduced subsidies and occasional threats to shut down all but about a tenth of the rail network (Canada, following the same approach, actually did close about half its passenger rail network in 1990).

* *Executive Director, Transport 2000, 10 Melton Street, London NW1 2EJ, England*

Even leaving aside environmental concerns, it is increasingly clear that these policies do not work in their own terms; they will not help traffic flow more freely. The Government doubled the trunk road programme in 1989; it now plans to spend £17b. on new trunk roads and motorways over the next ten years. This programme was justified by traffic forecasts predicting that road traffic would increase by 83 to 142 per cent between 1988–2025, a doubling in the number of vehicles. These forecasts are not just an academic exercise; they are used to justify each individual road scheme and cannot be questioned at public inquiries (though the Government continues to deny that the forecasts are Government policy in the sense of targets or options which the Government is aiming to meet). Yet it is quite clear that the country cannot cope with 83 to 142 per cent extra traffic (the figure is based on North American 'saturation' levels of car ownership); Dr John Adams of University College London has calculated that the extra traffic could only be accommodated if stationary on a 257–lane London-to-Edinburgh motorway. Local studies of the effects of such traffic levels combined with the roads proposed show severe congestion long before 2025. Business interests and others continue to support more road building on the grounds that 'essential traffic' (goods, and so on) must be given priority; they fail to recognize that since there is no system for designating 'essential' traffic, there is nothing to stop the new roads filling up with local traffic, as happened to the M25.

THE ENVIRONMENTAL PROBLEMS

The road-building programme and the road traffic forecasts have potentially severe environmental consequences. First, there is concern about pollution. Road traffic is already the fastest growing source of greenhouse gases and accounts for 18 per cent of the United Kingdom's carbon dioxide emissions, 45 per cent of nitrogen oxides, 28 per cent of hydrocarbons, and 85 per cent of carbon monoxide. It is clear that the growth of road traffic envisaged in the forecasts will add to this pollution considerably, even allowing for changes in technology like catalytic converters which will cut some emissions from individual vehicles. The forecasts predict a 30 to 50 per cent growth in traffic between 1990 and 2005, yet over the same period the Government has committed itself to stabilizing emissions of carbon dioxide (for which there is no 'technical fix' in road transport). Clearly one or other policy has to give, or other sources of carbon dioxide (industry and energy production) will have to cut rather than simply stabilize their emissions to meet the overall stabilization target.

There are also more local pollution problems caused by motor vehicles, notably the smog caused by some of the pollutants reacting with sunlight. This smog creates serious health problems, especially for those with respiratory problems. Again, while catalytic converters may help to address this, any benefits will be overwhelmed by the growth in traffic. Los Angeles, with some of the world's worst vehicle-related smog problems, has had catalytic converters on its vehicles for years.

The second main area of environmental concern with transport is with the impact of *road-building* itself. As already mentioned, the Government has its own large programme for motorways and trunk roads; a third of the motorway network is to be widened from six to eight lanes, while many A roads are to become dual carriageways or motorways. Local councils, responsible for the non-trunk roads (96 per cent of all roads), have their own sizeable road-building schemes. All this road construction has a huge environmental impact. New roads are one of the main sources of damage to sites of special scientific interest (SSSIs), Britain's best wildlife areas, and while each road scheme may only have a limited impact, the cumulative effect is enormous. The Nature Conservancy Council estimates that the trunk road schemes alone could threaten up to 160 SSSIs, while a report commissioned by the South East Wildlife Trusts estimated that 372 areas of wildlife importance could be damaged by roads. Countryside designated as 'areas of outstanding natural beauty' (AONB) and areas of archaeological importance are also under threat. Occasionally, road planners score a bullseye and produce a road like the M3 at Winchester which affects an archaeological area, an SSSI, and an AONB all at once. A report for Friends of the Earth and the London Wildlife Trust, again by Dr John Adams, suggests that the technique of valuation used by the Government actually uses the presumption against development conferred by designations such as SSSIs to give such land a low or even nil value; if true, this would actually give an incentive to route roads through such areas. Even without this incentive, it is clear that savings in drivers' time and in accidents, which are costed, take precedence in practice over designated environments, for which no value is given. Dorset County Council's preferred route for the Melbury Abbas bypass affects an SSSI and National Trust land, but an alternative, less damaging route was ruled out because it would take three minutes longer and therefore not achieve a 'positive net present value' in the cost-benefit analysis system.

Road-building also puts pressure, if of a less direct kind, on other valued countryside and wildlife habitats, through quarrying the aggregates for road-making materials. The expanded road programme is justifying extraction in areas such as the Mendips and the beaches around Dungeness. Alongside these rural impacts, there are still a number of roads planned through towns. Glasgow has a huge urban motorway programme, while 'relief road' plans are to be found in a number of places like High Wycombe and Norwich. Such schemes often involve severance of communities, destruction of housing and schools, and a general worsening of the quality of urban life, yet without any improvements in travel for motorists.

But the environmental impact of new road schemes does not stop at their construction. The third main environmental concern in transport is the way in which roads attract *new car-based development*, 'suburbanizing' the country-side in the process. This process, the impact of roads on surrounding land uses, is entirely outside any formal public control. The traffic forecasts and the roads programme they support are prepared with little reference to land-use planning; the two systems are completely separate and the evidence is that the

Department of the Environment, which nominally oversees road inquiries and also guides local authority planning policies, has not given any priority to linking the two. The result is that road planning fails to allow for development alongside the roads (road planners still do not accept the idea of 'generated traffic'; instead, they use a 'fixed trip matrix' for most road schemes which assumes that new roads will not change journey patterns). The Oxford-Birmingham M40 motorway which opened in January 1991 has already attracted one million square feet of office space alongside it at Banbury alone.

More generally, new developments (housing estates, out-of-town shopping centres, business parks, school and hospital amalgamations, and so on) have been given planning permission without considering either their impact on local traffic or the potential of access by those without cars. The result is that average journey lengths from home to work, school, shops, hospitals, and other facilities have all grown in the last thirty years, making it more difficult to make such trips without a car. Yet the number of journeys made has not increased greatly. In other words, *mobility* has increased, but *access* (the purpose of mobility) has worsened.

The Government's funding and planning of roads is only one 'intervention in the transport market'; tax relief on the purchase, use, and parking of company cars, now running at £2.8b. a year, represents a huge subsidy to the richest motorist. Further Government support to motoring is provided by funding for the National Health Service to look after traffic accident victims (at a cost approaching £6b. a year) and for the policing of traffic law, at a further unidentifiable cost.

Alongside this, alternatives to cars and lorries have in general become less rather than more attractive. Walking and cycling have become more dangerous; this is not necessarily reflected in accident statistics because the danger forces people to stay off roads. Attention is only now being given to the needs of pedestrians and cyclists, after years of neglect. Buses, potentially the most flexible public transport substitute for the car, have been deregulated, with mixed results, but with a general instability in services and a decline in already low standards of passenger information and waiting facilities. The lack of bus priority in traffic has made buses in towns even more unreliable and unattractive. Passengers have voted with their feet, or wheels; passenger mileage on buses dropped by 13 per cent from deregulation in 1986 to 1990.

Railways have also suffered as a result of consistent underfunding. Subsidies to British Rail have been cut over the last few years; InterCity and freight services are now expected to make money; London Underground and Network SouthEast are due to lose their subsidy by 1993, and 'Regional Railways' (other local passenger services) is to cut its grant by 20 to 25 per cent. This continued reduction in public funding has affected service quality in a number of ways, including through staff cuts at stations. The financial strait-jacket applied to British Rail has also affected investment levels; though Government ministers proclaim the high level of investment, in reality this is mainly about replacing outworn trains, track, and signalling, not about improving the services offered or making new services available.

It is easy to criticize current policies, less easy to propose replacements. However, consensus on alternative transport policy approaches is emerging in the academic world and among transport and environment groups, all of which now accept that it is impossible to build enough roads to meet demand, and that the emphasis must now be on reducing the demand (or at least the growth in demand) for road transport, both through various types of restraint and through improved alternatives.

Any new approach must start by replacing current policies, which give priority to forecast-led roads spending, with national and local objectives for transport as a whole. These objectives might be in terms of sustainability – improving air quality, for instance – and in safety. New policies also need to give priority to improving accessibility – easing people's access to facilities – rather than mobility (which is, after all, a means to an end and rarely an end in itself). For both this and environmental objectives, we need to re-invent *transport planning* (rather than the current approach which seeks to address specific delays facing users of roads and public transport), to make sure that this transport planning embraces all modes of transport (not just private motor vehicles), and to link this transport planning to the general land-use planning system.

The aim of this planning will be, in the short term, to provide a coherent framework within which transport problems and possible solutions can be examined. In the medium to long term, transport and land-use planning can be used to reduce the need to travel, by locating developments and new facilities so that people can reach them easily on foot, bicycle or public transport.

If objectives-led planning is the first main change that is needed, the second is reform to *transport taxation and funding*, where the signals sent by the current system work entirely in the wrong direction. Company-car tax relief, noted above, offers a large incentive to car use and also to the ownership of larger, more polluting cars, while tax-free parking at work gives a direct incentive to car commuting. But market distortions go wider than this; the current motoring tax system makes car ownership expensive and car use relatively cheap; the marginal cost of using a car is low compared with public transport where marginal costs are a direct proportion of total costs. Shifting the tax burden from ownership to use would help correct this; in the longer term, increased taxes on fuel ('carbon taxes') may be needed to reflect the environmental and other costs of motoring. At the same time, the system of appraising public funding for transport projects needs to be reformed so that wider environmental, economic, and social costs and benefits of projects can be considered on an equal basis, and they can be assessed according to the objectives already outlined.

As well as reforming transport taxation, *transport regulation*, another method of intervening in the market, could be tightened up. Speed limits can be used to reduce accidents and pollution; vehicle maintenance and road haulage operating regulations can help reduce pollution, improve energy efficiency, and make vehicles safer; and laws covering parking and other road traffic management measures can be used to discourage traffic from particular areas or routes and to affect road usage. But all of this depends on the regulations and laws being observed; they are not at present.

These changes would change the framework within which decisions about transport are taken, whether by individuals, officials or politicians. At a local level, the new approach should change local transport planning from the present investment programmes for individual modes (roads, railways, cycleways, and so on) to overall transport strategies, with a range of measures making up *transport packages*. These have already developed for cities such as Birmingham, Oxford, and Edinburgh and for counties like Surrey. Elements in these packages are likely to include:

- traffic restraint measures in urban areas and in sensitive leisure areas like the National Parks. These measures could include parking controls and charges, bans on some or all vehicles at certain times and possibly forms of road pricing in the longer term;
- park and ride services linked to areas of traffic restraint;
- priority for cycling and walking, especially in urban areas;
- improved public transport of various types: bus, rail, and light rail, with community transport services for remoter rural areas.

Councils pressing forward with policy and investment packages are currently coming up against the Government's rather rigid rules for funding transport spending, which impose different criteria and different grant regimes for spending on different modes. As already noted, these rules will have to change and more flexible, wide-ranging, and objectives-based funding will be needed to enable councils to implement these packages and to maximize the contribution of all modes to meeting transport needs and other objectives.

More generally, public transport must be radically improved; the main change needed is to see it and plan it as a whole network, rather than as a series of individual rail and bus services; the Passenger Transport Authorities in the big cities have succeeded in doing this and in making public transport attractive for car drivers as well as for existing users. Specific improvements in public transport, including rail electrification, re-opening of some freight lines to passenger traffic, expansion of rail freight facilities, and greater co-ordination and priority for bus services are also needed.

A new strategy for freight might also be considered. As with passenger traffic, most freight journeys are very short distance, but the growth in average length of haul has outstripped the growth in tonnage carried. Use of rail and water for the long haul parts of freight trips could reduce the environmental damage done by the biggest and heaviest lorries, especially if investment is made available to maximize the potential of combined transport systems, which allow easy transfer between modes. The Channel Tunnel offers opportunities for moving more freight by rail, though again a planned strategy will be needed to maximize this. The damage done by unsuitably large and heavy vehicles in urban areas and villages also needs to be addressed, through measures such as lorry bans and management measures, designated lorry routes, and perhaps trans-shipment centres at edges of built-up areas.

With all this, most freight and passenger mileage will still be travelled in motor vehicles by road. Road improvements will still be needed, but they must be assessed within the clear transport policy objectives already mentioned. Priority needs to be given to small-scale local improvements and bypasses, which are likely to meet real environmental and safety problems, rather than to general expansions in trunk road capacity

ACHIEVING CHANGE: THE ROLE OF THE LAW

Given that change is needed in transport policies, what role might the law play in this? In seeking solutions to transport problems, the law has perhaps a modest role to play, since, as noted above, many of the measures needed involve changing financial and administrative structures rather than adjusting the legal framework. The main exception to this is in the area of traffic regulation, as noted already, but even here the problem seems to be as much the lack of enforcement of existing laws as the need for new ones. Indeed, the lack of enforcement and respect for existing laws relating to road traffic poses a big issue for the law as a profession: of 150,000 parking offences in London every day, 149,000 go undetected, speed limits are widely ignored, and road haulage operators flout regulations covering drivers' hours, overloading, and vehicle maintenance. Effective enforcement of these laws is not just a matter of maintaining respect for the law; it is one key way to reduce the attractions and cost advantages of private road traffic. Dr John Whitelegg of Lancaster University has estimated that the lack of enforcement of road haulage regulations across Europe makes road haulage some 20 per cent cheaper than it otherwise would be. A more certain enforcement of motorway speed limits would increase the attraction of inter-city rail travel; urban speed limits, bus lanes, and other traffic restrictions could help give priority to other road users and reduce the attractions of car commuting. So law enforcement in the area of road traffic could contribute to a more environment-friendly transport policy.

The law can help create an environmental transport policy in a second main area: *safeguarding environmental and community interests* during the planning of transport infrastructure. Currently, the 'line orders' and compulsory purchase orders that authorize new roads are subject to public inquiries; new railway and light rail lines are authorized by private Bills in Parliament at present, but changes are likely in this over the next few years and a procedure more like the one already applied to roads is likely to emerge. The problem with the present highway inquiry system is that it is structured to enable negotiation on matters of detail with individual landowners, and cannot cope with wider issues, or even with proposals for alternative routes. The system is biased still further by the Transport Secretary's being involved both in

132

proposing road schemes and in judging the outcome of public inquiries; attempts to involve other departments (the Lord Chancellors's Department in appointing inquiry inspectors, the Department of the Environment as joint arbiter on the outcome) seem to have made little difference. Unlike the development planning system, where structure or local plan consultations allow at least some debate about the desirability of a particular development or land use, there is no national and local procedure by which the desirability and impact of a particular road scheme can be debated. The integration of transport planning with land-use planning (which would by implication mean devolving much of the responsibility for planning new transport infra- structure to local or regional authorities) would be one way of providing such a procedure.

Meanwhile, however, objectors faced with a system which they feel does not give their views a fair hearing are increasingly likely to resort to law to challenge decisions made. Environmental groups are also increasingly likely to take legal action since they have found that the public inquiry system is consistently failing to protect valuable environments from damage by road building. European law offers a whole new dimension to this sort of action, since most main road schemes are subject to environmental assessment under European Community legislation, and there is scope for legal argument about the extent to which current United Kingdom road-planning procedures conform to the spirit or the letter of EC requirements. In the short term, therefore, we can expect more legal involvement in road (and perhaps rail) planning decisions. In the longer term, reform of existing highway planning laws should be sought to give local communities a fairer hearing and to provide greater safeguards for designated and valued environments. The legal framework should aim to ensure that local, environmental, and road traffic interests are involved in genuine negotiation over clear objectives, rather than the needs of increased road traffic taking complete and automatic precedence as at present. As already hinted, this debate may get bound up in discussion about constitutional reform, since there is a strong argument that transport policy at present is distorted by the Department of Transport's detailed involvement in planning and building roads, and that only by devolving this away from the department can other interests at local and national level be considered fairly. In this case, a legal framework may be needed whereby the Transport Secretary can set transport policy objectives for regional or local transport authorities and can use these objectives as the basis for funding transport projects.

The issue of public involvement may arise at more detailed local levels, where parking and traffic management measures arouse strong feelings. A small but useful change here would be enabling clearer and less legalistic consultation by local councils on proposed changes. At present, councils find that they are bound to issue traffic notices in prescribed forms incomprehensible to lay people and that this often provokes fears and controversy about proposals which clearer consultation could mitigate or avoid.

The third main area where the law is involved in transport policy is in setting a framework for the operation of *public transport systems*. In this area, laws have been radically changed in recent years, with the promise of more to come. In particular, bus services outside London have been deregulated and privatized within an entirely new legal structure, as noted above. Leaving aside the debate for or against privatization, the current system and the application of fair trading laws seems to forbid any co-operation between different companies, even to the extent of arranging fares structures or timetables which are clearly in passengers' interests. Meanwhile British Rail is working to a broad remit, given originally by the Railways Act 1974, of providing broadly the same level of service as that existing at present. This is not very useful as the basis for forward planning, but it also does not fit the experience of some rail-users where services are declining or being withdrawn outside peak hours. If British Rail is privatized, as suggested both by Conservatives and some Liberal Democrats, this will demand safeguards for users and for local communities (especially given experiences of asset-stripping from bus deregulation). The problem with public transport privatization, however, is that from an environmental perspective it will be more difficult to implement policies designed to reduce car use.

Whether or not public transport is privatized, legal reform might be needed to strengthen the rights of those using public transport and give wider duties to operators and local authorities to co-ordinate services. At present, rail users have only limited rights of redress when things go wrong, and bus users have no statutory consumer organization at all. A passengers' charter, with associated codes of practice, is being negotiated by the Consumer Congress so that passengers have a clearer idea of operators' commitments, but this is not likely to have any legal force.

CONCLUSION

Transport policy changes are almost inevitable, given the problems with current policies and the environmental damage being caused by increased road traffic and road construction. Alternative, more environmentally sensitive policies, which allow people to be less dependent on using cars and lorries, are both possible and desirable. Though the main changes needed are administrative and financial, the law has a number of potentially useful roles to play in this alternative:

- better regulation of the operation of road vehicles and road systems;
- securing greater consideration for community and environmental interests in transport planning;
- providing a new framework for transport planning and for the operation of public transport.

European Community Environmental Policy and Law

DAVID FREESTONE*

The environmental policy of the European Community is, in many ways, a paradox. The original Treaty of Rome made no provision for an environmental protection policy and the Treaty certainly did not provide an explicit basis for Community legislation in the field of the environment. Nevertheless over 100 legal instruments have been enacted in this area by the Community, the European Court of Justice has described environmental protection as '. . . one of the Community's essential objectives',[1] and it could now be counted as one of the more successful policies of the Community, both in terms of the areas of activity that it covers and the degree of popular support which it is beginning to command. It is indeed a monument to a pragmatic or flexible approach to the interpretation of the aims of the EEC Treaty.[2]

ORIGINS

The origins of the Community environmental policy can be found in the 1972 Stockholm Conference.[3] This coincided with the formal end of the transitional period[4] and the negotiations for enlargement of the Communities.[5] The end of the timetable laid down by the Treaty for the transitional period left a lacuna in policy. Although by no means all the Treaty objectives had been met,[6] most of what was then thought politically achievable was thought to have been achieved. The challenge of protecting the human environment laid down so dramatically by the Stockholm Conference provided a higher profile policy for the EC. At the famous Paris Summit of October 1972 the Heads of State and of Government (the predecessor of the European Council[7]) officially ackowledged the message of the Stockholm meeting, at which of course the EC member states had participated. Despite the overwhelmingly economic objectives of the text of the Rome Treaty, the Paris Summit Communiqué acknowledgced that economic expansion was 'not an end in itself' but that economic growth should be linked to 'improvement in living and working conditions of life of the citizens of the EC.' This phrase, drawn not from the

* *Senior Lecturer, Law School, University of Hull, Hull HU6 7RX England.*

I would like to acknowledge the assistance of Han Somsen in the preparation of this and other work in this field. The final text is my sole responsibility.

text of the Treaty but from its Preamble,[8] formed the somewhat tenuous basis for the development of a Community environmental policy. The basic principles of this policy were laid down by the Paris Summit and persist to the present.[9]

The Summit further called on the Commission to draw up a Community environmental policy and on 22 November 1973 the Council of Ministers approved an ambitious four-year Community Action Programme on the Environment.[10] This designated three areas of activity: reduction and prevention of pollution and nuisances; improvement of the environment and quality of life; Community action, or common action by member states, in international organisations dealing with the environment. Not all the objectives of the action programme were met in the four year period, but there have been four successive action programmes[11] – the fourth of which, covering the current period from 1987, expires at the end of 1992.

LEGAL BASIS FOR EUROPEAN COMMUNITY ENVIRONMENTAL POLICY

Under the Treaty of Rome

As indicated above, the Paris Summit found a mandate, albeit a somewhat tenuous one, for environmental protection action in the commitment of the parties to the Treaty of Rome, contained in the Preamble, to 'the constant improvement of the living and working conditions of their peoples.' This has been interpreted (somewhat expansively it must be said) to mean the improvement in the 'quality of life' and thus the environment. In addition it has been argued that discrepancies in national environmental protection laws could result in distortions or obstructions to trade in that differing national environmental standards could be used as means of discriminating against goods from other member states, resulting in 'unfavourable competitive conditions', adverse effects on the interests of the consumer and the obstruction of free trade.[12] On the basis of such arguments, the Commission has felt itself able to propose, and the Council of Ministers has felt itself able to agree to, environmental legislation based on either (or sometimes both) Articles 100 and 235. Article 100 authorizes directives approved unanimously 'for the approximation of such provisions laid down by law, regulation or administrative action in the member states as directly affect the establishment or functioning of the common market.' The wording clearly signifies a link with economic policies and while it has provided a satisfactory basis for legislation in a number of spheres, such as water quality[13] or noise emission,[14] where different national standards could confer unfair trading advantage on certain enterprises, in other spheres it has proved too difficult to demonstrate that such discrepancies affected the 'establishment or functioning of the common market.' Then recourse has had to be made to Article 235 under which legislation not envisaged elsewhere is authorised if it is 'necessary to attain in the course of the operation of the common market, one of the objectives of the Community'. Here the Preamble was invoked to justify the

136

argument that protection of the environment was one of the objectives of the Community.[15] This laudable enthusiasm for Community competence in environmental matters has led to some strange results, notably the claim that the conservation of species of wild birds is necessary for 'the harmonious development of economic activities throughout the Community and a continuous and balanced expansion.'[16]

Under the Single European Act

The coming into force of the Single European Act[17] in July 1987 obviated the need for this juristic artifice. The SEA gave formal recognition to the Community environmental policy and provides for the first time a clear and unambiguous legal basis for EC environmental law. The main features of it are set out in the new Article 130, paragraphs R, S, and T.

Article 130R defines the objectives of EC environmental policy: to preserve, protect and improve the quality of the environment; to contribute towards protecting human health; to ensure a prudent and rational utilization of national resources. Article 130R(2) then sets out the principles on which Community action to achieve these objectives should be based, namely that preventive action should be taken, environmental damage should, as a priority be rectified at source, and that the polluter should pay. It also requires that environmental protection requirements shall be a component of the Community's other policies.[18]

Title II of the Single European Act envisages that environmental legislation will be based on one of two main legal grounds. Article 130S, by providing specifically for the enactment of environmental legislation, frees it from the requirement noted above that it should serve economic ends,[19] but such legislation must be adopted by unanimous agreement of the Council of Ministers, unless (by unanimity) it chooses to define those matters as ones on which decisions are to be taken by a qualified majority.[20] Action taken under Article 130 is subject to the principle of subsidiarity,[21] namely that:

> The Community shall take action relating to the environment to the extent to which the objectives [of EC policy] can be attained better at the Community level than at the level of the individual Member States.

and to the general safeguard provision in Article 130T that:

> The protective measures adopted in common pursuant to Article 130S shall not prevent any Member State from maintaining or introducing more stringent protective measures compatible with this Treaty.

An alternative basis for environmental legislation is provided under Article 100A – the basic provision under which the Single Market legislation is enacted. This article provides for action by majority vote in the Council of Ministers and, presumably in recognition of the fact that the pressures to achieve the Single Market might result in environmental considerations being pushed into second place, the Commission is obliged when presenting proposals for environmental action under this article to 'take as its basis a high level of protection' (Art. 100A (3)), and in addition when such action is taken by majority vote, member states are specifically permitted to adopt stricter measures of domestic environmental protection.[22]

Despite the adoption of these provisions, which appear designed both to confirm the value of action which has already been taken and to ensure that environmental considerations occupy a central role in Community decision making, a recent commentator has suggested more cynically that:

> The inclusion of environmental provisions in the Treaty cannot be said to have led to an increased importance in environmental objectives. Action in the field of the environment will continue to be weighted against trade objectives and when a conflict arises there is little in Title VII of the Treaty which will contribute to tipping the balance towards environmental considerations. On the contrary the principles listed in Article 130R(3) . . . when rigidly adhered to, will often prove to be an insurmountable obstacle.[23]

THE ROLE OF THE EUROPEAN COMMUNITY POLITICAL INSTITUTIONS

The four action programmes[24] represent an important statement of general policy, but it is also noticeable that in the last ten years environmental protection has moved steadily up the EC political agenda in the same way that it has at a national level. A brief consideration of the roles of the main political actors on the EC scene may illustrate this.

The European Council

The European Council, as the Summit of Heads of State or of Government has been called since 1975, has on a number of occasions stressed the importance to be given to environmental protection within and by the EC. These have largely been 'disaster driven' in the sense that they are responses to *causes célèbres* – but then few major policy initiatives in any field, national or EC, appear spontaneously. In 1978, shortly after the wreck of the Amoco Cadiz, the European Council agreed a specific programme on sea pollution. In 1983 when the acid rain effects on the Black Forest were first highlighted, the Stuttgart European Council decided that environmental protection policy should be a priority within the Community, emphasising the need particularly to reinforce the fight against pollution and the dangers to European forest areas. In 1985, as 'green' concerns moved into the fore in a number of continental European countries, the Brussels European Council decided that environmental protection policies should become a fundamental part of economic, industrial, agricultural, and social policies. The March 1985 Summit also designated 1987 as the European Year of the Environment.[25] More recently, in the now famous Rhodes Declaration, the European Council pledged itself to 'play a leading role in the action needed to protect the world's environment' and to continue to strive for 'an effective international response . . . to such global problems as depletion of the ozone layer, the greenhouse effect and the ever growing threats to the natural environment.'[26]

The Council of Ministers

The Council of Ministers is the cutting edge of the EC legislative process. It is thus inevitable that it is within the Council that national differences of perspective, culture, and approach, or, as it is now called, 'style', should come to the fore. This occurs in many areas of EC policy, and environmental policy has not escaped. Notorious and sometimes bitter disputes have held up progress in a number of areas. It has been pointed out that the northern European states – Denmark, The Netherlands, and Germany which were earlier and more enthusiastic converts to the 'green movement' – contrast vividly with the Mediterranean countries which are often accused of putting development (even non-sustainable development) before environmental concerns. The United Kingdom has in the Thatcher years presented a strange face to the Environmental Council. Its well-publicized and arguably initially well-founded objection to uniform emission standards in water quality control, while taken aboard by the EC in the 1976 aquatic environment directive,[27] has, with the passing of the years and the privatization of the water industry, been increasingly perceived as a defence of lower standards. The vigorous opposition by the UK to the use of catalytic converters in favour of a 'lean burn' engine solution to car exhaust emissions, which was eventually compromised in 1985,[28] was also perceived as special pleading. Similarly, a number of other British government stances, such as its failure to designate more bathing beaches even than Luxembourg under the bathing water directive,[29] its position on the ocean dumping of sewage sludge,[30] and on the use of best available technology to prevent pollution[31] (to which it insists on adding an economic cost/benefit analysis which some experienced commentators feel impossible to put into practice[32]) have been widely seen as a defence of British industry's 'dirty' practices, rather than genuinely scientific alternative policies.

A number of attempts have been made to analyse the dynamics of agreement or consensus formation within the Environment Council meetings. Von Moltke[33] has put forward an interesting 'consensus cycle' theory under which national policy proposals invariably provide the initial impulse for Community proposals;[34] these proposals although not adopted by the Council are often taken aboard by other member states which then introduce them into their own national law. The Community proposal, albeit perhaps in modified form, then emerges as a consensus position. Dashwood's more cautious 'radiator effects' theory[35] suggests that the substance of a novel Community proposal is often taken over as a national policy; this national adoption will often 'radiate' back to the Community process, thus making the Commission proposal more acceptable. It is probably true, as Rehbinder and Stewart suggest,[36] that both theories are over-simplistic; nevertheless, it is without doubt the case that the process of environmental policy formation at both national and Community levels is symbiotic. National environmental policies are relatively young and undeveloped, certainly compared with fiscal or economic policies, and the early involvement of the European Community dimension in a number of spheres has appeared to permit the formation of an often surprisingly large degree of consensus among member states, even in the presence of conflicting economic interests.[37] Thus, although there is always a danger that a consensus approach will result in 'lowest common denominator' policies, and as we have seen, the SEA specifically recognizes that stricter national policies may well be permissible, the evidence does not support the view that EC environmental policy moves at the pace of the slowest. It may not always meet the aspirations of the 'greenest' but it has and surely will continue to act as a major spur to most national environmental policies.

The Commission

As initiator of legislation and guardian of the treaties,[38] the Commission has a special role in the development of the action programmes and the implementing legislative proposals. In the implementation of policy it is noticeable that the Commission has pragmatically chosen where possible to base proposals for legislation on Article 100A – a legal basis for harmonization action to achieve the Single Market – which requires a majority vote, rather than the specific 'environmental' legal base of Article 130.[39]

In the performance of its role as enforcer of Community legislation it is also noticeable that it has, in the environmental field as in other fields, begun to initiate more actions against member states under Article 169 for breaches of the treaty by failure to implement the obligations of environmental directives. Up to the end of 1989 362 actions had been brought against member states.[40] Already the strain on the restricted number of Commission staff of such a policy, which is clearly intended to 'de-politicize' violation proceedings, is beginning to show.

The Council may have recently approved the Commission proposal for the establishment of a European Environmental Agency,[41] but the initial proposal was radically scaled down in the process of agreement. It was initially conceived as the European equivalent of the United States of America's Environmental Protection Agency (EPA) with a monitoring and enforcement role supplemented by the possible appointment of Community environment inspectors.[42] The role of the EEA in its agreed form will be restricted to research and monitoring; it will have no enforcement powers. The EEA will no doubt be of indirect assistance to the Commission by providing information which will be of assistance to the latter in its enforcement role, but it does not suggest that the Council supports the radical enforcement role for the Commission which Commissioner for the Environment, Carlo Ripa di Meana, appeared to envisage when he suggested recently that sanctions should be imposed on member states found habitually to be in violation of Community environmental norms by excluding them from access to the EC

140

environmental funding schemes such as Action by the Community on the Environment.[43] There is increasing evidence that the public agrees with him in this vision of the role of the Commission as supranational 'guardian of the environment'. In its task of apprehending breaches of Community environmental law (as with any breaches of EC law) the Commission is dependent on a number of main sources – MEPs questions and complaints, Article 177 EEC references from national courts, and direct complaints by individuals. In 1984 there were 11 such complaints by individual citizens about violations of EC environmental law in member states, in 1988 there were 190, and in 1989, 460.[44]

The European Parliament

Despite a series of Treaty amendments which have progressively increased its powers and influence in the Community decision-making system,[45] in the field of policy making the European Parliament is still a consultative body. Nevertheless it is a consultative body comprised of a large number of able and ambitious politicians. It is therefore not surprising that the European Parliament has taken advantage of the political capital to be made from a greater environmental awareness among its electorates. One of its earliest, well-publicized, successes in the field was the adoption by the Council in 1983[46] of a ban on the import of seal pup skins into the Community, after a series of Resolutions by the Parliament drawing attention to the hunting methods used in the 'culling' of baby seals.[47] This ban, which was extended to 1989 and then indefinitely,[48] was hailed as a major success by the European Parliament in mobilizing opionion within the EC. Since then major parliamentary initiatives have generally been been the result of the work of the Environment, Public Health, and Consumer Protection Committee (currently chaired by Ken Collins, MEP for Strathclyde East) which has established itself as an important, high-profile political force in the field. Armed with the detailed work of the committee, Parliament has been able to provide sophisticated inputs into debates on legislative proposals on a variety of issues including environmental impact assessment and transfrontier transport of hazardous waste,[49] to establish its own inquiries into controversial issues such as the handling of waste,[50] and to flag up important issues not yet receiving attention, such as sea-level rise.[51] Environmental policy has also benefited from general moves by Parliament to strengthen its own position within the Community decision-making process, including the strengthening of areas of non-obligatory expenditure[52] and its successful pressure on the Commission to present an annual report to Parliament on the Commission's work in the monitoring of the application of Community law, which includes a great deal of information on the application of Community environmental legislation by member states.[53]

THE SCOPE OF COMMUNITY ENVIRONMENTAL POLICY

Space here does not permit an exhaustive survey of the range of activities covered by the various instruments of the EC environmental policy. However some indication of its substantive content is important to enable any form of assessment of its success and significance to be made. In 1987, the European Year of the Environment, the Commission published four volumes of EC Environmental Legislation, 1967–1987. These were grouped under four heads: general policy and nature protection; air and noise; chemicals and waste; and water.[54] From this wide-ranging programme, two areas – nature protection and water – will be taken as examples.

Nature Protection

In the field of nature protection the EC has responded with common action on matters which have attracted public attention through the efforts of non-governmental organizations, such as the ban on the import of the skins of certain seal pups and their products, and the ban on the import into the Community of whale products for commercial purposes.[55] More fundamental measures on the protection of indigenous species of wildlife are contained in the important directive 79/409 on the conservation of wild birds,[56] described by Lyster as 'an important step forward' from previous similar international instruments.[57] This directive imposes strict obligations on member states to maintain populations of wild birds, to protect and maintain their habitat, to regulate hunting and trading and to prohibit certain methods of killing and capture. There is a centralized system of monitoring and the Commission is responsible for enforcement. It has proved difficult to change the habits of generations, particularly of hunting in the Mediterranean region, but the Commission's enforcement policy has demonstrated that the directive has teeth. The United Kingdom was persuaded to abandon proposals for expanding whisky production in the Isle of Islay on a designated site after a visit from a member of the Commission[58] and Germany is currently the subject of violation proceedings under Article 169 EEC for building a dyke in an important wetland site adjacent to the Wadden Sea.[59] The EC has also used its external relations powers in this field to enter into a number of important wildlife protection treaties, notably the 1979 Berne Convention on the conservation of European wildlife and natural habitats,[60] the 1979 Bonn Convention on the conservation of migratory species of wild animals,[61] the 1973 Washington Convention on international trade in endangered species of wild flora and fauna[62] and the 1980 Convention on Antarctic marine living resources.[63] Currently under consideration is a major Commission proposal for a habitat directive which will key in with and expand the approach of the wild birds directive. Under the current proposal member states will within two years have to identify the ten most important sites in the Community for designated species of wild flora and fauna listed in the annexes. These sites will require protection under national law to maintain the habitat and populations of these species. After ten years the number of sites for each species will have been increased to 100 and the network of sites, together with the wild bird directive sites will form a European network of special protection areas to be called Natura 2000.[64]

Water pollution policy is, in the words of Johnson and Corcelle, 'the oldest and most complete sector of Community Environment Policy'.[65] It was given priority status by the first action programme, significant proposals were made and adopted in the first two years of the programme[66] and more than twenty-five legal instruments have been adopted in this sector.

The dual approach of the Community's policy in this sector has been, on the one hand, to establish 'water quality objectives' which must, by a given time, be met for waters used for specified purposes: drinking, bathing, pisciculture, and so on, and, on the other hand, to regulate the quality of contaminated emissions from fixed installations. In order to ensure that member states meet both the water quality objectives and impose the required emission controls, detailed and legally binding standards are elaborated, setting maximum contamination levels and compulsory monitoring standards.[67]

To date, water quality objectives have been established for the following types of water: surface water for drinking,[68] bathing water,[69] water for freshwater fish life[70] and shellfish waters.[71] This first group of directives has a number of common features: they designate basic parameters (for example, for physical, chemical, and microbiological characteristics) which those waters must meet or aspire to meet; the competent authorities of member states are responsible for sampling and monitoring in accordance with the directive, but, most importantly, it is the member state itself which is responsible for designating the waters to which the directive applies (although of course the member state cannot in good faith use this discretion in order to defeat the objectives of the directive).[72] The only exception is the 1980 drinking water directive[73] which established mandatory standards for all water intended for human consumption. These standards have caused problems for the member states. A number of Article 169 actions are pending before the European Court of Justice for non-compliance and Somsen reports that 'more private individuals have approached the Commission about non-compliance with the drinking water directive than any other piece of EC environmental law.'[74]

The second group of directives seek to control emission standards. This approach has been the subject of a long and much reported controversy between the United Kingdom and the rest of the Community which has been well analysed by Boehmer-Christiansen who suggests that the controversy 'was never primarily technical, but political'.[75] The United Kingdom, which had a relatively established practice of regulating the pollution caused by emissions by ambient water quality,[76] objected to a system of EC standards for all emissions from fixed installations. This dispute came to a head with the enactment in May 1976 of the framework directive 76/464 on the discharge of dangerous substances into the aquatic environment[77] with the result that the directive adopts a mixed regime. Dangerous substances, selected on the basis of their toxicity, persistence, and bioaccumulation, are to be placed on List I (the black list), while List II substances 'are characterized by the fact that their deleterious effects on the aquatic environment are confined to a given area and dependent on the characteristics and location of the waters into which they are discharged.'[78] Member states are obliged to eliminate pollution from List I substances by enforcing a system of limit values which establish either the maximum permissible concentrations of these substances in discharges or in receiving waters (that is, either a 'uniform emission standards' (UES) or 'environmental quality objectives' (EQO) approach). Pollution from List II substances is to be controlled by an EQO approach, enforced on the basis of the quality of the receiving waters. There have been a number of problems with the implementation of the details of this directive. Although some 129 dangerous substances have been proposed for inclusion on List I only four directives establishing limit values were passed until 1986[79] when the framework directive was amended to expedite decision making.[80] Since then progress has still been very slow and a current Commission proposal is that the process of adding substances to the lists be changed to the majority voting procedure.[81]

The Community has also sought to play an active role in the international regulation of water pollution. In tandem with measures for the regulation of water pollution within the EC have developed the environmental activities of the EC on the wider international stage. Under the doctrine of 'parallelism' developed by the Court of Justice in a line of cases starting with the classic *ERTA* case,[82] the external relations powers, or competences, of the Community mirror, or parallel, its internal competences. The development of internal Community environmental law from 1973 has resulted in the corresponding expansion of the external competences of the EC to represent the member states. Nowhere in the environment field has this tendency been more pronounced than in the water pollution sector. The EC is a party to the 1974 Paris Convention on land-based pollution,[83] and thus participates, alongside its contracting member states in the Paris Commission (Parcom). It is party to the 1983 Bonn Agreement for co-operation in dealing with pollution of the North Sea by oil and other harmful substances.[84] It has also signed the 1982 Law of the Sea Convention[85] and participates in the International Maritime Organization. It is a party to the International Rhine Convention,[86] the 1976 Rhine Chemical Convention[87] and participates in the Rhine Commission. The EC has observer status at the Oslo Commission as, for competence reasons, it has not ratified the Oslo Convention[88] and has also participated at the three international conferences on the protection of the North Sea.[89] The EC also participates in UNEP conventions and is a party to a number of relevant UNEP regional seas conventions.[90]

Commentators are divided on the value of the EC's input into these fora.[91] Because of the parallelism concept Community external relations competence is continually developing and expanding. Hence it is difficult, if not impossible (and from the EC perspective certainly undesirable) for it to state categorically at any time the exact limits of its external relations competence. This causes difficulties: sometimes measures cannot be approved at international meetings because the EC currently lacks internal competence to put them into effect (that is, it acts as a brake) whereas in other situations the existence of

Community competence, and the presence of EC member states with a united and progressive position, may well provide an important impetus to the success of international negotiations. Here too the process can be symbiotic. The three international conferences for the protection of the North Sea have provided objectives for the participating states in an area in which the EC is probably the most important single actor. Agreements within Parcom[92] as well as proposals for EC legislation[93] stem directly from the declarations issued by these meetings.

POLICY IMPLEMENTATION

The Use of the Directive

The historical origins of Community environmental policy still have an influence over its form, because they largely dictated the legal instruments which it has utilized. Article 189 EEC authorizes two main methods of Community legislation: the *regulation* and the *directive*.

A regulation is of general application throughout the territories of the member states and is directly applicable – that is, it becomes automatically part of the law of the member states without the need for implementation;[94] a directive, on the other hand, specifically requires implementation. Article 189 (3) reads :

> A directive shall be binding, as to the result to be achieved upon each Member State to which it is addressed, but shall leave to the national authorities the choice of form and methods.

The regulation is a device of uniformity, but the directive, which imposes an obligation of *result* rather than form, is ideally suited for the achievement of harmonized, or (in the jargon of the EEC Treaty) approximated policies.

The necessity of relying heavily on Article 100 as a legal base in the early development of environmental legislation dictated the use of the directive, for that article, concerned as it is with harmonization, only authorizes action by directive. Although Article 235 does not impose a similar restriction it has been suggested that the Commission, anxious not to be challenged as going beyond its legal power, has been very cautious in its use of Article 235 and other forms of legal instrument.[95]

Having said this however, the way in which the directive has been used in environmental policy areas is not strictly in accord with a rigorous distinction between regulations and directives. Rehbinder and Stewart have pointed out that the obligations imposed on member states by environment policy directives fall into three broad categories and that often these different categories of obligation are found within the same directive.[96] Their three categories are as follows: first, the 'typical' directive which imposes a clear result obligation, genuinely leaving the means to the member states[97] – in practice such obligations are often procedural, as in the enforcement of obligations imposed elsewhere in the instrument. Second, the 'regulation-

145

type' directive which imposes detailed substantive obligations, such as prohibitions, standards and tolerances, and provisions for implementation such as testing and measurement. These obligations, which are often contained in annexes with simplified amendment procedures, give no effective leeway or discretion to member states in implementation.[98] Third, the framework directive, such as the classic aquatic environment directive[99] which simply provides a framework for future supplementation by more detailed 'regulation-type' directives. Provided that the requirements of these later specialized directives can be met, there is often no need for the framework directive itself to be incorporated into national law. Rehbinder and Stewart conclude that 'with respect to substantive law the distinction between regulation and directive has been blurred, although it has retained most of its validity in the field of procedure.'[100] The Court of Justice has implicitly confirmed this elision of legislative forms,[101] and although a challenge has been brought against a directive on the grounds that it was inconsistent with Article 189, the action was abandoned as a result of a political arrangement and never went to court.[102]

Direct Effect of Environment Directives

Largely as a result of the regulatory way that directives are phrased, the European Court of Justice has on a number of occasions found that certain provisions of directives fulfil the requirements of the doctine of direct effectiveness, in that they are 'complete and legally perfect'.[103] The practical implications of this are that an individual (whether natural or legal) may rely on such provisions in the national courts in proceedings against the Government,[104] in suits arising from failure to implement or faulty implementation of such a provision. This doctrine, which is a judicial development by the European Court of Justice, has made a significant impact in other sectors of Community law, but not yet in the environmental area. It is noticeable however that a number of recent directives and proposals are drafted in unequivocal terms which might well be found by the Court to fulfil the requirements of direct effectiveness.[105] The doctrine is however subject to an important limitation: namely that such provisions may not be relied upon in proceedings against other individuals; however where a national court is called on to interpret national implementing law, the European Court has also ruled that it is under an obligation to interpret that national law so as to give full effects to the text of the directive itself.[106] Of course, article 177 also provides a general mechanism whereby the national court can refer questions of interpretation to the European Court to assist it in this task, but the Court will only give rulings on the interpretation of EC law, not on issues of national law or of application.[107]

The Regulatory Approach

The regulatory approach which manifests itself in the specificity of the obligations imposed by directives in this sector is in fact a hall mark of the nature of EC environmental instruments as well as their form. Taking its lead perhaps from the majority of domestic policies of the member states, it is notable that the overall approach of Community environmental law is regulatory: harmonized standards, such as environmental quality standards, and product and process (for example, emission) standards, are imposed on member states which have the responsibility to implement and enforce them under the supervision of the Community. Very little use has been made to date of other types of powers; indeed the EC has seldom taken anything other than a *passive* regulatory approach, that is, amending existing laws to keep up with technological advances rather than seeking to force technological develop-ments by setting progressive standards – an approach sometimes taken in the United States of America (where it is known as 'technology-forcing'). Again, it may in the past have been the use of the harmonization devices of Article 100 which inhibited such approaches.

Commentators have pointed out that a number of devices other than passive regulation are available for the development of environmental policies,[108] and in many member states public opinion may well have swung, or be in the process of swinging, towards support for evironmentally progressive taxation such as the differentiation which now exists on lead-free petrol in the United Kingdom and other European states. The directive on waste oils does require member states to organize and subsidize the collection, regeneration, and combustion of waste oils, and current proposals on waste encourage recycling and national self-sufficiency,[109] but the systematic use of subsidies always threatens to fall foul of the prohibition on state aids in Article 92. In the fourth action programme some priority is attached to the development of appropriate instruments for environmental protection, in particular the 'development of efficient instruments such as taxes, levies, state aid, authorization of negotiable rebates with a view to implementing the principle that the polluter pays . . . .'[110]

In the light of serious concerns about methods to reduce carbon dioxide emissions within the member states, the United Kingdom has also made proposals for tradeable emission permits modelled on the United States of America Clean Air Acts, which the Commission is thought to be considering.[111]

CONCLUSIONS

It is, naturally, difficult to make a comprehensive assessment of the whole of the Community environmental policy in the compass of a short article. As was said at the outset, from an internal Community perspective, environmental policy has certainly come a long way since 1973. It is one of the Community's more successful policies, in terms of the quantity and range of the legislation enacted under its auspices, and in terms of its increasing popular support.

From an external perspective, however, one is entitled to ask whether the

147

existence of a Community environmental policy, as opposed to twelve national environmental policies, represents an added advantage for environmental protection in Europe or indeed the world. Here the answer may be more equivocal. Commentators on individual sectors feel that the Community – as a bloc of developed states with a common position – can represent an important positive force in regional and international negotiations, but because of its problems of competence and the very need for it to agree a uniform policy, it can also act as a brake on regional and international developments.[112]

From the point of view of substance, even the environmental policy's strongest proponents accept that there is a down side.[113] As its policies cut deeper there are increasing problems of enforcement, and the number of treaty violation procedures is increasing. Political compromises sometimes result in 'a certain incoherence' in some texts.[114] Nevertheless, the achievements should not be underestimated. There have been a number of major changes in environmental practices within the Community as a direct result of its environment policy, most notably in water quality control in member states. The wild birds directive also, while not a model of compliance, has necessarily resulted in fundamental changes in habits in some member states, particularly in the Mediterranean. The policy has generated significant public law developments, such as the recent directive on freedom of access to information on the environment, and major proposals on wildlife habitat, disposal of waste, and carbon emissions are in the pipeline. Some member states – most notably Denmark – have not been reticent to voice the view that common standards will mean lower standards, but there can be little doubt that, delinquencies aside, the common policy does more to encourage the laggards than to hold back the leaders.

The Community environmental policy, like most national equivalents, is only lately coming of age, in the sense that it demands as much attention as other sectoral policies, and indeed is taken into account in the development of those policies. It is clear that the Commission, in line with European public opinion, recognises the need for the integration of environmental policy with other policies. This view is, for example, increasingly being felt (albeit somewhat late in the day) in the common fisheries policy, but has yet to make any noticeable impact on the common agricultural policy. There is also some justifiable cynicism that it may be being pushed into second place in the race to complete the single market. Nevertheless the fact that it functions in tandem with other Community policies means that the system of cross-sectoral compromises and trade-offs may act equally to its benefit as against it. Major proposals such as the recently announced Commission concept of a carbon tax will have to be negotiated in the context of package deals on other issues within the Council, as of course will an EC policy on carbon emissions for the climate convention negotiations. As environmental issues assume more importance in the global, as well as the national and regional, political arenas, a credible Community policy must be able to maintain flexibility and coherence. To do this requires not only pressure from the European Parliament and energy and innovation from the Commission, but also commitment from the member states. As the Intergovernmental Conference on Political Union, which began in December 1990, progresses with its work, it will be instructive to see how important environmental matters are taken to be in this next phase of European integration.

NOTES AND REFERENCES

1 Case 240/83 [1985] ECR 531.
2 See S.P. Johnson and G. Corcelle, *The Environmental Policy of the European Communities* (1989); P. Birnie, 'The European Community's Environmental Policy' in *The UN Convention on the Law of the Sea: Impact and Implementation*, eds. E. D. Brown and R. R. Churchill (1987) 19 *Law of the Sea Inst. Proceedings*, 527–556; E. Rehbinder and R. Stewart, *Environmental Protection Policy*, Vol. 2 of *Integration Through Law* (1985); N. Haigh, *EEC Environmental Policy and Britain* (2nd ed. 1987). Also N. Haigh et al., *European Community Environmental Policy in Practice*, 4 Vols. (1986 onwards). For an early assessment see H. Booth and A. Green, 'The European Community Environmental Programme and UK Law' (1976) 1 *European Law Rev.* 444–63, 535–53.
3 United Nations Conference on the Human Environment (UNCHE) held in Stockholm, 5–16 June 1972, UN Doc. A/CONF.48/14/Rev.1.
4 Under Article 8 EEC, the transitional period was designed to run for 12 years, 1958–70.
5 The proposed accession of Denmark, Eire, Norway, and the United Kingdom; Norway of course withdrew after a referendum voted against membership.
6 For example, the failure to develop a common transport policy, which was the subject of an Article 175 EEC action (for 'failure to act in infringement of [the] Treaty') by the European Parliament, see *European Parliament* v *Commission and Council*, Case 13/83 [1985] 1 CMLR 138.
7 Now formally recognised by Article 2, Single European Act.
8 Note also that Article 2 EEC designates 'an accelerated raising of the standard of living . . .' as one of the tasks of the Community.
9 These are set out at length in the First Programme (OJ 20.12.73 C 112), reproduced in Johnson and Corcelle, op. cit., n. 2, pp. 12–14 and summarised well in Birnie, op. cit., n. 2, p. 534 and *The European Community and the Environment* European Documentation, 3/1987.
10 OJ 20.12.73 C 112. Booth and Green, op. cit., n. 2, summarize the five objectives as follows: to abolish the effects of pollution; to manage a balanced ecology; to improve working conditions and the quality of life; to combat the effects of urbanization; to co-operate with states beyond the EC on environmental problems (p. 445). Of the eleven implementing principles – 'prevention at source' and 'the polluter pays' have been the most significant.
11 For texts see: Second Programme (1977–81), adopted 17 May 1977, OJ 13.6.77 C139; Third (1982–86), adopted 17 February 1983, OJ 17.2.83 C46; Fourth (1987–92), adopted 19 October 1987, OJ 7.12.87 C328.
12 These arguments are very fully discussed in Rehbinder and Stewart, op. cit., n. 2, pp. 15–30.
13 See further below.
14 See Johnson and Corcelle, op. cit., n. 2, pp. 220–36.
15 See n. 1, also *Commission* v *Italy (Re Detergents Directive)* [1981] 1 CMLR 331.
16 Directive 79/409, 10th preambular para., but note also that 'harmonious' and 'balanced' have been interpreted to imply respect for conservation and natural resources – see Johnson and Corcelle, op. cit., n. 2, ch. 1.
17 UKTS 31 (1988), Cm. 372; EC 12 (1986), Cmnd. 7958; 25 ILM 506. On the environment policy after the SEA, see J.S. Davidson, 'The Single European Act and the Environment' (1987) 2 *International J. of Estuarine and Coastal Law* 259–63; P. Kromarek, 'The Single European Act and the Environment' (1986) 1 *European Environment Rev.* 11.
18 Article 130R (3) also obliges the Community, when preparing its action relating to the environment to take account of: available scientific and technical data; environmental

conditions in the various regions of the Community; the potential benefits and costs of action or lack of action; the economic and social development of the Community as a whole and the balanced development of its regions.

19 See further H. Somsen, 'EC Water Directives' (1990) 1 *Water Law* 93.
20 Article 130S (second indent). The Commission is currently proposing that the procedure for adding new substances to the annex of directive 76/464 on dangerous substances be changed (by unanimous vote) to a majority approval procedure, see further below n. 81.
21 In fact the EC appears to have adopted such an approach in the past regarding environmental legislation: see *Progress made in connection with the the environmental action programme and assessment of the work done to implement it* (Communication from Commission to Council) COM (80) 222 final, 7 May 1980, cited Birnie, op. cit., n. 2, p. 551.
22 Subject, that is, to the procedure of Article 100A(4): 'If, after the adoption of a harmonization measure by the Council, acting by a qualified majority, a Member State deems it necessary to apply national provisions on grounds of major needs referred to in Art. 36, or *relating to protection of the environment . . .* , it shall notify the Commission of these provisions (emphasis added). The Commission shall confirm the provisions involved after having verified that they are not a means of arbitrary discrimination, or disguised restriction on trade between Member States.' Note also the Danish declaration attached to the SEA (quoted in Davidson, op. cit., n. 17, p. 259) and A. Toth, 'The legal status of the Declarations attached to the Single European Act'(1986) 23 *Common Market Law Rev.* 802.
23 Somsen, op. cit., n. 19.
24 See n. 11.
25 Johnson and Corcelle, op. cit., n. 2, p. 20.
26 EC Bull. 12 1988, point 1.1.11; reproduced in D. Freestone and T. IJlstra (eds), *The North Sea: Basic Legal Documents on Regional Environmental Co-operation* (1991) 232.
27 Directive 76/464, see further below at n. 77.
28 See Johnson and Corcelle, op. cit., n. 2, pp. 126–136 for a detailed account of the negotiations and the final approval of the directives on 3 December 1987, for texts see OJ 9.2.88 L36/1.
29 The United Kingdom initially proposed 27 instead of the 600 or so actual sites, see further below n. 69 and n. 72.
30 The United Kingdom is the only North Sea state which dumps sewage sludge. After considerable pressure from the other North Sea states it, announced immediately prior to the 1990 Hague Conference that it would end sewage dumping by the end of 1998. See further D. Freestone, 'The Third International Conference for the Protection of the North Sea' (1990) 1 *Water Law* 17, 18.
31 The United Kingdom has insisted on adding the rider that 'best available technology' means 'not entailing excessive cost' (BATNEEC), see the footnote to this effect in The Hague Declaration, 1990, (reproduced Freestone and IJlstra, op. cit., n. 26, p. 6) reported to have been included at the insistence of the United Kingdom. Note also the 1990 Environmental Protection Act.
32 See Richard Hawkins, 'EPA 1990 Part II: waste on land', *Environmental Law and Practice*, *passim*.
33 K. von Moltke, *Institute for European Environmental Policy, Annual Report 1981*, 4ff, cited Rehbinder and Stewart, op. cit., n. 2, p. 265.
34 There would be historical reasons for this in the 1973 Council 'Standstill' Agreement, OJ 15.3.73 C9/1, under which the member states agreed to inform the Commission as soon as possible of their intention to introduce national environmental measures, and then to suspend such national action for at least two months to allow the Commission to decide whether it should propose Community measures instead.
35 A. Dashwood, 'Hastening slowly: the Community's path towards harmonisation' in *Policymaking in the European Communities*, eds. H. Wallace, W. Wallace and C. Webb (1973) 195–6. His theory is not restricted to environmental issues.
36 op. cit., n. 2, p. 266.

37 See further, for example, S. Saetevik, *Environmental Co-operation between the North Sea States* (1988).

38 See Article 155 EEC, and D.A.C. Freestone and J.S. Davidson, *The Institutional Framework of the European Communities* (1988), 57–66.

39 For example, Commission proposal for a Council directive on civil liability for damage caused by waste, OJ 4.10.89 C251/3; Proposal for Council directive amending directive 75/442 on waste, OJ 19.11.88 C295/3; Proposal for Council directive on hazardous waste, OJ 19.11.88 C295/8. Although 130S is being used, see, for example, the habitat directive proposal (see below n. 64) and the recent directive 90/313 on the freedom of access to information on the environment, OJ 23.6.90 L158/56.

40 Tabular annex to statement by Commissioner Ripa di Meana, 8 February 1990, Brussels; (1990) 1 *Water Law* 4.

41 OJ 1989 C217, although at the time of writing the site of the agency has yet to be settled.

42 See Johnson and Corcelle, op. cit., n. 2, p. 341.

43 (1990) 1 *Water Law* 4; Belgium is reported to be the worst offender, see concerns expressed in *Seventh Annual Report to the European Parliament on Commission monitoring of the application of Community law*, 1989, COM(90) 288, 22 May 1990, p. 36. Note also proposal for a directive on the harmonization of reports on the implementation of environmental directives, OJ 1990 L214/6. The basic regulation for action by the Community on the environment (ACE) is No 1872/84, OJ 3.7.84 L176/1 (as amended).

44 See *Seventh Annual Report* op. cit., n. 43, p. 34.

45 The Budgetary Treaties of 1970 and 1975, the 1976 Direct Elections Act, the 1986 Single European Act, and note also the important decision of the European Court of Justice in the *Isoglucose* cases (Cases 138 and 139/79 [1980] ECR 3333) on the obligation to consult the European Parliament, see generally Freestone and Davidson, op. cit., n. 38, pp. 71–84.

46 Initially by a resolution of 5 January 1983 OJ 18.1.83 C14, calling on Norway and Canada to examine the issue further, and subsequently by directive 83/129, OJ 9.4.83 L91/30.

47 See Johnson and Corcelle, op. cit., n. 2, p. 241.

48 Directive 85/444, OJ 1.10.85 L259/70.

49 Rehbinder and Stewart, op. cit., n. 2, p. 269.

50 EP Report 1–1376/83, Resolution OJ 14.5.84 C127/67.

51 EP Report Doc A 2–87/89 on the consequences of a rapid rise in the sea level along Europe's coasts, 19.4.89.

52 In the 1991 Draft Budget the European Parliament at its first reading increased the environmental allocation from the initial Commission proposal of 74m ECU (reduced by the Council to 56m) to 119m ECU, of which it wishes to see 36m go to a new 'Environment Fund'. The remainder would go to existing schemes: environment and regional development (ENVIREG), 125m; Mediterranean (MEDSPA), 13m; biotypes and nature improvement (ACNAT), 15m; and action by the Community on the environment (ACE), 5m, see (1991) 2 *Water Law* 4.

53 See *Seventh Annual Report*, op. cit., n. 43, p. 34. In addition the European Parliament has passed a number of resolutions on the monitoring of the application of environmental law which the Commission is following up: for example, on water, OJ 11.4.88 C94/155; air, OJ 11.4.88 C94/151; habitats, OJ 14.11.88 C290/137.

54 Commission of the EC, Directorate-General for Environment, Consumer Protection and Nuclear Safety, *European Community Environmental Legislation, 1967–1987*. Brussels, (1987). Four Vols., Doc. No. XI/989/87.

55 Council regulation 348/81 on common rules for import of whales and other cetacean products, OJ 12.2.81. L39/1.

56 OJ 10.2.82. L103/1.

57 S. Lyster, *International Wildlife Law* (1985) 67.

58 See (1990) 1 *Water Law* 105.

59 An application for an interim order preventing further building work – the first application of its kind – was however unsuccessful. See *Seventh Annual Report*, op. cit., n. 43, p. 34.

60 Council decision 82/72, OJ 10.2.82 L38/1.

151

61 Council decision 82/461, OJ 19.7.82 L210/100.

62 Implemented originally by Council regulation 3626/82, OJ 31.12.82 L384/1, (now much amended).

63 Council decision 81/691, OJ 5.9.81 L252/26.

64 For text of original proposal see OJ 21.9.88 C247/3, and for text of proposed annexes see COM (90) 59 final. Under this proposal the environmental impact directive 85/337 will be amended to extend to work affecting designated sites (draft article 11).

65 See Johnson and Corcelle, op. cit., n. 2, p. 25.

66 id. By contrast, the first air pollution legislation was in 1980.

67 These requirements are so strict they are in reality more like regulations, see further below.

68 Council directive 75/440 concerning the quality of surface water intended for the abstraction of drinking water, OJ 15.7.75 L 194, as amended by Council directive 79/869, OJ 29.10.79 L271/44.

69 Council directive 76/160 concerning the quality of bathing water, OJ 5.2.76 L31/1.

70 Council directive 78/659 on the quality of fresh waters needing protection in order to support fish life, OJ 14.8.78 L222.

71 Council directive 79/923 on the quality of shellfish waters, OJ 10.11.79 L281/47.

72 See, for example, bathing water directive, above n. 69, article 1.

73 Council directive 80/778 relating to the quality of water intended for human consumption, OJ 30.8.80 L229/11.

74 H. Somsen, 'EC Water Directives' (1990) 1 *Water Law* 96.

75 S. Boehmer-Christiansen, 'Environmental Quality Objectives versus Uniform Emission Standards' in *The North Sea: Perspectives on Regional Environmental Co-operation*, eds. D. Freestone and T. IJlstra (1990) 139.

76 Somsen, op. cit., n. 74, points out that the United Kingdom as an island state with short, relatively fast-flowing rivers derived some competitive advantage from such a system, and that the use of UESs conflicted with the British 'tradition of decentralised and pragmatic pollution control'; see further D. Vogel, *National styles of regulation: environmental policy in Britain and the United States* (1986).

77 Council directive 76/464 on pollution caused by certain dangerous substances discharged into the aquatic environment of the Community, OJ 18.5.76 L129/23.

78 Somsen, op. cit., n. 74, p. 97.

79 For mercury : Council directives 82/176, OJ 27.3.82 L81/29 and 84/156, OJ 17.3.84 L74/49; cadmium: Council directive 83/513 , OJ 24.10.83 L201/1; HCH: Council directive 84/491, OJ 17.10.84 L274/11. Note that the 129 substances were listed in Council resolution of 7 February 1983, OJ 17.2.83 C46, and that Council directive 80/68 on the protection of groundwater against pollution caused by dangerous substances, OJ 26.1.80 L20/43 was enacted pursuant to article 4 of directive 76/464 and follows the general approach of that directive.

80 By Council directive 86/280 on limit values and quality objectives for discharges of certain dangerous substances included in List I of the annex to directive 76/464, OJ 4.7.86 L181/16.

81 See COM (90) 9 final for original version of proposal and for comment, H. Somsen, (1990) 1 *Water Law* 9–10. Of course, under the procedure of Article 130R EEC, such a proposal must be approved unanimously by the Council.

82 *Commission* v *Council* (*Re European Road Traffic Agreement*), Case 22/70 [1971] ECR 263. See also A. Nollkaemper, 'The EC and international environmental co-operation–legal aspects of external Community powers' (1987) 2 *Legal Issues of European Integration* 55.

83 1974 Paris Convention for the prevention of pollution from land-based sources, UKTS 64 (1978; Cmnd. 7251); 13 ILM 352 (1974); and with amending Protocol, see Freestone and IJlstra, op. cit., n. 26, pp. 128 ff.

84 1983 Bonn Agreement for co-operation in dealing with pollution of the North Sea by oil and other harmful substances; UKTS Misc 26 (1983; Cmnd. 9104); and with 1989 amending decision, see Freestone and IJlstra, op. cit., n. 26, pp. 171 ff.

85 For the text of the EC Declaration on signature of the Law of the Sea Convention on 7 December 1984, listing its legislation in the field, see Freestone and IJlstra, op. cit., n. 26, pp. 228 ff.

86 1963 Berne Agreement on the International Commission for the protection of the Rhine against pollution, 994 UNTS 14538 (1976), supplemented by 1976 Bonn Agreement; see further A. Nollkaemper, 'The Rhine Action Programme: A Turning-point in the Protection of the North Sea ?' in Freestone and IJlstra, op. cit., n. 75, p. 123.

87 1976 Bonn Convention on the protection of the Rhine against chemical pollution, 27 ILM 625 (1988), and see OJ 19.9.77 L240.

88 1972 Oslo Convention on the prevention of marine pollution by the dumping from ships and aircraft, UKTS 119 (1975); Cmnd. 6228; 11 ILM 262 (1972); for text with amending protocols, see Freestone and IJlstra, op. cit., n. 26, pp. 91 ff.

89 For the full texts of three Declarations, see Freestone and IJlstra, op. cit., n. 26, Bremen, 1984, pp. 62–90; London, 1987, pp. 40–61; The Hague, 1990, pp.3–39.

90 See generally, P. Sand, *Marine Environment Law* (1988); for example, 1976 Barcelona Convention for the protection of the Mediterranean Sea against pollution (and protocols) 15 ILM 290 (1976); also the 1983 Cartagena Convention for the protection and development of the marine environment of the wider Caribbean region (and first protocol) 22 ILM 221 (1983).

91 See for example, S. Saetevik, op. cit, n. 37. and J.-L. Prat, 'The role and activities of the European Communities in the protection and preservation of the marine environment of the North Sea' in Freestone and IJlstra, op. cit., n. 75, p. 101.

92 See, for example, Parcom recommendations 89/1 on the precautionary principle, and 89/2 on best available technology, reproduced in Freestone and IJlstra, op. cit., n. 26, pp. 152 and 153 respectively.

93 For example, the current EC Commission proposal for a directive concerning the protection of fresh, coastal, and marine waters against pollution caused by nitrates from diffuse sources. Original text at COM (88) 708 final, as amended in light of EP proposals COM(89) 544 final, and see (1990) 1 *Water Law* 6.

94 Indeed such implementation is contrary to Community law: see, for example, *Commission* v. *Italy (Slaughtered Cow Case II)*, Case 34/73 [1973] ECR 101.

95 Rehbinder and Stewart, op. cit., n. 2, pp. 245–252.

96 id., pp. 33–36, 137 ff.

97 For example, directive 90/313 on freedom of access to information on the environment, OJ 23.6.90 L158/56.

98 For example, the water quality directives, above at n. 79 and n. 80.

99 Directive 76/464, above n. 77.

100 Rehbinder and Stewart, op. cit., n. 2, p. 36.

101 Case 91/79, *Commission* v. *Italy* [1980] ECR 1099; Case 92/79, *Commission* v. *Italy* [1980] ECR 1115.

102 Brought by the two British titanium dioxide producers, Case 78/79, *BTP Tioxide* v. *Commission* and Case 79/79, *Laporte Industries* v. *Commission*, OJ 20.6.79 C153/5. Both were dormant for many years and never went to court.

103 There is an enormous literature on this concept. Notably see J.A. Winter, 'Direct applicability and direct effect: two distinct and different concepts in Community law' (1972) 9 *Common Market Law Rev.* 425 and A. Dashwood, 'The Principle of Direct Effect in European Community Law' (1978) 16 *J. of Common Market Studies* 229. See also T.C. Hartley, *The Foundations of European Community Law* (2nd ed. 1988) 183 ff., and Freestone and Davidson, op. cit., n. 38, pp. 27–44.

104 Which includes 'an emanation of the State' (per ECJ in *Marshall* v *Southampton and Southwest Area Health Authority*, Case 152/84 [1986] 1 CMLR 688. This means 'any body providing a service under the State's control' ECJ in *Foster* v *British Gas* [1990] 2 CMLR 833, (1990) 1 *Water Law* 54.

105 For example, Directive 90/313 on freedom of access to information on the environment, above n. 97; see also the Commission proposal for a directive on civil liability for waste, OJ 4.10.89 C251/3.

106 *Von Colson and Kamann* v. *Land Nordrhein-Westfalen*, Case 14/83 [1984] ECR 1891 and *Harz* v. *Deutsche Tradax Gmbh*, Case 79/83 [1984] 1921, provided that this does not breach

normal rules of legal certainty by, for example, making the national law retrospective, *Officier van Justitie* v. *Kolpinghuis Nijmegen*, Case 80/86 [1989] 2 CMLR 18.

107 See for example, *Pretore di Salo* v. *Persons Unknown*, Case 14/86 [1989] 1 CMLR 71.
108 For example, Rehbinder and Stewart, op. cit., n. 2, pp. 226–231.
109 Directive 75/439 on the disposal of waste oils, OJ 25.7.75 L194/23 (as amended). Note also the recent proposals on waste, OJ 19.11.88 C295/3 and 8, which adopt similar approaches.
110 See Council resolution on the implementation of a European Community policy and action programme on the environment (1987–1992) of 19 October 1987, (87/C328/01) item(s).
111 See also the recent announcement by Commissioner Ripa di Meana that the Commission will propose a carbon tax, *The Independent*, 20 December 1990.
112 See sources above at n. 91.
113 Johnson and Corcelle, op. cit., n. 2, p. 9.
114 id.

International Environmental Law and the United Kingdom

ROBIN CHURCHILL*

INTRODUCTION

Some environmental issues are purely national in scope. Many others, however, have an international dimension. Thus, to the extent that law has a role to play in dealing with environmental issues, international law as well as national law is required. The aim of this paper to look at the development and implementation of a number of selected areas of international environmental law in relation to the United Kingdom (UK). The UK's international legal obligations are an important factor, although only one of several factors, in shaping the domestic environmental policy and legislation of the UK. At the same time domestic policy considerations also affect the degree to which the UK is prepared to assume international legal obligations – and, as we shall see, the assumption of such obligations is almost entirely voluntary. The paper thus has a double focus – looking both at the contribution the UK has made and is making to the development of international environmental law and at the impact of international environmental law on domestic environmental policy and law in the UK.

The remainder of this introductory section will explain, particularly for the benefit of readers without any knowledge of international law, how international environmental law (a branch of international law) is developed, and then list the areas of international environmental law which have been chosen for examination and explain the reasons for this choice. The rest of this paper will then examine the areas chosen from the point of view of the double focus just referred to.

THE DEVELOPMENT OF INTERNATIONAL ENVIRONMENTAL LAW

The main vehicle for the development of international environmental law is the general multilateral treaty, that is, a treaty (or agreement or convention – the terms are synonymous) between three or more states, either on a regional

* Cardiff Law School, University of Wales College of Cardiff, PO Box 427, Cardiff CF1 1XD, Wales.

or world-wide basis. In examining the role of any particular state in the development and implementation of an international environmental treaty, one can examine that state's role in four stages:

(i). Its role in the preparation and negotiation of the treaty concerned. Such an examination is not always easy, because not all treaties have publicly available records of their negotiation.

(ii). Signature and ratification by that state of the treaty concerned. Signing a treaty does not bind a state, but indicates that it is considering ratifying the treaty. It is only the later act of ratification that leads to a state being legally bound by the treaty. Normally multilateral treaties require a specific number of ratifications before they enter into force. Once in force, they are only binding on those states that have ratified.

(iii). Formal implementation, whether by legislation or otherwise, of the treaty concerned once it has been ratified. For so-called dualist countries such as the UK (which view international law and national law as two separate systems of law), treaties, even when ratified, have no status in domestic law: they only become part of domestic law when they have been implemented by legislation. Thus, a treaty which is intended to affect matters at the domestic level must be implemented by legislation if it is to have such effect. In so-called monist countries (which view international law and national law as both part of a single system of law) such implementation is not normally required: once the treaty has been ratified it is automatically part of the law of the land.

(iv). The way the formal methods of implementation actually operate in practice. It is not unknown for a treaty to have been formally implemented by legislation but for it not actually to be applied in practice in the state concerned because of defects in the implementing legislation or because the legislation is not properly given effect to.

(a) Although the general multilateral treaty is the main vehicle for the development of international environmental law, there are two other, subsidiary, ways in which such law is being developed. The first of these is decisions of international organizations. Some international organizations have legislative or quasi-legislative powers because they can make decisions which bind their member states. The best example of such an organization is the European Community (which is discussed in the previous paper). Other examples include the International Maritime Organization (the UN's specialized agency for shipping), the Oslo and Paris Commissions (concerned with pollution of the North Sea and North-East Atlantic from the dumping of waste and land-based sources, respectively), a number of international fisheries commissions, and the International Whaling Commission. The final (b) way in which international environmental law is being developed is through the decisions of *ad hoc* international conferences, such as the three conferences on pollution of the North Sea (held in 1984, 1987, and 1990) and a series of conferences on global warming. Although the decisions of such conferences are primarily political in character, they are not without some legal significance. First, undertakings given by states at such conferences, even though essentially political in nature, may in some circumstances become legally binding, either because they are regarded as unilateral declarations intended to be binding or through the doctrine of estoppel.[1] Secondly, even if such undertakings are not legally binding, they may in time be translated into treaties or decisions of international organizations and so become legally binding in this way. Decisions of international conferences of this character are often known as 'soft law'.

CHOICE OF TOPICS FOR STUDY

Although it is one of the youngest branches of international law, international environmental law already comprises a very substantial body of law. It is obviously not possible in a short essay to look at international environmental law in relation to the UK other than in a few selected areas. The areas chosen for study in this paper are the following: (i) depletion of the ozone layer and global warming; (ii) acid rain; (iii) pollution of the sea as a result of the dumping of waste; (iv) conservation of fauna and flora, focusing particularly on the Berne Convention.

These areas have been chosen because they cover a reasonable spread of major international environmental issues, most of these issues are topical and fairly well understood by non-specialists, and finally the international law applicable to them illustrates all the stages and forms of international environmental law-making described above as well as being susceptible to the double-focus examination of each topic proposed above. Nevertheless, the selection of areas for study is open to the charge of eclecticism: some may also feel that issues have been selected which show the UK in a worse light than other environmental issues which have not been chosen for study. Some attempt will be made to answer these charges in the conclusion to this paper.

DEPLETION OF THE OZONE LAYER AND GLOBAL WARMING

Although in some ways depletion of the ozone layer and global warming are separate issues, they are nevertheless interlinked, which is why they are treated together in this paper. The ozone layer in the upper atmosphere (stratosphere) prevents most of the dangerous ultra-violet radiation from the sun getting through to the earth's surface. In the 1970s it was discovered that the ozone layer was thinning, and in 1985 a large hole in the ozone layer was discovered over the Antarctic. Subsequently, this hole has increased in size and has at times drifted northwards over Australia. In 1989 a hole was discovered over the Arctic. The thinning and holes in the ozone layer are caused by the chlorine in chlorofluorocarbon gases (CFCs), which are used as propellants in aerosol sprays, refrigerants and coolants in air-conditioning plants, and also in insulation products, cleaning agents and plastic foam packaging. The consequence of depleting the ozone layer is an increase in ultraviolet radiation reaching the earth. This in turn causes an increase in skin cancer and cataracts and other eye diseases, and may also suppress the immune system in humans and slow plant growth.

It is thought that global warming, about whose existence and, especially, its likely extent there is still considerable uncertainty, will result from increasing concentrations of certain gases in the atmosphere from man-made emissions, whose effect (like the glass in a greenhouse) is to let in the sun's radiation but to allow little heat to escape from the earth. This effect is known as the greenhouse effect and the gases causing it are known as greenhouse gases. The connection between global warming and the depletion of the ozone layer is that the gases causing the latter, CFCs, are powerful greenhouse gases, currently responsible for about fourteen per cent of the greenhouse effect. The other greenhouse gases are carbon dioxide (fifty per cent), methane (eighteen per cent), ground-level ozone (twelve per cent) and nitrous oxide (six per cent). Furthermore, depletion of the ozone layer allows, as explained above, more of the sun's ultraviolet radiation to reach the earth's surface, which not only warms the earth thus adding to the global warming resulting from the greenhouse effect, but also may damage the phyto-plankton under the ocean surface, which in turn will reduce the oceans' capacity to absorb carbon dioxide from the atmosphere, thus adding to the amount of carbon dioxide in the atmosphere and contributing to the greenhouse effect.

Although the two issues are interlinked, we will consider international efforts to prevent further depletion of the ozone layer through controlling emissions of CFCs first, before turning to the control of other greenhouse gas emissions: for reasons of space it is not possible to consider other aspects of global warming, such as preventing further destruction of tropical forests.

Emissions of CFCs are controlled at the international level by the Vienna Convention for the Protection of the Ozone Layer of 1985[2] and the Montreal Protocol on Substances that deplete the Ozone Layer of 1987.[3] The Vienna Convention is largely a framework treaty: it does not lay down any specific measures for controlling emissions of CFCs but leaves these to be elaborated through subsequent protocols (that is, supplementary agreements) to the convention. The Montreal Protocol is the first, and so far only, such protocol. It provides that the consumption and production of CFCs must be frozen at 1986 levels as from 1989, and then reduced to eighty per cent of 1986 levels by 1994 and fifty per cent by 1999. In addition, the consumption and production of halons (also ozone-depleting gases) must be frozen at 1986 levels by 1992. In both cases there is some relaxation of these timetables for developing countries.

In considering the role of the UK in the development and implementation of the Vienna Convention and its Montreal Protocol, we will use the four-stage framework outlined at the beginning of this paper, examining in turn the UK's role in the negotiation of the convention and protocol, its ratification of these instruments, and their formal and practical implementation. As regards the first of these, negotiations, it is difficult to evaluate the UK's role in the negotiation of the Vienna Convention and Montreal Protocol. This is because in these negotiations EC member states negotiated as a bloc (the subject matter of the negotiations falling partly, although not totally, within the competence of the EC), and there is no public record of how the Community reached its negotiating position. It has been suggested, however, that the UK, possibly under pressure from ICI, thought to be the largest CFC producer in the EC, may have put a brake on the Community's negotiating position.[4] Nevertheless, the EC did play a reasonably constructive role in the negotiations on the Montreal Protocol through its insistence that the production of CFCs must be controlled (whereas the United States of America and some other western countries had initially argued strongly that only certain forms of consumption should be controlled), although it had to accept a stricter timetable of cuts in production than it had originally proposed.[5]

Along with all other EC member states and the Community itself, the UK has ratified both the Vienna Convention and the Montreal Protocol. As explained above, ratification of a treaty which has implications for matters at the domestic level (as the Montreal Protocol clearly does) normally in the UK requires the enactment of implementing legislation. In fact there has been no such UK legislation: instead, because the EC itself is a party to the Montreal Protocol, the Protocol has been implemented for EC member states at the Community level by a regulation.[6] As far as practical implementation is concerned, it is too early to make any complete judgment. This is because all that the Montreal Protocol at present requires of its parties is that they have stabilized their consumption and production of CFCs at 1986 levels. As far as the writer is aware, no figures for UK consumption and production of CFCs for 1989 are yet publicly available, so that it is not possible at present to say whether the Montreal Protocol has so far been complied with. Nevertheless, it is likely that it has been, since the Government stated in February 1990 that it believed that British industry had reduced its use of CFCs by fifty per cent.[7]

As far as the second aspect of the double focus of this paper is concerned, namely the impact of international environmental law on UK domestic law and policy, the fact that the UK has probably already gone as far as, if not considerably further, than the requirements of the Montreal Protocol is probably not due very much to the protocol, which was signed only in September 1987 and came into force only on 1 January 1989. Rather, it is due to a number of other factors. These include: consumer pressures, which have led to a significant reduction in the use of CFCs in aerosols; voluntary schemes for recycling CFCs operated by local authorities and retailers in conjunction with ICI; an EC decision of 1980 which required a thirty per cent reduction in the use of CFCs in aerosols by 1981 as compared with 1976;[8] and voluntary agreements negotiated by the Commission with various sectors of industry for a reduction in the use of CFCs. It will be observed that conspicuous by its absence from this list of factors is any Government administrative or legislative action. This is no coincidence. The Government's view is that CFC emissions should be controlled through targets being set internationally, and then leaving it to industry to determine the means by which such targets are to be achieved.[9] This is in keeping with the present Conservative Government's general philosophy of keeping the regulation of industry to a minimum.

Almost as soon as it was signed, the Montreal Protocol was widely criticized for not going far enough in controlling emissions of CFCs. In the steps that have recently been taken to tighten up the provisions of the Montreal Protocol, it is possible to detect a more active role by the UK. This is no doubt in part a result of Mrs. Thatcher's recent display of a strong personal interest in global climate change (discussed below). Thus, in March 1989 the UK hosted the Intergovernmental Conference on Protection of the Ozone Layer, at which widespread political agreement was reached on the need to tighten up the Montreal Protocol. Just over a year later, in June 1990, the UK again acted as host for the meeting which formally amended the Montreal Protocol. These amendments require the production and consumption of CFCs to be phased out completely by 2000. Along with its fellow EC member states, the UK had proposed that the final phase-out date should be 1997, but this was not acceptable to the United States of America, the Soviet Union, and Japan. It is likely nevertheless that the EC will unilaterally adopt 1997 as the phase-out date, as a draft regulation to this effect, proposed by the Commission,[10] is currently being considered by the Council of Ministers. In any case, the new timetable of the Montreal Protocol is to be examined with a view to possible further revision in 1992.

Turning from CFCs to other greenhouse gases, international efforts to control the emissions of such gases are only just beginning. It will be much more difficult to reach agreement on control measures for such gases than it was for CFCs, both because of the greater uncertainty over the consequences of greenhouse gas emissions and because of the much greater cost and difficulty in reducing such emissions. As mentioned above, the main greenhouse gases, apart from CFCs, are carbon dioxide, methane, ozone, and nitrous oxide. The main sources of man-made emissions of carbon dioxide are the burning of fossil fuels (oil, gas, coal) in power stations, factories and car exhausts, and the burning of wood, especially tropical forests. The most feasible ways of reducing such emissions are increased energy efficiency; using gas instead of coal in power stations (gas emits only sixty per cent of the carbon dioxide emitted by coal for the same amount of energy); generating more electricity from renewable sources (wind, waves, tide, sun) and possibly, and more controversially, from nuclear power stations; developing more efficient engines for cars and discouraging private motoring by better public transport; and less burning of forests. The main sources of emissions of methane are agriculture (from the guts of ruminants – cattle, sheep, camels – and from water-logged fields such as rice paddies), rotting organic matter in refuse tips, the burning of wood and other vegetation, and leakages from gas pipes and mines. The main sources of nitrous oxide emissions are car exhausts, fossil fuel combustion, nitrogenous fertilizers, ploughing fields, and burning vegetation. The most feasible ways of reducing emissions of nitrous oxide and methane are by burning less fossil fuels, wood, and vegetation, reducing the use of nitrogen in fertilizers, and dumping less rubbish in tips and recycling or burning it instead. Emissions of ground-level ozone come largely from vehicle exhausts. They can be reduced by fitting catalytic converters to cars, although this increases emissions of carbon dioxide and nitrous oxide.

International efforts to deal with the greenhouse effect have been focused initially in the Intergovernmental Panel on Climate Change (IPCC), set up jointly by the World Meteorological Organization (WMO – a UN specialized agency) and the UN Environment Programme (UNEP) in November 1988. The IPCC has three working groups. Working group I has been concerned with the scientific aspects of global climate change, working group II with the effects of climate change, and working group III with strategies to limit or adapt to climate change. The IPCC was due to publish a report in time to be discussed at the Second World Climate Conference, held in November 1990. Thereafter it is hoped to begin negotiating and drafting a climate change convention, with protocols setting emission limits for various greenhouse gases. It is further hoped that these negotiations will be completed in time to allow such a convention (if not its protocols) to be opened for signature at the UN Conference on Environment and Development, due to be held in Brazil in June 1992.

Mrs. Thatcher has taken a strong personal interest in the question of global climate change. This question featured prominently in the important speech she made to the Royal Society in September 1988 in which she first revealed an increased awareness of environmental issues. In April 1989 she hosted a seminar on global warming at 10 Downing Street. This personal interest of Mrs. Thatcher's no doubt explains, at least in part, why the UK has played a fairly prominent role in the work of the IPCC, in particular by chairing working group I. In addition, the UK, together with Canada and Malta, has acted as a co-ordinator for the legal measures topic group of Working Group III, which is considering elements for inclusion in a climate change convention. The Government has also increased funding in the UK for scientific research on climate change, at a time when state funding for scientific research generally is declining, and the results of this research are being fed into the work of the IPCC.

Although, as indicated above, real negotiations on controlling emissions of greenhouse gases have yet to begin, the question of such controls has been discussed, and the need for them generally recognized, at a number of inter-governmental conferences held during the past two years. The UK has attended most of these conferences. The major exception was a conference held at The Hague in March 1989 organised by France, the Netherlands, and Norway (which in many ways has been the most radical of these conferences in the approaches it has canvassed), when Mrs Thatcher declined an invitation for the UK to attend as a deliberate snub to the organizers. The reason for this snub appears to be because she thought the organizers were upstaging a conference she had hosted the previous month and because it was known that the conference was to discuss the need for new international machinery of which Mrs Thatcher (at that time at least) disapproved. At the conferences the UK has attended, its attitudes to the control of greenhouse gas emissions have gradually changed. While initially the UK was not prepared to commit itself to such controls, it now accepts that such controls are necessary. Importantly, it also accepts (unlike the United States of America) that further research is not necessary before targets are set as a precautionary measure – an attitude it had rejected as recently as November 1989. In May 1990 Mrs Thatcher made a speech in which she said that the UK would stabilize carbon dioxide emissions at 1990 levels by 2005.[11] This undertaking is a modest one when compared with some of its fellow EC member states: Denmark, France, and Italy have said that they will stabilize carbon dioxide emissions by 2000 (as has Japan), the Netherlands that it will do so by 1995, and West Germany has undertaken to reduce carbon dioxide emissions by twenty-five per cent by 2005. The UK's undertaking is also modest when one considers that carbon dioxide emissions in the UK have been fairly stable for the past fifteen years or so, fluctuating between a high of 180 million tonnes of carbon emitted in 1979 and a low of 147 million tonnes in 1984.[12] The reason for the lack of ambition in the UK's target is thought to be the Government's desire not to hit the profits of the newly privatized electricity industry (power stations being a major source of carbon dioxide emissions) and the Government's policy of encouraging private transport, which it foresees as more than doubling in amount by 2025. On the other hand, the UK's undertaking to stabilize emissions of carbon dioxide compares favourably with the United States of America, the Soviet Union and Saudi Arabia (all leading emitters of greenhouse gases), none which is (yet) prepared to acknowledge the need for controlling emissions of greenhouse gases.

It is obviously too soon to say what the UK's ultimate role will be in negotiating a convention and protocols to limit emissions of greenhouse gases, let alone predict whether it will ratify any instruments that may eventually be agreed. From what was said earlier about how emissions of greenhouse gases can be reduced, it is clear, however, that if the UK were to become a party to any instrument controlling emissions of greenhouse gases, it would have a major impact on UK energy, transport, industrial, agricultural, and waste disposal policies and practices – an impact far greater than the phasing-out of CFCs is currently having.

ACID RAIN

Acid rain is caused principally by emissions of sulphur dioxide from the chimneys of power stations and factories combining with water vapour in the atmosphere to form weak sulphuric acid which is then precipitated as rain or snow. A lesser cause of acid rain are nitrogen oxides, emitted from vehicle exhausts, power stations, nitrogenous fertilizers, and the burning of forests and tropical grasslands, which mix with water vapour to form nitric acid. Acid rain kills fish and other aquatic life in lakes, ponds, and streams; causes

162

damage and death to trees; and attacks the stone and brickwork of buildings. Because of the wind and the use of tall chimneys on power stations and factories, many states (and the UK is a notable example) export acid rain to other states. For this reason acid rain is an international problem, and therefore is most likely to be successfully tackled if this is done at the international level.

The first international legal step to deal with acid rain was the negotiation and adoption in 1979, under the auspices of the UN's Economic Commission for Europe (whose members include not only all European states but also Canada and the United States of America), of the Convention on Long-Range Transboundary Air Pollution.[13] Under this convention parties are obliged gradually to reduce and prevent air pollution, but because of opposition from some states (notably the UK and West Germany) during negotiation of the convention, no timetable is laid down in the convention as to what extent or by what date this is to be done. This major defect has largely been remedied by the subsequent adoption of two protocols to the convention. The first of these,[14] adopted in 1985, provides that states parties to it are to reduce sulphur dioxide emissions by thirty per cent of 1980 levels by 1993. The second,[15] adopted in 1988, commits its parties to restrict emissions of nitrogen oxides to their 1987 levels by 1994, to apply national emission standards for major new sources, and by 1996 to have adopted control polices based on the critical loads which the environment can tolerate.

Turning now to the role of the UK in the development and implementation of these three instruments, we will use the four-stage framework outlined at the beginning of this paper and used when discussing the Vienna Convention and the Montreal Protocol on the protection of the ozone layer. The UK, as a member of the UN Economic Commission for Europe, took part in the negotiations that led to the adoption of the 1979 convention. As we have seen, the UK was largely instrumental in the convention's containing no specific provisions for dealing with acid rain. The UK claimed that more proof was needed of the connection between sulphur dioxide emissions and acidification of rivers and lakes, and damage to trees before it could agree to a timetable for the control of sulphur dioxide emissions – even though by the mid 1970s such a connection was widely recognized. This position was one consistently taken by successive UK governments since the early 1970s when the Scandinavian states had first begun to complain about the amounts of acid rain reaching them from the UK. No doubt not far from the front of the minds of the UK's negotiators was the cost to the UK, especially to its electricity industry (the main source of sulphur dioxide emissions) and ultimately that industry's customers, of controlling and reducing emissions of sulphur dioxide. And no doubt because the convention contains no specific measures for controlling acid rain, the UK felt able to sign it and subsequently, in July 1982, to ratify it. Because the convention has no specific effect at the domestic level, there has been no need for any implementing action.

Turning now to the sulphur dioxide protocol of 1985, the UK played little part in the negotiation of this protocol. The first negotiations took place between the ten (later twenty-one) countries of the 'Thirty Per Cent Club', so called because its members had pledged to reduce their emissions of sulphur dioxide by at least thirty per cent of 1980 levels by 1993 at the latest. The UK was not a member of this 'Club' nor did it attend its meetings. The later stages of the negotiations took place in a working group of the executive body of the convention. In view of its attitude during the negotiation of the convention, it is not surprising that the UK has neither signed nor ratified the protocol (although nineteen of the thirty-two parties to the convention had ratified it by the end of 1989). The UK is not the only major acid-rain exporting state party to the convention not to have ratified the protocol: the United States of America, East Germany, and Poland have also not ratified. Interestingly, West Germany, which as we have seen had been, along with the UK, a major opponent of strict emission controls when negotiating the convention, has ratified the protocol: in 1982 it completely changed from its former position when it became clear that it was a major victim of acid rain. The reasons given by the British Government for not ratifying the protocol are that the base year and reduction target are arbitrary and take no account of the substantial reduction in sulphur dioxide emissions in the UK achieved during the 1970s. The Government has also claimed that it would be impossible for the specified reduction in emissions to be met by the 1993 deadline because of the complexity of fitting the necessary flue gas desulphurization (FGD) equipment in power stations and the time taken to get planning permission for this[16] – a claim disputed by the House of Commons Select Committee on the Environment.[17] Since the UK is not a party to the protocol, the question of its implementation does not, of course, arise. Nevertheless, it is interesting to note that it is not entirely inconceivable that the UK may in fact meet the protocol's obligation of a thirty per cent reduction of sulphur dioxide emissions by 1993: in 1988 emissions were just over twenty-four per cent down on 1980 levels[18] (although much of this reduction is due to the economic recession of the early 1980s rather than to any conscious effort to limit emissions). The Government itself in 1988 estimated that its FGD programme would achieve a thirty per cent reduction by the late 1990s.[19]

Even if the UK is not a party to the protocol, a combination of diplomatic pressure and EC obligations is forcing it in the same direction as the protocol's targets. As mentioned above the Scandinavian states have complained for many years about the export of acid rain from the UK to Scandinavia. On the eve of an official visit by Mrs Thatcher to Norway in 1986, it was announced – and surely the timing of this announcement was not purely coincidental – that the Government had authorized the Central Electricity Generating Board to spend £1 billion on retrofitting three 2000 megawatt power stations with FGD equipment, fitting low nitrogen oxide burners to twelve major coal-fired power stations, and requiring all new coal-fired power stations to be fitted with acid gas emission control technology. Further impetus has come from the EC, which in 1988 adopted the large combustion plants directive.[20] This directive requires the UK to reduce emissions of sulphur dioxide from existing combustion plants of 50 megawatts or more (which include most power stations) by twenty per cent of 1980 levels by 1993, by forty per cent by 1998 and by sixty per cent by 2003. Although the Government originally reckoned it would be necessary to double the FGD programme to meet these targets, early in 1990, following the privatization of the electricity generating industry and undoubtedly as a consequence of it, it was announced that there would be no doubling of the FGD programme: instead the existing programme would be completed and a combination of the use of gas and imported low-sulphur coal would be utilized to meet the obligations of the directive.[21] It remains to be seen whether this approach will be successful: the Select Committee on Energy has, however, questioned whether this approach is legitimate, given that the targets for the UK in the directive were set on the understanding that they would be met primarily through the use of FGD.[22]

Returning now to the 1979 Convention and its protocols, it remains to examine the 1988 protocol on nitrogen oxides emissions. The writer has not been able to discover what role the UK played in the negotiation of this protocol. The UK signed the protocol when it was opened for signature in November 1988, but as at the end of 1989 had not ratified it (although eight other states had done so). Because the UK is not (yet) a party to the protocol, the question of its implementation does not arise. Although the UK signed the protocol when it was opened for signature, it declined to sign a declaration adopted at the same time as the protocol, which, although not legally binding, urges its signatories to reduce nitrogen oxides emissions in the order of thirty per cent from a baseline of any year between 1980 and 1986 by 1998, on the grounds that the Government 'did not think it right to commit ourselves both to an arbitrary percentage date for 1998 and to the quite different 'critical loads' approach of the protocol for the earlier date of 1996.'[23]

Even though the UK is not a party to the protocol and has not signed the declaration, as with the sulphur dioxide protocol EC obligations are pushing it in the same direction. The large combustion plants directive (already referred to) requires the UK to reduce emissions of nitrogen oxides from existing large combustion plants by fifteen per cent of 1980 levels by 1993 and by thirty per cent by 1998. Secondly, Directive 89/458[24] sets strict standards for the emission of nitrogen oxides in the exhausts of all new cars with engines of less than 1400 cc built after 1992: similar standards are planned for larger cars.

To sum up the position on acid rain: the UK's role in developing international law to combat acid rain has been almost entirely a negative one. Because the UK is not a party to either of the relevant protocols, the international law that has so far been developed has had no impact on law and policy in the UK. Instead, external factors influencing UK policy have been various EC obligations and, to a lesser extent, diplomatic pressure from Scandinavian states not members of the Community. Internal factors which have shaped UK policy are, of course, beyond the bounds of this paper.

For many years states have disposed of some of their waste by dumping it directly in the sea from ships. Although not the most important source of marine pollution, dumping is nevertheless a significant source, and has given rise to a good deal of controversy in western Europe in recent years, particularly in relation to the dumping activities of the UK. Dumping is particularly interesting as an object of study, not only for this reason, but also because it illustrates all three types of international environmental law-making referred to at the beginning of this paper and the relationship between them.

Dumping has been regulated at the international legal level in the North Sea and north-east Atlantic since 1972 by the Convention for the Prevention of Marine Pollution by Dumping from Ships and Aircraft[25] (usually known as the Oslo Convention). The convention prohibits the dumping of some of the more noxious kinds of waste, and provides that other kinds of waste may be dumped only if a permit has been obtained and, in the case of some wastes, only in certain areas. The convention also established an international commission (the Oslo Commission) to oversee the operation of the convention. The UK ratified the convention in 1975, implementing it by means of the Dumping at Sea Act 1974, which was subsequently repealed and replaced by Part II of the Food and Environment Protection Act 1985.

At this point we must introduce a new international forum. In 1984 the North Sea states, concerned at the increasing pollution of the North Sea, met in Bremen and drew up a declaration on the protection of the North Sea. A second conference of North Sea states was held in London in 1987 and produced a further declaration. More recently, in March 1990, the third conference was held in The Hague and again issued a declaration. These three North Sea declarations all call for various forms of action to be taken to reduce pollution of the North Sea. It is generally considered that the declarations are not as such legally binding, but are a form of 'soft law' referred to at the beginning of this paper.[26]

As far as the dumping of waste is concerned, the North Sea declarations focus particularly on the dumping of industrial waste and the dumping of sewage sludge. While the Bremen declaration contains a general but rather imprecise exhortation to reduce dumping, the London declaration contains much more precise and detailed provisions for reducing these two forms of dumping, even though, it is important to note, such dumping was at the time of the adoption of the London declaration perfectly lawful under the Oslo Convention. We will consider the London (and Hague) declarations' provisions on industrial waste and sewage sludge separately and in each case look at the UK's response.

Paragraph 22(a) of the London declaration, though not without some ambiguity,[27] essentially provides that the dumping of industrial waste in the North Sea must be phased out by the end of 1989 except for wastes for which there is no practical alternative disposal on land and which pose no risk to the marine environment. This provision was reinforced by a decision of the Oslo Commission adopted in June 1989 to the same effect,[28] which added that the exceptional wastes whose dumping could continue must be shown to the commission to meet the necessary conditions (no alternative disposal, no risk to the marine environment) through a procedure, called the prior justification procedure, under which a state proposing to dump waste of this category must notify the commission and give other states an opportunity to put their point of view as to whether the proposed dumping complies with the stipulated conditions.

The UK dumps two main types of industrial waste – fly ash from power stations and liquid industrial waste. In the case of fly ash, a licence to continue dumping in 1990 was granted, and such dumping actually began in January 1990. At that time no report had been made to the Oslo Commission as required under the prior justification procedure. This was clearly contrary to the Oslo Commission's decision of 1989 and against the spirit, if not the strict wording, of the London declaration. Whether the matter has subsequently been resolved in accordance with the prior justification procedure the writer has not been able to establish. In the case of liquid industrial waste, the UK had by the end of 1989 reduced the number of operations licensed for dumping to eight (as compared to twenty in 1987). These licences, unlike the fly ash licences, were notified to the Oslo Commission in accordance with the prior justification procedure and drew objections from other North Sea states: nevertheless, dumping took place in early 1990 before all the steps under the procedure were completed. Again, this was a breach of the Oslo Commission's decision and of the spirit of the London declaration. The UK Government has announced that it intends to phase out industrial waste dumping by the end of 1992, apart from two licences which will be extended into 1993 (which in fact happen to be for the largest amounts of waste).[29] This appears to pre-empt use of the prior justification procedure in future years. The other North Sea states appear to have acquiesced in this, since the Hague declaration (in paragraph 18) simply notes the UK's undertaking, though it does add that continued dumping will be subject to paragraph 22(a) of the London declaration (referred to above).

Turning now from industrial waste to sewage sludge, the latter is the residue left after the treatment of the liquid and solid wastes discharged into sewers. Because many industrial premises discharge their waste into sewers, sewage sludge contains not only matter originating from domestic use of the sewerage system but also remains from industrial wastes, many of which are toxic. In recent years the UK has been the only state dumping sewage sludge in the North Sea: altogether the UK disposes of about thirty per cent of its sewage sludge by dumping it at sea (the remainder is spread on agricultural land (forty-five per cent), goes to landfill (twenty per cent) or incinerated (five per cent). Paragraph 22(c) of the London declaration provides that the contamination of sewage sludge by persistent, toxic, or bioaccumulable materials should be not increased above 1987 levels and should eventually be reduced. At the time of writing, only limited figures exist to show whether this

167

obligation is being met.[30] In 1988 the amounts of mercury, cadmium, copper, lead, and zinc dumped with sewage sludge were all significantly less than in 1987.[31] In the longer term it will no longer be necessary to look at these figures, as in March 1990, a few days before the third North Sea conference began in the Hague, the British Government announced that the dumping of sewage sludge at sea would be terminated by the end of 1998.[32] This undertaking was noted in the Hague declaration (paragraph 15). The reason for the UK's decision to phase out the dumping of sewage sludge, even though not required by the London declaration, is undoubtedly because of the pressure it has come under, and criticism it has received, from other North Sea states.

Looking at the question of pollution of the North Sea from dumping with the double focus outlined at the beginning of this paper, it is clear, first, that the UK has made no positive contribution to the development of the law in this area through the work of the North Sea conferences and the Oslo Commission – rather its efforts to resist such development have largely been responsible for the ambiguities that abound in the conference declarations and the Oslo Commission's decision of 1989. Secondly, it is also clear that the developments referred to have had and will have a significant impact on British waste disposal practices. The reason why the UK is the odd man out on this issue (and why it has not properly complied with the London declaration) would seem to be because of a fundamental difference of pollution control philosophy between itself and its North Sea neighbours. The UK regards it as permissible to dump waste in the sea unless and until it can be scientifically proved that it causes harm to the marine environment, whereas the other North Sea states espouse the precautionary principle, and argue that waste should only be dumped if it poses no risk to the marine environment. It may be that the Government's stance over dumping can also be explained by its desire not to impose on companies dumping waste the additional expenditure which would have been necessary in order to have secured full compliance with the London declaration and the Oslo Commission's decision.

WILDLIFE CONSERVATION

There are a considerable number of treaties, both regional and global, concerned with the conservation of wildlife. This section focuses on what has proved to be the most significant treaty for the conservation of wildlife in Europe, the Berne Convention on the conservation of European wildlife and natural habitats.[33] The convention has two broad aims, the conservation of flora and fauna and the preservation of habitats. As regards the first, parties must prohibit the deliberate picking or collecting of the species of flora listed in Appendix I of the convention; must prohibit the deliberate killing of the species of fauna listed in Appendix II; and regulate the exploitation of the species of fauna listed in Appendix III so that their population levels are not endangered. As regards habitats, Article 4 imposes a general obligation to take the necessary 'measures to ensure the conservation of the habitats of the

168

wild flora and fauna species, especially those specified in the Appendices I and II, and the conservation of endangered natural habitats', while Article 6 prohibits deliberate damage to or destruction of the breeding or resting sites of Appendix II species.[34]

In looking at the role of the UK in relation to the Berne Convention, we will use the four-stage framework suggested at the beginning of this paper, examining in turn its role in respect of the negotiation of the convention, participation, formal implementation, and practical implementation. As regards the first of these, there appear to be no public records of the negotiation of the convention (which occurred under the aegis of the Council of Europe), so that it is impossible to say what role the UK played in the drawing up of the convention. As regards participation, the UK signed the convention when it was opened for signature and ratified it on 28 May 1982. The main legislation implementing the convention is the Wildlife and Countryside Act 1981,[35] though a number of other pieces of legislation, such as the Conservation of Seals Act 1970 and the Badgers Act 1973, are also relevant to the implementation of the convention. Both the formal implementation of the convention in the UK and especially its practical implementation have defects and deficiencies. For reasons of space, only a few examples can be given of such defects and deficiencies.[36]

The UK's record of compliance with the obligations of the Berne Convention relating to the conservation of flora and fauna is, on the whole, reasonably good, though there are some deficiencies. These include the failure to regulate the killing of certain Appendix III species (e.g. adders, frogs, and toads), contrary to Article 7; deficiencies in the licensing system for the sale of Appendix III species and the almost wholly ineffective enforcement of this system; and allowing seals to be killed for interference with fisheries, and in ways that do not seem to be wholly in accordance with the convention.

The major problems have come in relation to the convention's obligations concerning habitat protection. British legislation provides two main forms of protection for wildlife habitats – nature reserves (of which there are about 400) and sites of special scientific interest (SSSIs) (of which there are about 5,300). While nature reserves give complete protection to all the habitats they cover, SSSIs have a number of drawbacks. While it is normally an offence to damage or destroy an SSSI (though in practice prosecutions for this offence, which appears to have be committed on numerous occasions, are rare), there are a number of ways in which it is perfectly legitimate to damage or destroy an SSSI: for example, if planning permission to develop a site has been granted by the relevant planning authority (and this has happened on dozens of occasions) or under a private Act of Parliament. A further weakness in the protection of habitats in the UK is that habitats outside nature reserves and SSSIs are relatively unprotected: they can legitimately be destroyed or damaged if this is the 'incidental result of a lawful operation and could not reasonably have been avoided'.[37] Such unprotected habitats include a number of habitats of major importance to various Appendix II species. Many of these habitats have in fact in recent years been legitimately damaged or destroyed:

for example, many breeding ponds of great crested newts, the nests and habitats of corncrake in the Hebrides as a result of changes in farming practices, and Dorset heaths which are the home of the smooth snake. Overall, there is little doubt that the UK has failed to comply fully with its obligations under the Berne Convention to protect habitats. However, it is only fair to put this failure in to some kind of international context, and point out that every party to the convention, to a greater or lesser extent, is guilty of the same failure.[38] The reason why the UK has not complied sufficiently with its obligations under the Berne Convention to preserve habitats is due at least in part to the fact that environmental considerations do not enjoy any priority when public authorities decide whether to permit the development of land: as a senior civil servant in the Department of the Environment explained to a House of Lords Committee recently, a balance between economic and environmental interests must be struck and there is no 'preconception of which way the balance must fall'.[39]

So far we have looked at the Berne Convention in terms of the UK's participation in the convention. We must now turn to consider the second aspect of the double focus used in this paper – the impact of the convention on policy and practice in the UK. This has in fact been relatively limited. Many species of fauna and flora were protected before the Wildlife and Countryside Act 1981 under earlier legislation, although the 1981 Act has added new species for protection as required by the convention. The main forms of habitat protection, nature reserves and SSSIs, were already in place well before the convention was adopted.

CONCLUSIONS

The four environmental issues discussed in this paper – global warming and protection of the ozone layer, acid rain, the dumping of waste at sea, and the Berne Convention – show a rather mixed record in terms of the UK's contribution to the development of international environmental law, ranging from the moderately positive in the case of global warming and protection of the ozone layer to the distinctly negative in the case of acid rain and the dumping of waste at sea. A supporter of the British Government might argue that the author has concentrated on too many issues where the UK's record is poor and thus has given a distorted picture. It is true that there are some international environmental issues where the UK has a good record, such as whaling (though the good record here is not unconnected with the fact that the UK has no economic interest in whaling) and, possibly, pollution from ships. Equally, however, there are a number of other issues where the UK's record is poor, such as radioactive discharges from Sellafield and marine pollution from certain land-based sources. The author would contend, though of course without a full study of every issue he cannot prove, that the picture given of the UK's international environmental record in this paper is not an unrepresentative or misleading one. From that picture it can be seen that in any kind of international league table the UK's performance in relation to the four issues considered in this paper falls short of its most obvious comparators, the other states of north-west Europe and particularly its fellow members of the EC. On the other hand, the UK does have a better record than one or two other developed states, notably the United States of America.

As with domestic environmental issues, the British Government's actions in relation to international environmental issues fall well short of its rhetoric. Statements such as 'Britain has taken the lead [on global warming] and will continue to do so'[40] and 'Britain is playing a major role in international steps to control acid rain'[41] are, on the evidence of this paper, exaggerations: indeed, the second statement is so far from the truth as to be downright dishonest. The reasons for this gap between actions and words are largely the same as with domestic issues: the Government's general aversion to regulation; its desire not to increase costs to industry, particularly of industries that have recently been privatized; a philosophy of pollution control that requires rigorous scientific proof before action is contemplated (though an exception is made for global warming); and, more generally, an inability to accept that current patterns of economic life, transport, and so on in the UK require far-reaching changes if there is to be a real commitment to the environment.

Where by its actions the UK has accepted international obligations, its record in implementing them has often been defective (as in the case of the Berne Convention) and in some cases where the record is good (as with the Montreal Protocol on the ozone layer) the Government cannot take the credit. Whatever the record of implementation, it is clear that the UK's international environmental obligations have had and continue to have a significant impact on domestic environmental law and policy in the UK.

NOTES AND REFERENCES

1 For a fuller discussion of this point, see Y. van der Mensbrugghe, 'Legal Status of International North Sea Conference Declarations' in *The North Sea: Perspectives on Regional Environmental Co-operation*, eds. D. Freestone and T. IJlstra (1990) 15–22.

2 Text in (1987) XXVI *International Legal Materials* (hereafter ILM) 1516.

3 Text in id., p. 1541.

4 N. Haigh, *EEC Environmental Policy and Britain* (2nd ed. 1987) 269. Jachtenfuchs suggests that largely because of British pressure EC states were not prepared in the negotiations on the Vienna Convention to agree to any specific proposals to control the production and consumption of CFCs. He also says that the UK (and France) were responsible for giving the Commission a very restrictive mandate to negotiate on behalf of the EC in the negotiations on the Montreal Protocol. See M. Jachtenfuchs, 'The European Community and the Protection of the Ozone Layer' (1990) XXVII *J. of Common Market Studies* 261 at 263, 265–6. He also suggests that the position of the UK Government was largely influenced by the views of ICI: see, e.g., pp. 268, 270.

5 House of Lords Select Committee on the European Communities, Seventeenth Report, *The Ozone Layer: Implementing the Montreal Protocol, Session 1987–88* (1988; H.L. 94) 10–12.

6 Regulation 3322/88, *Official Journal of the European Communities* (hereafter OJ) 31.10.88 L297.

7 Lord Reay, 515 *H.L. Debs.*, col. 779 (6 February 1990).

8   Decision 80/372, OJ 3.4.80 L90.
9   op. cit., in n. 7, col. 780; Department of the Environment, *Air Pollution*, (1988; Cm. 552) 5, 14.
10 OJ 4.4.90 C86.
11 *The Guardian*, 26 May 1990. This undertaking was repeated in the Government's White Paper of September 1990, *This Common Inheritance: Britain's Environmental Strategy*, (1990; Cm. 1200) 64, 68. For the strategy to achieve this goal, see pp. 68–78, 283–291. On the other hand, in November 1989 a Government minister had said that 'we believe that, as a first step, we should be looking to the year 2000 as the date by which CO_2 emissions are stabilised': Mr. Trippier, 159 *H.C. Debs.*, col. 1305 (10 November 1989).
12 Department of the Environment, *Digest of Environmental Protection and Water Statistics*, No. 12 1989 (1990) 24.
13 Text in (1979) XVIII ILM 1442. For an analysis of the convention, see A. Rosencranz, 'The ECE Convention of 1979 on Long-Range Transboundary Air Pollution' (1981) 75 *Am. J. of International Law* 975–82. See also id., 'The Acid Rain Controversy in Europe and North America: A Political Analysis' in *International Environmental Diplomacy*, ed. J.E. Carroll (1988) 173–87.
14 Text in (1988) XXVII ILM 698.
15 Text in (1989) XXVIII ILM 212.
16 82 *H.C. Debs.*, col. 202 (Written Answers) (4 July 1985); op. cit., n. 9, p. 9.
17 Select Committee on the Environment, First Report, *Air Pollution, Session 1987–88* (1988; H.C. 270) xxix.
18 op. cit., n. 12, p. 12.
19 loc. cit. in n. 16.
20 Directive 88/609, OJ 7.12.88 L336.
21 Select Committee on Energy, Third Report, *The Flue Gas Desulphurisation Programme, Session 1989–90* (1990; H.C. 371) ix, xi.
22 id., pp. xix–xx.
23 142 *H.C. Debs.*, col. 278 (Written Answers) (30 November 1988).
24 OJ 3.8.89 L226.
25 UK Treaty Series 1975, No. 119.
26 For detailed studies of the history, legal status, and content of the North Sea declarations, see Freestone and IJlstra, op. cit., n. 1.
27 See, further, J. Gibson and R.R. Churchill, 'Problems of Implementation of the North Sea Declarations: A Case Study of the United Kingdom' in Freestone and IJlstra, op. cit., n. 1, p. 47 at 58–60.
28 Oscom Decision 89/1 of 14 June 1989 on the Reduction and Cessation of Dumping Industrial Wastes at Sea. It is a moot point whether this decision is legally binding: see Gibson and Churchill, op. cit., n. 1, pp. 59–60.
29 167 *H.C. Debs.*, cols. 898–9 (Written Answers) (22 February 1990). See also Mr. Curry, 165 *H.C. Debs.*, cols. 1165–70 (25 January 1990).
30 One problem is that for some of the contaminants figures for the amounts dumped prior to 1988 do not exist.
31 op. cit., n. 12, p. 33.
32 168 *H.C. Debs.*, col. 487 (Written Answers) (5 March 1990).
33 UK Treaty Series 1982, No. 56.
34 For a detailed discussion of the convention, see S. Lyster, *International Wildlife Law*, (1985) ch. 8.
35 The Act applies only to Great Britain. For the corresponding legislation for Northern Ireland, see the Wildlife (Northern Ireland) Order 1985 and the Nature Conservation and Amenity Lands (Northern Ireland) Order 1985.
36 For a fuller account, see S. Lyster, *European Wildlife Convention: Report on Problems in the UK*, (1985).
37 Wildlife and Countryside Act 1981, ss. 4(2), 10(3), and 13(3). An exception is made for bats whose habitats are completed protected.

38   International Union for Conservation of Nature and Natural Resources, *Implementation of the Bern Convention* (1986) 10–11, 13–15.

39   House of Lords Select Committee on the European Communities, Fifteenth Report, *Habitat and Species Protection, Session 1988–89* (1989; H.L. 72) 10.

40   Mrs. Thatcher's speech to the 1989 Conservative Party Conference, quoted in (1990) 9 *Earth Matters* 10.

41   op. cit., n. 11, p. 148.